TRAIL OF FOOTPRINTS

TRAIL OF FOOTPRINTS

A History of Indigenous Maps
from Viceregal Mexico

ALEX HIDALGO

UNIVERSITY OF TEXAS PRESS   AUSTIN

An earlier version of chapter 1 appeared as "A True and Faithful Copy: Reproducing Indian Maps in the Seventeenth-Century Valley of Oaxaca," *Journal of Latin American Geography* 11 (Special Issue, 2012): 117–144. Reprinted with permission from the University of Texas Press.

An excerpt from chapter 3 appeared as "How to Map with Ink: Cartographic Materials from Colonial Oaxaca," *Ethnohistory* 61:2 (2014): 277–299. Reprinted with permission from Duke University Press.

This book is a part of the Recovering Languages and Literacies of the Americas publication initiative, funded by a grant from the Andrew W. Mellon Foundation.

LATIN AMERICAN AND CARIBBEAN ARTS AND CULTURE

⊗ The paper used in this book meets the minimum requirements of ANSI/NISO Z39.48-1992 (R1997) (Permanence of Paper).

Library of Congress Cataloging-in-Publication Data

Names: Hidalgo, Alex, 1971– author.
Title: Trail of footprints : a history of indigenous maps from viceregal Mexico / Alex Hidalgo.
Description: First edition. Austin : University of Texas Press, 2019. Includes bibliographical references and index.
Identifiers: LCCN 2018029665
    ISBN 978-1-4773-1751-8 (cloth : alk. paper)
    ISBN 978-1-4773-1752-5 (pbk. : alk. paper)
    ISBN 978-1-4773-1753-2 (library e-book)
    ISBN 978-1-4773-1754-9 (non-library e-book)
Subjects: LCSH: Cartography—Mexico—History.
    Indian cartography—Mexico—History.
    Mexico—History—Spanish colony, 1540-1810.
    Aztec cartography. | Manuscripts, Mexican.
Classification: LCC GA481 .H53 2019 | DDC 912.7209/03—dc23
LC record available at https://lccn.loc.gov/2018029665

doi:10.7560/317518

Para Gabilú

CONTENTS

ILLUSTRATIONS

NOTES ON TRANSLATION

I have retained the spelling of cities, towns, and settlements used by the Archivo General de la Nación (AGN) to classify the maps in this study in the notes and captions but have modernized them whenever possible in the main body of the text. Although this results in divergent spellings of a patronym or toponym ("Cuestlavaca"/"Cuestlaguaca"), following the AGN's classification scheme will allow readers to locate sources with greater ease. In modernizing place-names, I have chosen to include accents of town names with their origin in Nahuatl ("Xoxocotlán," "Zimatlán," "Ocotlán"), but I have omitted diacritics from all other Nahuatl words. Spanish passages cited in the notes have been modernized. Where direct translation or transcription was not possible, I have rendered text as I read it in the source. Unless otherwise noted, all translations are my own.

ACKNOWLEDGMENTS

In researching the lives of maps, I have acquired countless debts and benefited from the support of many advisers, colleagues, and friends. Ramona Pérez introduced me to Oaxaca as a master's student in Latin American studies at San Diego State University, and she opened doors for me that led directly to the world of indigenous mapmaking. In Alan Sweedler I found a mentor whose encouragement steered me to pursue advanced studies in history at the University of Arizona, where, as a doctoral candidate, I completed a substantial portion of the research that informs this book. Their support has left the deepest imprint on my career.

At the University of Arizona, I wish to acknowledge support from the Group for Early Modern Studies, the Medieval, Renaissance, and Reformation Committee, the College of Social and Behavioral Sciences, the Graduate College, and the Department of History for their support to carry out preliminary research. A Fulbright García-Robles Grant allowed me to spend extended time in Mexico City and Oaxaca in 2010. The Centro de Investigaciones Históricas at El Colegio de México kindly hosted me during my stay, and Juan Pedro Viqueira Albán offered valuable advice while I conducted research in the capital. I wish to thank the dedicated archivists, librarians, and curators at the Archivo General de la Nación and the Mapoteca Orozco y Berra in Mexico City, and at the Archivo General del Estado de Oaxaca and the Biblioteca Francisco de Burgoa in Oaxaca, for their generous time and knowledge.

My deepest appreciation to the Kluge Center at the Library of Congress for a Kislak Short-Term Fellowship in American studies. Tony Mullan, Mary Elizabeth Haude, Mark Dimunation, Clark Evans, and Mary Lou Reker made my experience in Washington, DC, memorable. Grants from the American Historical Association and the Program for Cultural Cooperation between Spain's Ministry of Culture and US Universities helped subsidize a visit to the Benson Latin American Collection at the University of Texas at Austin and other costs associated with research. I am most grateful for a Ford Foundation Dissertation Fellowship and an Excellence in Social Science Fellowship from Arizona's Confluencenter for Creative Inquiry that provided invaluable support for two consecutive years of writing.

As I transformed my research into a book, funding from the Conference on Latin American History's Lewis Hanke Prize allowed me to return to Mexico for additional research at the Archivo General de la Nación. Likewise, a pair of Junior Faculty Research Grants and a Research and Creative Activities Fund from the Graduate College at Texas Christian University, where I have taught since 2013, allowed me to revise three chapters over the course of two summers. The Department of History and College of Liberal Arts at TCU have provided generous funds to support conference travel, research materials, collaborations with scholars, and costs associated with publication.

At Arizona, Kevin Gosner, my main adviser, encouraged my interest in maps and provided crucial guidance that helped me assemble and interpret the varied sources that inform this book. I am grateful for his sharp eye and his breadth of knowledge, as well as for his generous nature and kind disposition. In Martha Few I found a fierce ally, a wonderful role model, and the most creative historian I know. Bert Barickman's critical observations and attention to detail proved most helpful when considering the theoretical implications of using maps as sources. Stacie Widdifield taught me about the importance of detailed visual analysis, and she provided valuable feedback as I stumbled when interpreting my evidence. I also wish to thank Helen Nader, Linda Darling, Dale Brenneman, Michael Brescia, and Emily Umberger for graciously sharing their knowledge and expertise.

A diverse network of scholars tied to Latin America, maps, and visual culture has donated substantial amounts of time and resources to seeing this project come to fruition. Dana Leibsohn has been a tireless champion, carefully reading multiple versions of the manuscript and offering critical insight at different points along the way. Barbara Mundy's sharp wit and discerning eye have had a significant impact on my understanding of indigenous mapmaking. Over the years, she has offered valuable guidance and generously shared multiple sources from her extensive digital archive. Raymond Craib kindly read my research and provided useful feedback at a crucial stage in the project. I am grateful to Ramón Gutiérrez, who made helpful suggestions on two early chapters and encouraged my pursuit of history. Likewise, I am thankful for David Robinson's lively commentary on an early version of the first chapter that appeared in a special issue of *Journal of Latin American Geography*. I have greatly benefited from the insights of Yanna Yannakakis and Stephanie Wood. Stephen Colston taught me to think about pictorial records and the colonial world. I wish to thank Ryan Kashanipour, Ignacio Martínez, Max Mangravity, and John López, with whom I have shared so many stimulating conversations and whose friendship and support I value greatly. Over the years, they have each read various drafts of this work, offering critical feedback and lending a helpful ear.

I benefited from presenting my work across several platforms in the United States and Mexico. I thank Stephanie Cole for inviting me to deliver a paper about authentication at the Dallas Area Social History group in 2014, and to Susan Ramirez and Jorge Cañizares-Esguerra for their discerning feedback on a subsequent draft of the same topic during the annual meeting of the Southwest Seminar in 2015. At the Southwest Seminar, José Carlos de la Puente, Jay Harrison, Alcira Dueñas, Joaquín Rivaya Martínez, Juan José Ponce Vázquez, Mark Lentz, Renzo Honores, and Caroline Garriott helped me to consider the way various forms of pictorial evidence informs our understanding of spatial relations and law. Presenting at the Museo Nacional de Antropología in Mexico City in 2015 for the second Congreso Internacional de Etnohistoria de América allowed me to sharpen aspects of my analysis of inks and indigenous knowledge. Joanne Rappaport, Alejandro Cañeque, Kelly McDonough, Scott Cave, and Rocío Quispe Agnoli provided valuable suggestions for my discussion of painters during the 2015 meeting of the TePaske Seminar at Georgetown University. I found Dana Leibsohn's and Aaron Hyman's comments for a panel on archives during the College Art Association's annual meeting in 2016 especially useful as I attempted to outline the book's epilogue. A visit to Penn State in fall 2016 to deliver a public lecture on paper and secrecy helped me enhance aspects of the third chapter. I am grateful to Martha Few,

Matthew Restall, Kei Hirano, Zachary Morgan, Kate Godfrey, Christopher Valesey, and Samantha Billing for being such gracious hosts.

My appreciation to Angelina Trujillo, Juan Julián Caballero, and Maarten Jansen for their help translating colonial Mixtec. Thanks also to Alejandra Odor Chávez at the Archivo General de la Nación and to David Wright for sharing sources and insight about ink and paper.

At Texas Christian, an exciting community of scholars, educators, and public intellectuals has welcomed me into their fold. I have benefited from the encouragement and support of my colleagues in the History Department, including Peter Szok, Gregg Cantrell, Hanan Hammad, Todd Kerstetter, Celeste Menchaca, Rebecca Sharpless, Kara Vuic, and Gene Smith. I am grateful to Alan Gallay and Peter Worthing for their careful guidance and to Jodi Campbell for her support and enthusiasm. My thanks to Bill and Courtney Meier and to Max Krochmal and Courtney Wait for their hospitality and friendship. I would also like to thank June Koelker, Julie Christenson, Roger Rainwater, and Robyn Reid in the Mary Couts Burnett Library for facilitating the acquisition of key sources. Juan Carlos Sola Corbacho, Ryan Schmitz and Denise Landeros, Dan Gil, Karla and Brandon O'Donald, Sohyun Lee, Freyca Calderon and Ricardo Suárez, Adam Fung, and Mona Narain have ensured that my family and I always feel welcome in Fort Worth. My appreciation to Steve Sherwood and the William L. Adams Center for Writing for their meticulous editing as I worked through each draft of the chapters that make up this book.

Collaborating with the University of Texas Press has been an enriching experience. I am most grateful to Kerry Webb for her unwavering support and to Angelica Lopez-Torres, Amanda Frost, Lynne Chapman, and Jon Howard, who carefully reviewed every aspect of this book and helped guide me through publication.

On a personal note, I would like to thank the Guzmán and the Vallejo families for hosting me in Mexico City, as well as Richard Headly-Soto and Aleksander Mesa for their hospitality while I conducted research in Washington, DC. A special thank-you to Judith and Michael Britt for their generosity and kindness, and to Anne Marie Jakobson, Rhea Thompson, and Michelle Garmon for their support. My deepest appreciation to Brian Singleton, Nancy Jones, Hope Antrim, Michael Utt, and Chris Antrim for their encouragement and good cheer. Enrique and Socorro Carrillo have gone out of their way to help me finish this project and to try to ensure I did not lose my sanity in the process—*muchas gracias*. Carlos Carrillo, Enrique Carrillo Regino, Gaby Alvarez, Sandy Solis, and Paulo Carrillo Solis and Marifer Carrillo Solis have encouraged and supported my efforts in countless ways. I am grateful for the love and support I have received from my aunts, Leticia Focareta and Bella Floridia, and most of all, from my late grandmother, Emma Ponce. Bianka and Federico Escobedo, Alexis and Hermes Vega, Eric Villegas and Yajaira Ríos, Héctor Villegas, John Focareta, Filipo Floridia, and José Luis and Guadalupe Sánchez have enriched my life and provided the strongest support network one can have. My extended family—Clemente Villegas, Pato Gómez, Faride Gutiérrez, Lidia González, Pedro García de León, Martha González, Jamil and Alma Salum, and Asela Castaños—has made the journey to complete this book much sweeter; so has my friendship with Fausto Castañeda, Miguel Enciso, Farah Salum, Guillermo Valencia, and Manuel Fernández. I wish to thank Poncho Carrillo, with whom I have bonded over our shared passion for music, history, and politics, and Juan Carlos Rodríguez, for always having my back.

I would have never followed this path had it not been for the encouragement of my mother, Mariza Sánchez, who taught me to dream, to work hard, and to pay attention to the universal language that binds us. My daughters Alys, Siena, and Chiara inspire me every day with their joy and their laughter. Finally, I want to share credit for this project with Gabriela Carrillo, my partner in life, with whom I hold the strongest bond of all.

TRAIL OF FOOTPRINTS

INTRODUCTION

All maps state an argument about the world.

BRIAN HARLEY, *THE NEW NATURE OF MAPS*

In 2011, the United Nations Educational, Scientific, and Cultural Organization (UNESCO) accepted a proposal from Mexico's national archive, the Archivo General de la Nación (AGN), to register 334 indigenous maps made between the sixteenth and eighteenth centuries into the Memory of the World Program.[1] AGN officials made the case that the maps reflected the sophistication of indigenous pictorial traditions after the Spanish invasion of the Americas, and they documented the need to develop the building's infrastructure for the care and storage of the maps.[2] UNESCO's announcement triggered a series of measures to guide contact with patrons. The most significant change resulted in the removal of the maps from public use, a security precaution deployed by the AGN to prevent theft or irreparable damage to the World Heritage records. Patrons now turn to Mapilu, a web platform based on the painstaking work of archivists at the AGN who from 1977 to 1982 restructured the organization of the archive's massive graphic collection.[3] By bringing together visual records including plans, maps, drawings, shields, and codices scattered across several collections, archivists produced a strong genealogical index for the native records. This book analyzes a subset of the UNESCO maps from the southern Mexican region of Oaxaca.

What prompted the use of maps during Mexico's colonial period? How did conquered peoples learn to make maps, and for whom did they make them? How well could users read and understand the maps they viewed? And more important, what argument did Indian maps make about the world? While most maps served as visual evidence in the assignment, use, or defense of land and spatial boundaries, people also used them in different contexts, sometimes as historical records, as objects of admiration, or as mnemonic devices during ritual celebrations. As Susan Pearce observes, an object "can exist in a number of situations, or social discourses, through the (often lengthy) course of its physical life."[4] In our own time, people use indigenous maps from the colonial period in old and new ways, a practice tied to spatial conflict as much as to political and state affairs, care and preservation, research, and monetary gain.[5] But from the late sixteenth century to the middle of the eighteenth, Mixtec, Nahua, and Zapotec maps played important roles in the definition of spatial boundaries, functioning as visual aids to assign land for agriculture, ranching, mining, and subsistence farming, as well as in legal disputes when deployed by litigants as evidence. Provincial bureaucrats, notaries, and imperial authorities used the maps to assess natural resources, geography, political organization, and regional history, and intellectuals collected and studied them for their historic value years later. Even after their initial commission, maps continued to inform disputes one or two hundred years after their making, circulating in town councils, notarial workshops, and judicial archives, and they found their way into the personal papers of prominent indigenous leaders across the region.

Mapmaking, I contend, fostered a new epistemology among the region's Spanish, Indian, and mixed-race communities used to negotiate the allocation of land. The craft of making maps drew from social memory, indigenous and European conceptions of space and ritual, and Spanish legal practices designed to adjust spatial boundaries in the New World. Indigenous mapmaking brought together a distinct coalition of social actors— Indian leaders, native towns, notaries, surveyors, judges, artisans, merchants, muleteers, collectors, and painters—who participated in the critical observation of the region's geographic features. Demand for maps advanced material technologies that drew from Indian botany and experimentation and established notarial methodologies tied to Iberian legal culture and archival practice. The resulting corpus of maps reflects a regional perspective tied to Oaxaca's decentralized political structure, its strategic location along a complex network of trade routes that facilitated the flow of goods and people across the central and southern reaches of the viceroyalty, and a fractured and rugged geography that shaped settlement patterns in the region.

ON INDIAN MAPS

The study of indigenous maps sits at the intersection of several overlapping historiographical narratives that explain the significance of mapmaking within wider debates about colonialism, technology, literacy, social memory, and artistic innovation. J. B. Harley's

groundbreaking scholarship on the history of early modern maps questioned longstanding assumptions that for generations privileged topographical accuracy and mathematical precision when assessing spatial relationships. Harley suggested we peer instead into the "invisible social world" underneath the surface of every map to examine each as a multifaceted object that brought together people, tools, and knowledge.[6] Subsequent work by historians of cartography wrestled with Harley's propositions, paying close attention to the experts who served sovereigns, ministers, and other ranking members of imperial courts across Europe to plot, describe, and possess lands known and unknown.[7] These groups used maps to measure territory, trade routes, potential revenue, taxes, and mineral extraction and to design or redevelop infrastructure. By the early 1990s, the geographer Mark Monmonier's now classic *How to Lie with Maps* (1991) dispelled many of the claims traditionally made about the veracity of maps by examining the varied strategies used by modern cartographers to manipulate data through cartographic projections and subject choices.

In the 1980s and 1990s, scholars of colonial Latin America applied the lessons of the cultural turn to explain the role of indigenous mapmaking in New World society. Studies by Barbara Mundy, Serge Gruzinski, and Dana Leibsohn framed our understanding of shifting modes of pictorial representation and of the context and political conditions under which people made maps.[8] Closely tied to visual analysis and postmodern sensibilities, these groundbreaking works searched for the subsumed voices of traditionally marginalized groups. Tied to mid-twentieth-century debates about continuity and change from the Late Post Classic to the early colonial periods, these studies closely examined the transition between pictorial and alphabetic systems of writing, the implications of nonalphabetic literacy among Indian societies in the Americas, and the collapse of indigenous knowledge brought on by Western learning.[9] In this recovery process, we learn that native painters wrestled with what Barbara Mundy dubs "double-consciousness," the set of local expectations that mapmakers catered to when making a map coupled with rules imposed by Spanish authorities who commissioned and inspected the maps.[10] Painters, observes Dana Leibsohn, neither fully gave in to Spanish demands nor emphatically resisted Western culture and pictorial traditions.[11] This mixture of flexibility and obstinacy described by Leibsohn characterizes the history of Indian maps.

Invariably, the story of indigenous mapmaking culminates in rapid decline. For Mundy, the implementation of imperial policy surrounding the allocation of land through royal grants, known as *mercedes*, during the last quarter of the sixteenth century initiated a process of "dispossession," through which maps "became the backdrop for alphabetic text." Mercedes maps, she observes, stripped native painters of their unique indigenous vision by shifting their attention from "the spatial substrate of collective identity" to "a picture of parcels of property for the use of acquisitive Spaniards."[12] By the early seventeenth century, disease wiped out large swaths of the Indian population, painters included, while an emphasis by authorities on alphabetic text rendered pictorial records obsolete. Whatever maps of indigenous origin circulated in later years, they functioned primarily for communal purposes and did not carry much legal value in viceregal courts. The prominent French cultural historian Serge Gruzinski observed early in his career that "although at the end of the sixteenth century we still find 'classical' glyphs painted with accuracy, more often the drawing had lost its strength, elegance, and consistency." This represented a definitive rupture from the creative works of an earlier generation of native painters.[13] *Trail of Footprints*, by tracking the lives of a collection of sixty maps made in the Oaxaca region from the 1570s to the 1730s, invites a reassessment of mapmaking during the long middle years of the colonial period.

SOURCES AND METHOD

Maps usually entered the public record to facilitate claims to land. Drawn primarily from the maps in the UNESCO registry, the AGN sample documents the relationship between people, knowledge, and land across various parts of the region, including the Mixteca, Tehuantepec, northern sierra, central valleys, and the coast (Figure i.1). Patrons from indigenous and Spanish backgrounds commissioned maps from native painters to petition or regularize land, to dispute boundary claims, to seek social privileges, and even to supply geographical information for royal efforts to account for Spain's vast holdings in the New World (Table i.1). Individuals and corporate entities, including townships, missionary orders, and lay brotherhoods, secured maps to start a variety of ventures, including sugar mills, livestock and cattle ranches, and fisheries. In other cases, religious authorities sought maps to establish parochial boundaries.

To read indigenous maps, we must peel back the three layers of content: cartographic signs, alphabetic writing, and materiality. Cartographic signs—graphic elements used to represent geographic features and the built environment—followed pictorial conventions tied to Mesoamerican visual traditions and to European culture. Bell-shaped hills known as *tepetl* that represented towns, partial rectangles that designated farmland, crosses associated with religious temples, and water glyphs that identified aquatic environments are some of the most common signs found on maps. In addition, painters represented elements of the built environment: churches, houses, fences, stables, sugar mills, and municipal buildings along with smaller features such as stone mounds that were used to define territorial boundaries.

TABLE I.1. *Sampled Indian maps, 1570–1730*

Petition for estancia de ganado menor	16
Petition for estancia de ganado mayor	5
Petition for caballerías	4
Site of land-size unspecified	4
Casería, or settlement of houses	1
Boundary verification	8
Compliance with fondo legal of 600 varas	2
Establishment of religious boundaries	1
Establishment of fisheries	1
Evidentiary support for land dispute	8
Relaciones Geográficas survey	5
Novillero, or steer ranch	1
Sugar mill	1
Infrastructure	1

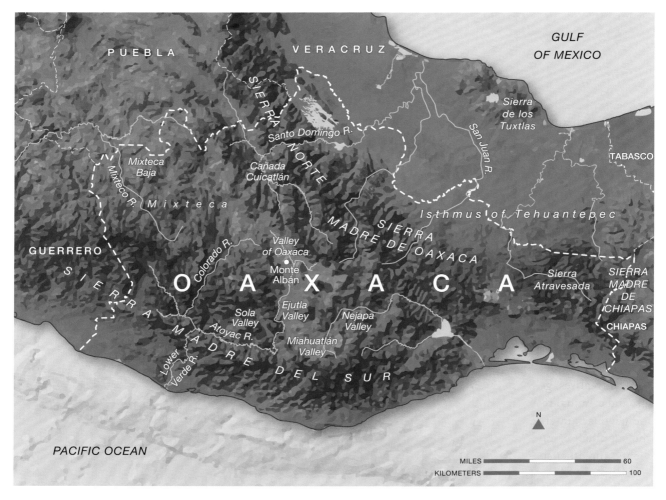

I.1. *Regions of Oaxaca. Map by Carol Zuber-Mallison, ZM Graphics.*

Likewise, they depicted natural elements: mountains, hills, rivers, trees, brush, flowers, and boulders as well as domesticated and wild animals such as horses, sheep, cows, jaguars, and serpents. Celestial bodies, most notably the sun and moon, regularly made appearances to designate cardinal directions or the movement of the stars; painters typically illustrated the features of a face on the body of the sun and moon, a visual strategy tied to European heraldry and alchemy. While not all elements appeared as regularly as others, painters found creative ways to represent what they needed, and they took care to explain their maps to those who read them.

The alphabetic glosses that appear on most maps reflect the intervention of scribes and authorities when they inspected a map to legitimate its content. Paleographic and diplomatic analysis, the study of ancient writing systems, and the critical reading of historical documents function as primary tools to unlock a map's second layer of content. Writing found on maps—the work of a scribe's detailed inspection—translated cartographic signs and visual imagery into words, established distances and directions to population centers and petitioned or disputed sites, and identified major trade routes, regional roads, and local trails. Writing legitimized cartographic records through annotation, dating, and signing, and it identified landholders, petitioners, and related parties. In some cases, writing in indigenous languages (including Mixtec, Nahua, and Zapotec) reveals the intervention of native painters and scribes seeking to establish authority over space and its visual representation.

To unearth a map's third layer of content, I analyze the materials used in the mapmaking process. Indigenous painters used a selection of organic and inorganic ingredients, including flowers, rocks, insects, dirt, bark, wood, and sap to produce a range of more than a dozen colors that regularly embellished the elements of a map. European rag paper, linen, animal skin, and native maguey paper served as the principal mediums on which indigenous painters articulated their visions of the geographic and political landscape. The study of materiality sheds light on indigenous knowledge in the natural sciences that contributed to the fabrication of substances used to paint a map and on the transformative influence of European ideas, tools, and ingredients on pictorial records. A unique source base composed of medical and natural treatises, general histories, orthography manuals, and criminal records references the extent to which indigenous painters engaged with the environment and the suppliers of raw materials to generate tools, pigments, and other supplies used to make maps.

Maps typically circulated with any number of legal records tied to agrarian issues.[14] They accompanied land grant petitions known as mercedes that flooded the courts in various parts of New Spain during the last few decades of the sixteenth century. Maps, along with topographical surveys, public announcements, and testimony from witnesses, allowed authorities to divide the land based on Iberian ideals of law and property. Edicts, legal codes, and notarial manuals help to contextualize the Crown's efforts to implement and regulate imperial policy in reference to land. In other cases, litigants introduced old maps as evidence of property ownership, especially starting in the second half of the seventeenth century when competition for natural resources in Oaxaca intensified. These dockets shed light on the highly contentious nature of land tenure, one exacerbated by ethnic tensions and the shifting health patterns brought on by disease. Likewise, a combination of chronicles, royal petitions, vocabularies, and firsthand reports known as *relaciones* help to contextualize the competing goals of indigenous leaders who negotiated on behalf of their families and the towns they represented. Indian maps often entered the archive under challenging circumstances, being viewed as objects of distrust and suspicion that underwent exacting scrutiny.

THE OAXACA REGION

Oaxaca serves as a fascinating case study to analyze mapmaking because of its rich pictorial traditions, decentralized political organization, important trade routes, and diverse human and geographic landscape. Pictorial writing and record-making in the era preceding the arrival of Europeans contributed to an active participation of Nahuas, Mixtecs, and Zapotecs in Oaxaca's manuscript culture.[15] Indigenous maps in Oaxaca circulated alongside codices of pre-Colombian and early colonial origin that have captivated North American and European scholars for generations. In most parts of Mesoamerica, screenfold manuscripts and other pictorial books and records recounted historical events, cosmology, genealogy, and calendrics. Codices disappeared by the second half of the sixteenth century under intense pressure from zealous Christian clerics fearful of their religious content, their tragic histories a constant reminder of the violent clash of civilizations that defined the age. The complexity of these records has kept art historians, archeologists, antiquarians, and collectors across time busy combing through the visual elements, changes in style, language patterns, and use of color.[16] Along similar lines, *lienzos* (genealogical and cartographic records painted on large cloth surfaces that combined logographic writing with pictorial imagery) also circulated during the sixteenth century when indigenous nobles and *caciques* (hereditary lords; leaders of indigenous groups) used them to recount historical events and petition land, goods, and privileges.[17] Neither genre circulated as widely, as often, or as forcefully in viceregal society as the maps used to allocate land, which make up the focus of this study.

The decentralized nature of sociopolitical organization in Oaxaca differed from the more urbanized and centralized political landscape in central Mexico. Ethnic states (known among Mixtecs as *ñuu*, among Zapotecs as *yetze*, and among Nahua as *altepetl*) formed the basic unit of organization, each one delimited by clear boundaries, a political structure, constituent units, temples and palaces, and an organized labor and tribute-producing system.[18] The Spanish-imposed *repúblicas de indios*—a blanket term based on the Castilian principle of land and municipal government—only partially coincided with the range of the ñuu or yetze, which incorporated elements of the sacred. Forced resettlements known as *congregaciones* during the sixteenth century and a series of epidemics that struck in the late sixteenth and early seventeenth centuries altered the social and political configurations of Indian landholdings in many regions of Oaxaca.[19] Affected by low numbers and extirpation campaigns, indigenous people in Oaxaca gradually adjusted to new regulations that continuously placed them at a disadvantage.

During the sixteenth century, the Crown, Spanish colonists, secular authorities, and the regular orders appropriated land previously controlled by the ruling native elite. In central Mexico, royal officials reassigned property, confiscated possessions, and limited the holdings of caciques, thereby reducing the amount of indigenous land in the region.[20] Officers from the Nahua altepetl—primarily *principales* (leaders of local affairs) and caciques—administered lands held in common, dividing and assigning plots as needed through the maintenance of communal and familial record-keeping. *Cacicazgos*—entailed estates held by generations of leading notables—diminished in size, earnings, and political prestige as a result of Spanish policies, labor drafts, and the seizure of land by other natives. In the sixteenth century, many caciques across central and southern Mexico enjoyed the labor of commoners who worked land to support the estate.[21] Alternatively, caciques in the Valley and the Mixteca held considerable land and access to labor even though a general decline in wealth defined many cacicazgos after the seventeenth century.[22] Some caciques capitalized on transitional periods to expand their holdings despite limitations in laws governing entailed estates. Renting cacicazgo lands, for instance, helped generate considerable income for caciques despite regulations that prohibited the practice.[23]

Spaniards settled primarily in major urban areas across Oaxaca during the sixteenth century, including Antequera, Teposcolula, and San Ildefonso de Villa Alta, though the number of colonists in Oaxaca was consistently small during the colonial period. Kevin Terraciano notes that little opportunity to prosper economically limited migration to Oaxaca, a region with "no great mines, few haciendas, and no *obrajes* (Spanish-run textile enterprises)."[24] During the first half of the century, the Crown awarded *encomiendas* (grants of Indian labor and tribute) to individual Spaniards in Oaxaca who used them to mine for gold or to extract cacao, cloth, dyes, maize, and cotton. *Encomenderos*—the holders of an encomienda—played prominent roles in local power relationships that also included Christian clerics, regional judges, and native caciques from whom they wrested power. The gradual decline of the system of encomienda during the second half of the sixteenth century, a planned effort on the part of the Crown to limit the ambitions of local strongmen, contributed to a heightened interest in land during the seventeenth century that continued into the eighteenth. Spaniards also controlled the legal mechanisms imposed by imperial authority to ensure social order. Bureaucrats, *alcaldes mayores* (chief magistrates of a region), *corregidores* (chief administrators of territorial units), scribes, lawyers, and a host of other officials worked and lived in Oaxaca, forming social networks with the rich cast of natives, Africans, Europeans, and individuals of mixed-race ancestry known as *castas*.[25]

The colonial trade routes (Figure i.2) that intersected Oaxaca's diverse human and ecological landscape, many dating to the pre-Hispanic period linking central Mexico with Central America, allowed for the circulation of a wide range of goods along the *caminos reales* that extended from Mexico City southward into Chiapas, Guatemala, and as far as Nicaragua. Along with the movement of dyestuffs for mapmaking, especially the prized blue colorant indigo, these same routes facilitated the circulation of legal and notarial records, knowledge, and information.[26] Those who engaged in long-distance trade also trafficked in documents, and some served as

1.2. *Principal roads of Oaxaca. Map by Carol Zuber-Mallison, ZM Graphics. Based on a map by Maribel Martínez and Cecilia Gutiérrez in María de los Ángeles Romero Frizzi, "Los caminos de Oaxaca."*

unlicensed legal agents for native communities.[27] The powerful link between flows of legal knowledge and the raw materials used to make maps owed much to Oaxaca's strategic location.

The imposing geographic landscape, one traversed by four different mountain ranges, contributed to Oaxaca's linguistic and ethnic diversity (Figure i.3). The region sits in Mexico's southwestern reaches and is dissected by the Eastern Sierra Madre, the Southern Sierra Madre, the Sierra Atravesada, and the Northern Sierra. Mountains not only provide cover against strong winds blowing

in from the Gulf of Mexico in the north and from the Pacific Ocean along Oaxaca's southern coastline; they also serve as sacred elements that helped to define social identities. Oaxaca's various regions—coastal, Isthmus, Mixteca, the central valleys, northern and southern sierra, Cañada, and Papaloapan—each enjoy varied climates, topographical features, flora, fauna, and aquatic life. The Isthmus of Tehuantepec in the southeast, the narrowest stretch of land between the Gulf of Mexico and the Pacific Ocean, is surrounded by mountains in the west and windy plains in the east and toward the

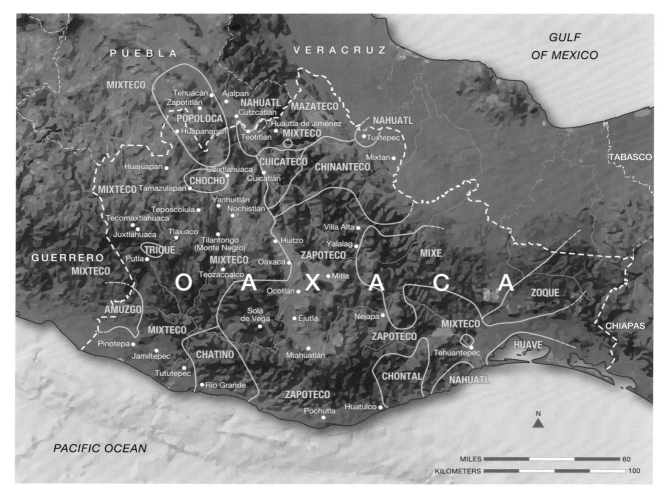

I.3. *Linguistic groups of Oaxaca. Map by Carol Zuber-Mallison, ZM Graphics. From John Paddock,* Ancient Oaxaca: Discoveries in Mexican Archeology and History *(Stanford: Stanford University Press, 1966).*

coast. The Atoyac River, one of the most extensive in the region, cuts across Oaxaca's central valleys, an area bound to the north by the Eastern Sierra Madre, to the south by the Southern Sierra Madre, and to the west by the Mixteca region. The Mixteca, a densely populated highland region that borders with the modern states of Puebla in the northwest and Guerrero to the west, shifts from arid and semidesert landscapes to steppes and wooded forests. Despite the broken and mountainous terrain that threatened to isolate the region from other parts of Mesoamerica, the peoples of Oaxaca maintained links with centers of power as a result of long-distance trade and commerce in the years before and after the wars of conquest in the sixteenth century. This duality, at once removed but also connected, allowed indigenous groups from Oaxaca to preserve a strong measure of independence, a salient characteristic that shaped indigenous land tenure in the region.

THE LONG SEVENTEENTH CENTURY

The temporal parameters of this book mirror the lives of the maps. Spread out over a period of 160 years

(1570–1730), the commission and use of indigenous maps in Oaxaca overlapped with the implementation of imperial mandates that guided colonization, new and revised policies that regulated land tenure, and fluctuation in the native population affected by disease, violence, and dislocation. Two major moments in time, from the 1570s to the 1600s and from the 1680s to the 1730s, frame my analysis of the routines—fieldwork and observation, technology and craft knowledge, transmission of social memory, and notarial validation—that shaped the map-making process.

In the years leading up to 1570, Spanish authority abroad faced a number of challenges. Outbreaks of violence in the Viceroyalties of Peru and New Spain led by local encomenderos threatened imperial power and exposed the vulnerabilities of governing a faraway empire. While encomenderos fought to retain their grants of labor in perpetuity, a reward they deemed appropriate for their service to settle the New World, royal authorities gradually dismantled the institution in order to prevent the rise of a powerful landed aristocracy. The Crown also had to contend with the evangelical project initiated in New Spain after the military defeat of the most powerful ethnic groups in Mesoamerica. Missionaries often clashed with the interests of an encomendero class more preoccupied with exploiting labor than providing spiritual education. The lack of personnel, dispersed settlement patterns, and diversity of languages made the spiritual life of native converts difficult to oversee, a process that led to the rise of syncretic rituals that scandalized church officials. Indians turned to the courts to litigate their cases directly with authorities, and they conspired against abusive judges, corrupt officials, and violent caciques. Behind closed doors, many still venerated the old gods, performing sacred rituals in caves and mountains. Natives negotiated with new leaders, learned to speak Spanish, and memorialized their histories in written, pictorial, and oral formats.

This difficult period exposed Spain's weaknesses for authorities to see. The historian Demetrio Ramos described this era in the late 1560s as the "crisis of the Indies," a pivotal moment when royal officials realized the policies that had guided colonization since the early

sixteenth century failed to properly address the needs of such a vast empire.[28] In response to the chaotic state of affairs, the King of Spain and his advisers launched a series of initiatives and issued new laws and policies designed to bring the Indies firmly under control. In the summer of 1568, the King convened his *junta magna*, a retreat that brought together top religious and secular advisers in Madrid, to draft new measures designed to maximize evangelical efforts in America and establish clear standards of social behavior. A few years later, authorities issued the *Ordenanzas* of 1573, a set of detailed orders for the discovery of new lands.[29] The ordinances included instructions about naming of provinces, mountains, and rivers, mandated the introduction and spread of Christianity, and regulated the circumstances under which people could launch expeditions by land or sea. More important, the new rules sought to improve the founding of settlements by providing specifications about the distribution of plots of land, the formation of town governments, and the implementation of urban design elements, including quadrilinear grids.[30] The laws regulated future expeditions into new lands and established guidelines that attempted to mitigate the violence associated with conquest.

The extent of King Philip's domains demanded detailed information about the New World's flora, fauna, geography, people, and history. Efforts to measure the region included an expedition by the Spanish physician Francisco Hernández, who spent seven years (1570–1577) in New Spain collecting detailed information about America's plants and their uses. With the appointment of Juan López de Velasco in 1571 as the cosmographer-chronicler attached to the Council of the Indies, Spain's principal unit of government that administered American affairs, the King hoped for a complete atlas and history of the region. Experts in astronomy and geography, the cosmographers for the Council of the Indies fulfilled an important role in the empire, defining the coordinates for places and boundaries and projecting them onto navigational charts.[31] To accomplish these tasks, López de Velasco first sent out an eclipse questionnaire in 1577 that sought to determine longitudinal measurements in order to map the various parts of the Hispanic world.

The following year, he sent out a survey to the Indies that asked provincial bureaucrats to inquire about the history of the region before the arrival of Europeans, the types of plants and animals found, and the major geographical features.[32] Known collectively as the Relaciones Geográficas, this effort mobilized regional bureaucrats, scribes, clerics, and translators who typically facilitated legal and commercial transactions across the Atlantic world to collect the desired information for the Crown. These types of projects relied on the bureaucratic structures that supported the administration of the empire as well as the well-developed commercial networks that allowed transatlantic commerce to flourish.

During the last quarter of the sixteenth century, the Crown intended to professionalize bureaucratic practices in the Indies by installing individuals who could place the empire's interests before their personal ambitions. The endless bickering and plotting of the conquistadors-turned-encomenderos who shaped the first phase of American colonization had taught authorities valuable lessons about the limits of empire.[33] Officials coupled this new stage of colonization with resettlement campaigns that attempted to congregate indigenous people from dispersed areas into tighter social units in order to make governing easier.[34] Mercedes de tierra, a system to distribute land institutionalized during the tenure of Viceroy Antonio de Mendoza, who governed New Spain from 1535 to 1550, gained renewed vigor in Oaxaca during the last three decades of the sixteenth century.[35] The land grant formed part of Iberian agricultural practices, and authorities used it in the New World to reward early settlers and to promote the cultivation of European crops and livestock. These new regulations gradually transformed the region's spatial boundaries.

Disease played another important role in the definition of space. By the first few decades of the seventeenth century, indigenous towns and settlements perished in droves as deadly pathogens rapidly spread across Mesoamerica. Oaxaca's central valley—the cultural and economic heart of the region—experienced dramatic loss. In 1570, Antequera registered nearly eight thousand tributaries, natives who paid a forced tax to Spanish authorities. By 1646, officials recorded only two thousand, a chilling loss that depleted three-quarters of the native population. The Cuatro Villas, an association of four powerful Indian towns (Cuilapa, Etla, Oaxaca, and Tecuilabacoya), reported similar patterns. A 1570 census listed more than seven thousand tributaries but only 849 by 1643.[36] Not surprisingly, the number of maps located in the archives made between 1610 and 1670 represents a fraction of those made during the last quarter of the sixteenth century.

The second half of the seventeenth century witnessed the gradual recovery of the native population in Oaxaca. Demographic growth intensified inter- and intraethnic tensions over land and spatial boundaries, longstanding markers of collective identity in the region. As a result, the courts witnessed a flood of complaints between Indians, Spaniards, and mixed-race people that often lasted for decades.[37] The composición de tierras decree of 1631, a policy intended to regulate land ownership, forced native communities to produce formal titles that they often did not possess.[38] Those who could not present a proper title lost their claim to land, while those with defective titles could pay a fee to correct the legal records; in each case, failure to comply reverted lands to the King.[39] In the 1680s, authorities increased the extension of the fundo legal, the minimum space allocated to each Indian community, from 500 varas, roughly 1,375 feet, to 600 varas, or 1,605 feet.[40] Although this measure benefited smaller settlements in need of agricultural land, it adversely affected larger towns that claimed bigger expanses of land. Royal authorities sought to generate funds and to regulate land tenure in order to manage it more effectively, at times reviving old rivalries or provoking disagreements between neighbors that often led to litigation. In his study of Mexican mapping routines of the nineteenth and early twentieth century, Raymond Craib has noted that "sharp lines of political and proprietary demarcation are neither timeless nor natural. . . . The result of requiring villagers to precisely fix their borders could often spur as many conflicts as it resolved."[41] The combination of factors described above contributed to the production of indigenous maps during this later period.

Although the output of native pictorials in the seventeenth century was not as substantial as the production of maps in the late sixteenth century, maps continued to circulate within the local and regional court system and among individuals and town governments. This practice allowed people of various backgrounds—especially Spanish officials and notaries as well as interpreters and witnesses—to come into contact with pictorial manuscripts, thus fostering a limited, but practical, knowledge of the region's cartographic vocabulary. Indigenous mapmaking sometimes served as evidence in territorial disputes, certifications of land, compliance with new ordinates, and the occasional infrastructure project. During this time, painters reinvented older pictographic conventions to fit contemporary social and political needs much like the earlier generations from the sixteenth century had done to accommodate Spanish colonization. These practices carried well into the eighteenth century.

The death of Charles II in 1700, the last Habsburg monarch, ushered in a new era of rule in the Americas. Much like their Habsburg predecessors, Bourbon officials deployed scientific expeditions to assess natural and human wealth, developed a new geographical survey project to gauge demographic growth and land tenure, and attempted to curb the rise of local elites by restructuring the organs of government. Bourbon policies often clashed with local power structures whose members faced exclusion from key administrative and judicial posts. The growth of the population and the competition for land and resources mandated a more precise system of representation to fulfill the needs that indigenous maps had once filled.[42] In this period, surveying by professional topographers and cartographers played a much more significant role in the definition of spatial boundaries across the viceroyalty. Despite these changes, indigenous mapmaking sometimes informed surveying, ritualized boundary-walking, and witness testimony, and they continued to circulate within the local and regional court system and among individuals and town governments.

TRAIL OF FOOTPRINTS

The footprint emerged in the sixteenth century as the most enduring element of mapmaking. Feet used in pre-Colombian codices symbolized journeys, a reminder that a great lord once embarked on a quest of marriage or to wage war in an effort to preserve a lineage or to expand a domain. The use of feet acquired new meaning during the last quarter of the sixteenth century when a new generation of painters adapted its use to make pictorial records, most notably community and regional maps used to petition and to defend land. Feet often accompanied an intricate system of roads through which people and goods circulated; more important, they connected settlements to one another by helping to establish spatial priorities. Tracking the imprints of the various actors who played a part in the production and circulation of maps across space and time represents this book's main objective.

Chapter 1 ("Patrons") analyzes the role of Oaxaca's indigenous communities, caciques, and others who commissioned maps. Why did these social actors require maps in the first place? What context defined the production of maps? An analysis of a lengthy dispute between Santa Cruz Xoxocotlán, a Mixtec town in the Valley of Oaxaca, and the owners of a neighboring ranch over five acres of arable land serves as a case study to contextualize land disputes and the sociopolitical organization of the region. "Thick description" of the lengthy dossier that documents the dispute offers an intimate portrayal of the way social actors maintained and generated collective memories about the past in their efforts to protect property. The case unfolded during a period of intense competition over land and geographic resources, one that privileged written titles and documents instead of Indian pictorials and maps. In 1686, officials introduced an old and tattered map as evidence to support their appeal over ownership of the contested land. Xoxocotlán claimed the map defined the boundaries, but over forty years of litigation officers of the Mixtec town had never used it as evidence, arousing suspicion among the opposing party. Mapmaking formed part of the tradition of spatial practices that engaged Iberian law and notarial culture as well as ritual boundary-walking and witness testimony. Maps interpreted the natural environment and its social relationships according to indigenous traditions. Natives demonstrated discerning tactics to navigate Spanish legal channels, although, as the case of

Xoxocotlán suggests, their efforts could sometimes go unrewarded.

In chapter 2 ("Painters"), I examine the role of indigenous painters, who acted as intermediary figures between the Spanish and native worlds. They formed part of several overlapping sectors involved in the division of land and the allocation of privileges and goods that generated the need for maps in the first place. As participating members of the region's vibrant manuscript culture, painters occupied unique positions of power alongside the loose association of scribes, notaries, lawyers, clerks, translators, caciques, and clerics involved in the production of written records. Chronicles, petitions to the Crown, and land dispute records help trace the footsteps of these illusive figures, individuals who exercised pictorial dexterity rooted in local traditions but who seldom signed their maps. Painters gained versatility as a result of their training with friars and native elders, their interactions with Spanish bureaucrats, their ventures into agriculture, and their participation in local political affairs. The ability to speak several languages allowed them to communicate with authorities who inspected and validated maps and with indigenous patrons claiming vested interests in land. Painters forged new signs and concepts and recast old ones to help articulate local geography and the subtleties that governed spatial relationships.

A striking feature of indigenous maps from Mexico's colonial past is the use of vibrant colors to represent geographic space. Rich shades of red and blue, earth tones, and glossy black ink gave meaning to the symbols of a map, yet seldom do we ask about the way in which painters made and obtained these colors. Chapter 3 ("Materials") probes the material dimensions of the maps to recover a body of knowledge centered on the transformation of plants and inorganic matter into working components. A combination of medical and natural treatises, general histories, orthography manuals, and criminal records suggests the extent to which painters engaged with the environment in their depictions of spatial relationships and the way commerce and trade shaped a map's features. Fieldwork and experimentation characterized cartographic technology, a practical art that included the collection of rocks, flowers, insects,

and soil in their natural state that mapmakers sampled to produce their rich palette of colors. The introduction of European materials transformed the range and function of pictorial records in New Spain. Rag-based paper and iron-gall ink—the handy tools of every Spanish scribe—pushed painters to consider the needs of the royal authorities who commissioned maps. Changes in material technology over time reflect the needs of native patrons increasingly involved in land dispute settlements to protect patrimonial assets and the devastating population loss that subjected indigenous learning and knowledge to change. The application of materials and dyeing techniques contributed to the distinct style of Indian maps, forcing users to engage with the priorities of indigenous visions of place.

Few records received more scrutiny and such heavy annotation as indigenous-made maps from central and southern Mexico. At the local level in the viceroyalty, the burden of mapping fell on Spanish bureaucrats and indigenous painters. Authentication, a multifaceted effort to legitimize the contents of a native map, which forms the subject of chapter 4 ("Authentication"), marks a critical site of knowledge where social actors defined and contested land and territorial boundaries. Fraught with tension due to differences embedded in the Spanish legal system that favored the European minority, authentication made maps legible by relying on written notarial formulas designed to shape and classify individuals and their activities. Conferring sameness to maps represented an official's most important task, as it facilitated communication between authorities and users at different stages of the process. "This is true and faithful," they certified on countless occasions after reviewing a map, branding it with their signatures in an act of possession that sought to convey authority in the state's eyes. But reducing signs and pictorial representation to alphabetic expression proved to be an imperfect process burdened by the mediation of translators and litigants, the effects of oppressive land-related policies, and the inconvenience of cultural dissimilarities.

The epilogue ("Afterlife") serves as a final comment on the significance of the map trade in viceregal society and the knowledge that emerged from spatial activities.

Using a series of inventories and correspondence that resulted from the 1743 imprisonment of an Italian historian named Lorenzo Boturini, we follow indigenous maps across time and space. For eight years, Boturini scoured monastic libraries, secular and clerical archives, native *cabildo* (a council for administrating local matters) holdings, cacique family papers, and individual collectors across central New Spain in search of original sources that would help him write a general history of the region. The Italian's holdings included Nahua calendar wheels, annals, painted tributary records, migration histories, and indigenous-language notarial documents along with cartographic histories, genealogical drawings, and more than a hundred native maps. What mechanisms allowed him to secure so many records despite strong efforts to suppress the circulation of Mesoamerican pictorials? What interest did authorities have in recovering, conserving, and annotating these valuable documents? The circulation of maps in the decades following their original commission suggests that, besides their legal status, maps acquired value as objects worthy of study. This afterlife—a moment divorced from their sixteenth- and seventeenth-century origin—extended the age of a map by plunging it into new social dimensions guided by interest in the past. In light of the five themes explained in the following chapters of *Trail of Footprints*, it is my contention that Boturini seized on the knowledge cultivated by cartographic activities to fulfill his goals.

1.1. *Map of Santa Cruz Xoxocotlán (1686), no. 625, Tierras, vol. 129, exp. 4, f. 249. Archivo General de la Nación, Fondo Hermanos Mayo, concentrados, sobre 363.*

CHAPTER 1

PATRONS

In the fall of 1686, Antonio de Abellán y Carrasco needed a map. As alcalde mayor of the Cuatro Villas del Marquesado, Abellán oversaw a range of civil and criminal cases involving the region's Indian, Spanish, and African members. Abellán mediated a case between a local Spaniard named Bartolomé Ruíz and Santa Cruz Xoxocotlán, a Mixtec town south of Antequera, the Spanish seat of power in the region.[1] The parties disputed ten measures (Table 1.1) of a livestock ranch known as an *estancia de ganado menor* effectively under Ruíz's control.[2] On October 3, two political officers from Xoxocotlán appeared before Abellán to present an ancient map they said described all of the town's land.[3] The two men suggested the map would facilitate the alcalde mayor's impending survey of Xoxocotlán's property, but because of its physical state, "worn by the passage of time," they petitioned a copy. Abellán evaluated the request and commissioned the task to a *maestro pintor*, or master painter. Three weeks later officials from the town accompanied an Indian *cacique* named Domingo de Zárate to meet with Abellán to examine the copy he had made of the ancient map (Figure 1.1).[4]

Why would a Spanish official commission a map from an Indian painter to help mitigate a land dispute in one of the most contentious regions of the viceroyalty?

This chapter analyzes the circumstances that prompted the use of maps and the people who commis-

TABLE 1.1. *Spanish units of measure.*

Vara	33 inches
League	2.6 miles
Medida	One-half acre; unit of agricultural land
Caballería	105 acres; unit of agricultural land
Estancia de ganado menor	Three square miles; livestock ranch
Estancia de ganado mayor	6.76 square miles; cattle ranch

Source: William Taylor, Landlord and Peasant in Colonial Oaxaca *(Stanford: Stanford University Press, 1972).*

sioned them and benefited from their use. Maps fulfilled the needs of authorities interested in identifying towns, plots, boundaries, rivers, mountains, and roads as they divided and exploited their domains. Individuals used them to petition officials for land and to protect personal and corporate interests. The new epistemology of maps took shape in response to the flood of litigation associated with land, a process that brought together networks of notaries, artisans, ranchers, caciques, merchants, and translators.

Indigenous maps usually entered the public record to facilitate claims to land. Michael Baxandall's analysis of early Italian Renaissance painting offers a helpful model to consider the commission of maps. He proposes that "a fifteenth-century painting is the deposit of a social relationship. On one side there was a painter who made the picture, or at least supervised its making. On the other side, there was somebody else who asked him to make it, provided funds for him to make it, and after he made it, reckoned on using [it] in some way or other."[5] While individuals in Italy commissioned paintings largely as luxury goods to enhance their status, in Oaxaca map commissions informed more utilitarian efforts associated with land tenure and agrarian issues. Over time, people often endowed some maps with great authority, communal treasures used to recount local histories during ritual celebrations and to defend town patrimony under threats of encroachment. Although marked differences exist between Renaissance patronage and indigenous cartography, the process by which maps entered into the public record also witnessed the "deposit of social relationships" among those involved with the commission and use of indigenous maps.

What sort of social relationships did the commission of indigenous maps help forge? The case of Xoxocotlán, a lengthy docket of over three hundred folios and the copied map, offers an intimate glimpse into rituals of space, political power shifts, generational affiliations, and legal strategies that individuals used to defend land. Untangling these "knotted" structures, a metaphor advanced by Clifford Geertz to explain the complex forms strongly tied to religious practice, language, and elements of everyday life, provides the necessary context to understand the need for maps in the first place.[6] The dossier includes a mixture of land titles, survey inspections, witness testimony, complaints and accusations, certifications, verdicts, and appeals. Because the records span a period of fifty years, roughly 1640 to 1690, tracing ownership of the disputed land includes several generations of indigenous and Spanish landholders. In addition, the extended timeline allows us to analyze the choices provincial bureaucrats made when presented with various forms of written, pictorial, and oral evidence. Like countless other cases that form part of the colonial archive, this one reveals the tenacity of indigenous litigants, changes in the standard of land ownership, the multiplicity of interests held by ethnically and economically diverse social actors, and the extremes to which these actors would go to protect their assets.

Unlike a majority of other land dispute cases, this one included an old and tattered map that reputedly linked the Mixtec town to the five acres of disputed land. A visual analysis of the copied map followed by an examination of the map's reception within the legal circuits where it circulated reveals the advantages and limitations of pictorial manuscripts in legal disputes. The copied map, a strategic representation of space used to describe the town's land as well as local social and political structures, formed a unique aspect of spatial practices in the Valley. Mapping forced viewers to wrestle with the continued, but not always welcome, use of pictorial records.

THE SETTING

The Valley of Oaxaca (Figure 1.2) sits on a 700-square-kilometer area where three major mountain ranges collide. During the colonial period, its rich soil, temperate climate, and thriving trade networks hosted a diverse population that included Zapotecs, Mixtecs, Nahuas, Spaniards, Africans, and *mestizos* (individuals of mixed-race ancestry).[7] Unlike other regions of New Spain, Indian towns and individuals retained control of two-thirds of the land in the region by the end of the eighteenth century. This situation contrasts sharply with northern and central Mexico, where natives progressively lost territory to Spanish-dominated *haciendas* (landed estates with a mixed economy of cattle and agriculture). Writing in the

1970s, William Taylor challenged the idea that haciendas functioned as the dominant form of land tenure in Mexico, a notion advanced in François Chevalier's *Land and Society in Colonial Mexico*. Although haciendas existed in Oaxaca, Taylor argued they were simply another type of landholding rather than the principal form of social organization proposed by Chevalier. Later studies further contextualized regional variances that challenged the hacienda model of an earlier generation of scholars.[8] The Valley's unique experience stemmed from a less violent conquest compared to central Mexico, a smaller number of Spaniards in the region, and a more effective enforcement of laws designed to protect Indians.[9] *Repúblicas de indios*—the Spanish category most often used to designate native townships—competed fiercely over spatial boundaries, contributing to the high rate of litigation in the region.[10] These "micropatriotic" efforts to protect social organization and defend land from ethnic rivals

1.2. Map of the Valley of Oaxaca. Map by Carol Zuber-Mallison, ZM Graphics.

characterized indigenous townships across Mesoamerica, a process also mirrored by Spaniards in New Spain.[11]

Land held exceptional value in the Valley. It yielded basic foodstuffs including maize, wheat, and sugarcane as well as a variety of fruits and vegetables including beans, avocados, maguey, onions, figs, and tomatoes. Land provided pasture for goats, sheep, cattle, horses, and swine and supplied wood for fuel and building materials.[12] Spaniards most commonly held haciendas, *estancias de ganado mayor* (cattle ranches), smaller livestock estates known as *labores*, and estancias de ganado menor.[13] In addition to farming and livestocking sites, indigenous groups placed a high premium on land because of its ritual value tied to cellular units of social organization known as *ñuu* in Mixtec communities and *yetze* among Zapotec ones.[14] Marcello Carmagnani suggests that, in the seventeenth and eighteenth centuries, land among Mixtecs and Zapotecs was tied to a revival of ethnic values and political organization, efforts that sought to curb the effects of colonialism.[15] "Territory," he writes, "was conceived as something altogether sacred and earthly. Sacred because it was the spatial dimension conferred by the gods to its children and earthly because it was the human and geographical space capable of synthesizing the fulfillment of everyday needs and the reproduction of future generations."[16] In the Valley, residents competed across ethnic lines to secure local boundaries, revealing in the process a web of interests that shaped spatial practices.

The region's rich manuscript culture—a coalition of scribes, clerks, lawyers, translators, mapmakers, and assorted Spanish and Indian officials—generated various types of handwritten documents for individuals and corporate entities engaged in commercial and legal affairs. Native lords and towns, the Catholic Church, Spanish landholders, and religious brotherhoods known as *cofradías* all procured titles, boundary surveys, maps, testimonies, and auction records to serve as evidence in matters related to land. A unique aspect of manuscript culture in Oaxaca involves the circulation of indigenous maps, pictorials, and alphabetic records written in native languages.[17] Individuals relied on the use of manuscripts to verify a claim and on witnesses to legitimate that claim through memory. Manuscripts as well as memory worked in tandem to secure a favorable judgment but were themselves subjected to the power dynamics of each locality.

Important roads converged in the central valleys, helping to move records, goods, and people but also to shape spatial boundaries. The *ruta mixteca* (Figure i.2), a pair of parallel roads that traversed a densely populated highland region that covered the western portion of Oaxaca, channeled the most important goods.[18] The two paths connected central Mexico, Oaxaca, and Guatemala to local and regional trade networks where important commodities including indigo, cochineal dye, silk, and cacao circulated alongside everyday items such as candles, paper, clothing, and wine. At Tehuacán, an important Nahua transportation hub that also connected to Puebla in the north and to Veracruz in the northeast, one of the roads made its way southward along the edges of the Sierra Madre. Travelers could choose a second road through Izúcar, a hot and dry region in southwestern Puebla, as they journeyed to Tezoatlán in the center of the Mixteca Baja in the Sierra Madre del Sur. From Tezoatlán, one could travel south to the coast toward Pinotepa, select a number of internal pathways that connected the region, or continue on to the central valleys.

In the sixteenth century, the introduction of draft animals, wagons, and carriages required wider pathways and gentler slopes than those that formed part of the rich network of roads used during the pre-Colombian era when *tamemes* (human carriers) provided the transportation of goods.[19] But Oaxaca's mountainous and rugged terrain limited the use of wheeled vehicles to the central valleys and the plains of Tehuantepec.[20] Elsewhere, carriers and, in some cases, mule trains navigated the treacherous and narrow corridors that connected settlements to one another.

The two roads from Izúcar and Tehuacán met at Huautlilla in the Mixteca Alta before descending into the central valleys. Travelers could then make their way south via Ocotlán and Ejutla to Huatulco, which served as the main port of entry in the sixteenth century for goods coming in from Asia, connecting the Pacific and Atlantic worlds, or they could travel southeast along

El Camino Real—the Royal Highway—that made its way to Guatemala via Tehuantepec in the Isthmus region. As María de los Ángeles Romero Frizzi has observed, despite the fact authorities had to care for the royal roads, the fractured nature of Oaxaca's terrain prevented the construction of more than "simple paths," most of which had existed for generations.[21] Nonetheless, these roads represented key arteries that funneled thousands of petitions, land disputes, and other important records that traveled back and forth between Oaxaca and Mexico City and, sometimes, via sea to Seville and Madrid.

NEGOTIATING LAND

Individuals and corporate entities in the Valley often turned to the courts in matters related to land. For a large part of the seventeenth century, Xoxocotlán and the owners of a neighboring hacienda west of the town quarreled over the limits of five acres of land defined by an assortment of trees (Figure 1.3). According to Xoxocotlán, the five acres formed part of its patrimonial lands since time immemorial. Three successive hacienda owners argued the five acres formed part of an estancia de ganado menor sold by a cacique from Cuilapa to Francisco Muñoz de Tejada, a Spanish landholder, to add to the property. Beginning in the 1640s, the town and the hacienda owners litigated on separate occasions over the course of fifty years for control of this property. During each instance, the parties involved presented written evidence, witnesses provided oral testimony, and officials surveyed the physical terrain, resulting in a verdict followed by a break in litigation. Tensions usually resurfaced when a new owner took over the hacienda property, each new tenant claiming the right to the estancia including the five acres of land and contesting the limits declared by Xoxocotlán. The records indicate the town relied on the testimony of elder Indian males and some influential Spaniards to attest to the town's claims. After decades of successful litigation, Xoxocotlán lost the right to the five acres in the early 1680s when it failed to provide a written title. The three phases analyzed below contextualize spatial practices used to divide, to defend, and to assign meaning to the natural environment, all of which led to the introduction of the copied map in 1686.

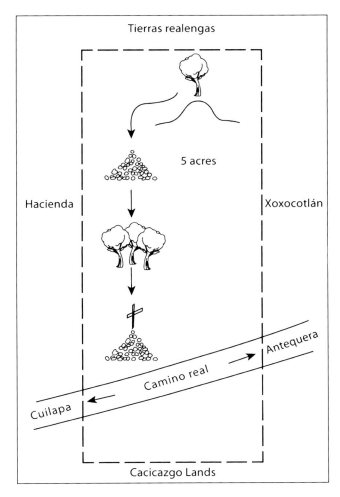

Tierras realengas

5 acres

Hacienda

Xoxocotlán

Antequera

Camino real

Cuilapa

Cacicazgo Lands

1.3. *Disputed land.*

The Red Roses Tree (1643–1649)

In 1643, officials from Xoxocotlán complained to the courts about the Spanish landholder Francisco Muñoz de Tejada. According to the complaint, Muñoz violently expelled Diego Juárez, Juan Jacinto, and other Indians on September 24 as they cut wood along a contested boundary northwest of Xoxocotlán's church. Muñoz, they argued, attempted to kill Juárez and the others with a spear and took away their axes, humiliating them and committing other unspecified offenses.[22] Muñoz had also prevented Xoxocotlán's horses and oxen from grazing freely, further angering the Indians and causing the

animals much harm. To prevent additional altercations, officers from Xoxocotlán petitioned Hernando Ortiz de Sepúlveda, the alcalde mayor of the Cuatro Villas, to affirm the limits of their town's land in a process known as *amojonar*, a survey of natural and manmade boundaries to define property limits.[23] Yanna Yannakakis contends that "ritual boundary marking emerged as a particularly salient spatial practice because of the degree to which indigenous people accepted Spanish notions of property, in which firm boundaries were critically important."[24] Amojonar comprised a key element to assign value to space in Oaxaca.

On September 28, the town's political officers and other members of the community, along with Ortiz, Muñoz, and Nicolás Rodríguez, a bilingual scribe fluent in Nahuatl, gathered at the top of a hill toward the western portion of Xoxocotlán's domains. The Indian officers pointed to a tree that blossomed with red roses (*árbol de rosas coloradas*) and said it was the first boundary marker, or *mojón*. They led the group southward down the hill, stopping along the way long enough to rebuild an ancient boundary stone (*mojón antiguo*) as they journeyed toward the next marker, which skirted El Camino Real. When they reached this ancient mojón, the source of the conflict, the scribe recorded the following passage: "When we arrived at the Royal Highway that comes from Antequera to the Villa of Cuilapa, we found another stone mojón the Indians said was ancient and they placed a cross there. They asked the alcalde mayor to witness the way they had arranged the markers."[25] This symbolic act of possession sought to preserve both the boundary marker and the memory of its renewal in written form. The act was designed to serve as a memory trigger, allowing later generations to reference it in their own disputes with neighbors.

Muñoz had purchased the estancia nine years earlier from Don Gerónimo de Lara y Guzmán, a powerful cacique from nearby Cuilapa. Lara, a Spanish-speaking Indian described as *ladino* who wore Spanish dress, boasted: "For some of us, selling them is of no consequence, [as] there are many more lands that form part of our *cacicazgo* [entailed Indian estate] which we farm and lease to others."[26] Caciques, the native hereditary lords, often held entailed estates, but their power varied from region to region. When called to testify about the limits of his estancia, Lara agreed with Xoxocotlán that the piece of land in dispute did not form part of the original sale. Five witnesses, including four Spaniards and an Indian cacique, confirmed Lara's reputable character and proper lineage, swaying the alcalde mayor to recognize the boundary claimed by Xoxocotlán. Except for Lara's testimony, no written title appears to have accompanied the Indian town's defense of its boundary, a fact not lost on Muñoz.

Muñoz urged the alcalde mayor to reconsider his decision. For Muñoz, the lack of a written title placed the Indians of the town, not himself, at a disadvantage, a point he made clearly in a deposition before a scribe on October 3, 1643. He asserted that his title, a *merced* (royal land grant) issued in 1591 to cacique Juan Guzmán, a relative of Don Gerónimo, specified the location of the estancia, and he petitioned authorities to measure the landscape.[27] He further argued that "the Indians had not presented authentic proof to confirm that the lands were theirs," adding that, in fact, he was one of the first holders (*primeros poseedores*) of the property, a testimony of time that sought to bind him to the land.[28] On the surface, Muñoz's appeal fulfilled the key elements for a successful lawsuit in New Spain, namely the presentation of a title of ownership. In 1644, judges at the Real Audiencia in Mexico City, the viceroyalty's highest judicial authority, reviewed the case and issued an *auto*, an official sentence, that instead confirmed alcalde mayor Ortiz de Sepúlveda's decision to uphold Xoxocotlán's claim to the five acres of land.

In Oaxaca, the notion of "time immemorial," especially among fiercely competitive ñuu, served to strengthen the bonds between individuals and place by according first settlers a privileged status. Royal decrees issued in 1588 and again in 1594 stipulated that "estancias and lands awarded to Spaniards should not be detrimental to Indians," embedding an element of time into the possession of land.[29] Recourse to this device, especially in the absence of a legal title, appealed to an official's sense of tradition and called into play the elements of custom and local rule. Joanne Rappaport and Tom Cummins

point out that, in the Andes, the use of time immemorial sought to "advance claims by transcending an imperfect paper trail through expanding the scope of written evidence by means of an appeal to oral tradition."[30] It served as an epistemological category of notarial culture used to scrutinize witness testimony, specifically the way people obtained knowledge they introduced into the written record.[31] People in early modern Spain, likewise, introduced similar rhetoric into litigation and petitions to the Crown when negotiating natural resources.[32]

When the natives from Xoxocotlán brought caciques and elder witnesses to testify on their behalf, they sought to establish an ongoing relationship between the past and present that had a direct bearing on land disputes by drawing from peoples' collective memories. Collective memories expressed a continual link to the past, pliable by those who used them and constantly in danger of disappearance.[33] Muñoz's claim as a first settler on the property near Xoxocotlán sought to challenge the Indians' own claim of time immemorial. Indeed, memories played an important role in shaping the contours of the Valley of Oaxaca's spatial boundaries, but they "represented a construct that masked competing claims through the political domination of a particular group of elites."[34] During this first moment of contention, a period that lasted roughly from 1644 through 1649, the natives from Xoxocotlán successfully retained the property that bordered the neighboring hacienda. They did so without a formal title, relying instead on powerful Indian witnesses such as Don Gerónimo de Lara to support their claim.

Xoxocotlán v. Antonio Rendón (1649–1660)

Francisco Muñoz's nephew inherited his uncle's hacienda and sold it in 1649 prior to his death to another Spaniard by the name of Antonio Rendón, a treasurer for the Church in Antequera. By 1655, Rendón made advances on the same portion of land, prompting Xoxocotlán to ratify the 1644 *amparo*, a judicial record that protected the boundaries defined during their litigation against Muñoz.[35] Brian Owensby observes that the amparo served as a legal instrument designed to fulfill the King's mandate to care for the realm's most vulnerable members. Beginning in the late sixteenth century, natives turned increasingly to amparos as a legal tool to mitigate boundary disputes. These records often followed certain prescriptions in which peaceful plaintiffs in rightful possession of land suffered at the hands of devious offenders who willfully intended to cause harm to their property.[36] The case of Xoxocotlán in this second phase of litigation followed a similar pattern.

According to their petition, individuals under Rendón's employ attempted to gain control of the land by sowing maguey plants and allowing Rendón's cattle to graze freely, a practice that greatly damaged the natives' parcels. Juan Pérez de Salamanca, Xoxocotlán's attorney, stated his clients held property that belonged to their community, which they had possessed since time immemorial.[37] Pérez de Salamanca emphasized the Mixtec town's relationship to the past by relying on the older manuscripts to establish a claim, especially since they included a boundary survey that described Xoxocotlán's *mojones*. The importance of memory and manuscripts can be gleaned from a declaration provided by the officials from Xoxocotlán two years later in 1657 while the case was still unresolved: "[Our lands are] here marked and surveyed as is clearly evident from these documents we present. . . . We request you order the limits and boundaries of our lands be respected, and to newly protect our borders with an amparo according to the aforementioned manuscripts."[38] Clearly, to the natives from Xoxocotlán the fact that their mojones were memorialized in written form in prior years acted as a shield to protect their property.

Manuscripts produced to defend land stand out as important sites that capture collective memories, revealing the way individuals interacted with the past. In the Valley of Oaxaca, notaries recorded a range of experiences including petitions and complaints, notification of witnesses, public announcements and auctions of land, presentations of written, pictorial, and oral evidence, and land surveys to measure spatial extension. Ultimately, the relationship between individuals, corporate entities, and land was ritualized and recorded in public acts of possession that brought together litigants,

townspeople, Spanish and Indian authorities, translators, witnesses, and painters to divide any given estate in the region. In each of these cases, mastery of the past in oral and written form supported the heavy burden of maintaining land in a contested environment such as the Valley.

In 1657, Spanish officials visited Xoxocotlán to inspect and protect the boundary markers in dispute. In this case, political officers from the Indian town engaged collective memories about their territorial limits through an examination of written documents, but also by recalling the physical landscape that bore evidence of earlier boundary inspections. On October 25, 1657, officials from Xoxocotlán led Spanish authorities as well as the hacienda's custodian (*mayordomo*), Manuel de Leyva, once again to the top of the hill toward the western flanks of the town where the survey commenced. The scribe noted a pile of large and small rocks next to a set of trees that included a wild fig and a crimson rose, the latter presumably the same one described over a decade earlier during the inspection with Francisco Muñoz. After the alcalde mayor protected (*amparó*) the boundary, the group followed southward until they reached another group of rocks the Indians described as "the ancient mojón referred to in said manuscripts."[39] By highlighting the earlier encounter, the town sought to establish a relationship between the boundary and the manuscript's content to strengthen their claim. The entourage passed a group of plum trees not mentioned in the previous survey on their way to the last mojón, a cross on the edge of the Royal Highway erected by former Indian officials during their boundary walk with Muñoz in September 1643. It is evident from the day's transcription that the representatives from Xoxocotlán and the Spanish officials relied on the older manuscript and the memory of each mojón to confirm the limits of the property. At the end of the day, the alcalde mayor protected Xoxocotlán's lands with an amparo instructing the hacienda's mayordomo not to trespass or let Rendón's cattle graze beyond the limits described in the document.

Three months later, on February 5, 1658, officials from Xoxocotlán returned to Antequera to present the alcalde mayor, Pablo Fajardo de Aguilar, a signed document by

New Spain's viceroy, Francisco Fernández de la Cueva, which ratified the earlier amparo. Fajardo followed prescribed rituals and guidelines when handling the folios, noting, "having seen it, I took it in my hands, kissed it, and placed the letter from my King and natural lord above my head to carry out [any orders] in compliance with His Majesty's wishes."[40] One year later, the natives from Xoxocotlán again petitioned an amparo to protect their boundaries: their *mojoneras* had started to disappear. The town's request stated that their mojones had "deteriorated with time" but also that some people intentionally removed them to cause them harm. On May 5, 1659, officials from Xoxocotlán, Spanish authorities, and other assorted guests gathered again at the hilltop with the fig tree and crimson roses to follow the trail of mojones that led toward the cross on the edge of the Royal Highway. We may infer from the records that Xoxocotlán's amparo succeeded in thwarting Rendón's encroachment, apparently allowing the town some measure of control, because the complaints stop in 1659. By the end of this cycle, the town of Xoxocotlán had secured its boundaries through an amparo ratified in Mexico City by the viceroy. They had done so by deploying a combination of written titles and collective memories tied to the natural world, the limits of their town, and their shared political experience.

The Plum Trees (1676–1692)

In 1676, ownership of the Muñoz hacienda passed to another Spaniard, a captain named Bartolomé Ruíz. By 1680, Ruíz reclaimed the five acres, now planted with corn and beans by a set of plum trees near the red rose tree identified in the previous survey. When Xoxocotlán complained to the courts, Ruíz's attorney, Diego Fernández de Córdoba, argued that the five acres in fact formed part of his client's property. According to him, it was Xoxocotlán's residents who had breached the boundary of the plum trees, the halfway point between the hill with the crimson roses and the cross by the Royal Highway. Ruíz's attorney recognized that amparos, the legal documents that sheltered its holder under the law, protected the boundaries in favor of Xoxocotlán, but he claimed the town had succeeded in retaining the land for so long

because of the "improper and impetuous ruling of the alcaldes mayores who against all justice" protected the natives in the first place.[41] This comment sought to discredit past legal verdicts that according to the attorney reeked of complicity between Spanish authorities and natives. Ruíz capitalized on the fact that Xoxocotlán had no legal title to the land, grounding his claim to it in the recognition of a legitimate bill of sale like his own.[42] Since he physically controlled the five acres of land in question, he believed the lack of a proper title did not work against him. To resolve the dispute, the alcalde mayor ordered both parties to present evidence of ownership in early 1682, including their legal records and witnesses.

Xoxocotlán assembled a group of elder males, mostly Indian lords with ties to the region, whom they called on to support their claim. It presented ten witnesses, eight Indian men and two Spaniards, who testified about the boundaries that divided the lands of the town from those of the Ruíz estate. Luis de San Juan, a ninety-five-year-old cacique, agreed that the plum trees marked Xoxocotlán's legitimate boundary; he knew this, he said, because he attended the amparo described above when serving as a political officer for Cuilapa. San Juan's testimony presents a dilemma because the plum trees were not mentioned during the 1643 boundary walk. It is possible Xoxocotlán's council members and Spanish officials chose not to reference the trees in writing but that local residents identified them as a natural marker. An alternative explanation suggests, as Ruíz's attorney later commented, that San Juan lied to authorities to support the town's claims. Andrés de Velazco, another cacique from Cuilapa, testified that he witnessed Ruíz's son, Francisco, enter to the east beyond the plum tree mojones that marked the property limits, ruining the Indians' sweet potato fields. Velazco had participated in an official boundary perambulation in 1657 and knew the borders well. According to the scribe who transcribed his deposition, Velazco, San Juan, and several other caciques who gave testimony wore Spanish clothing (*traje de español*) and spoke Spanish, both symbols of prestige usually recognized in notarial records.

The testimony of the two Spanish witnesses also hints at the way interests shaped testimony in the Valley. Juan de Almogabar, a thirty-eight-year-old landholder, reluctantly confirmed he had acted as a witness in a boundary survey during a former dispute between Xoxocotlán and another property owner. When questioned if he knew details about the conflict between Ruíz and Xoxocotlán, he stated simply, "No, I know nothing." When asked about the relationship between Ruíz and the Indian town, the witness said, "I only know that they contested [the estancia] this year." But Almogabar could not deny that during an earlier land survey he witnessed how the boundaries "started at a tree with crimson flowers leading to a triad of plum trees," the same marker currently under contention. Although he confirmed the boundaries, he made a point of emphasizing he had witnessed Bartolomé Ruíz use the five acres of land in the past and that this was the first time Xoxocotlán complained: "I have seen Antonio Rendón [the hacienda's prior owner] and then Bartolomé Ruíz sow beyond the boundaries but I have never known the Indians to do the same or to contest [this boundary] until now."[43] This was hardly the compelling testimony the Indians had hoped for. Weeks later, Xoxocotlán's legal counsel criticized Almogabar's deposition, suggesting he feared Ruíz and deliberately provided false testimony. A second Spanish witness, Marcial de Molano, also testified. Molano told authorities he knew the land belonged to Xoxocotlán because he had witnessed a boundary survey presided over by an alcalde mayor. Ruíz's attorney later challenged Molano's testimony, suggesting the witness had ulterior motives to verify Xoxocotlán's claim.

Ruíz's attorney brought together a group of individuals that included nine Spanish men and one Indian from a range of trades including farmers, cattlemen, butchers, scribes, and public officials. These witnesses emphasized their own connection to the past and to the hacienda to establish a legitimate claim. The testimony of two men, a Spaniard and an Indian cacique, added a layer of complexity to the suit when they suggested Don Félix de Mendoza, a powerful cacique from Xoxocotlán with a penchant for the fermented agave drink known as *pulque* and public displays of violence, also conspired to appropriate the five acres.[44] Francisco de Medina, a local scribe from Antequera, recalled that eight months prior to his testimony he had assisted the alcalde mayor of the Cuatro Villas in giving possession of lands to Simón de Chávez, another cacique from Cuilapa. Chávez was married to Doña María de Guzmán, a descendent of the original holders of the merced land owned by Ruíz and a relative of Don Félix; the couple sought to protect their assets. During the survey, Chávez and Don Félix gathered in Xoxocotlán with a cadre of nobles and other Indians to claim the land that bordered with Ruíz's property. According to Medina, Chávez and Guzmán intended to claim the entire estancia as part of their patrimony before Bartolomé Ruíz met them at the boundaries to protest the claim. Medina testified Ruíz challenged the two caciques, asking "How can you claim my estancia and lands that were sold legitimately by your wife's grandfather and which I possess with just title?" Chávez and Guzmán responded they no longer wished to take possession of the estancia and proceeded to survey other parts of the cacicazgo.[45]

The final witness, a forty-eight-year-old Indian male in Spanish dress named Juan de Aguilar, suggested a conspiracy in Xoxocotlán to deprive Ruíz of his property. Aguilar, a cacique from Xoxocotlán, assured the judge that the estancia—presumably including the five acres—belonged to Ruíz, having passed down legitimately from Francisco Muñoz. He stated that, because he believed Ruíz to be the rightful owner, the other native officials avoided and refused to speak to him lest he reveal the truth of their schemes. Aguilar's testimony exposed a clear rift within Xoxocotlán's indigenous elite, many of whom supported the powerful Don Félix. During the earlier dispute between the town and Francisco Muñoz in the 1640s, officials from Xoxocotlán relied on assistance from Don Gerónimo de Lara, the wealthy cacique from Cuilapa, to verify the limits of the estancia. Following the same strategy to litigate against Ruíz proved more complicated, for Mendoza's actions raised suspicion among his critics.

In a petition to the alcalde mayor in June 1682, Ruíz's attorney claimed Don Félix had persuaded the witnesses to provide false testimony to strengthen their case. He stated the witnesses testified at the behest of Don Félix, "an enemy of mine, who for this occasion incited this conflict persuading the other natives from the town to do it with his great authority ('*con la mucha mano*') as a powerful nobleman."[46] Reference to a "strong hand" served as a legal metaphor to describe "anyone who enjoyed wealth, office, or influence."[47] Fernández claimed Mendoza imposed *derramas*, forced payments that exceeded Spanish demands for tribute, on Xoxocotlán's residents and noted that Mendoza's father-in-law (the ninety-five-year-old cacique Luis de San Juan) and other kin made up the great portion of Xoxocotlán's witness list. The lawyer capitalized on the tension between Xoxocotlán's ruling elite, arguing that Aguilar's privileged position as a mayordomo confirmed his client's testimony.

The picture that emerges from the testimony of these witnesses describes a complex web of relationships tempered by competing interests in land and, in some cases, leading to hostile accusations and open enmity. "The question of boundaries," argues Yannakakis, "became a fraught one in which local knowledge of land tenure on the one hand, and of Spanish property law on the other, could be wielded as weapons by indigenous elites acting as witnesses in pursuit of varied objectives."[48] In the Valley, alliances took on various shapes that often pitted townspeople and lesser nobles seeking access to resources against more powerful caciques looking to retain traditional rights and privileges.[49] The fact that Juan de Aguilar, an Indian notable, testified against Mendoza and Xoxocotlán's officials underscores the differences of indigenous interests and memory in matters related to land. Fernández's comments about Mendoza's sphere of power suggest key Indian figures held influential positions in local affairs that threatened Spanish and indigenous interests alike. Likewise, individuals such as Bartolomé Ruíz played an active role in shaping the region's spatial contours.

In Mexico City, judges at the Real Audiencia reviewed the case in September 1682 and issued a verdict in favor of Bartolomé Ruíz. In Antequera, the alcalde mayor validated the disputed boundaries as described by Ruíz and warned the Indians not to disturb the Spanish landholder's possession.[50] During this phase of litigation, it was Ruíz who secured the five acres of land under dispute near Xoxocotlán. Although this moment marked a shift

in the relationship between Xoxocotlán and the neighboring hacienda, it did not deter the town from appealing the decision and further pursuing the claim. Four years later, the Real Audiencia in Mexico City granted Xoxocotlán an appeal.[51] The introduction of the old map in 1686 and the subsequent commission of its copy were directly related to the chain of events described above.

A TRUE AND FAITHFUL COPY

In some cases, patrons in litigation or who wanted to reinforce proper title in anticipation of a challenge to their claim of ownership commissioned copies of earlier maps. Extant examples suggest reproductions of late sixteenth- and seventeenth-century maps were made mostly in the central valleys after the 1680s, a pattern that continued into the late eighteenth century.[52] Copies of originals accounted for nearly half of the indigenous maps found after the late seventeenth century. Yet the copies themselves emerged as original productions that attempted to capture the details of the model but that also reflected the painter and the patron's contemporary sensibilities and needs. In some cases, copies served as models for newer commissions. Barbara Mundy and Dana Leibsohn have argued that, in late-nineteenth-century Mexico, copies of sixteenth-century codices "became foundations for new narratives" that allowed the state to portray an image of a powerful pre-Colombian past that superseded the colonial context in which they were made.[53] In the Valley of Oaxaca, those who commissioned copies attempted to establish a continuous thread with the past that often included negotiations with Spanish authorities to gain control over land.

Map reproduction fell on the shoulders of people such as Don Domingo de Zárate, a native lord from the Mixtec ñuu of Xoxocotlán. In early October 1686, Zárate accepted a commission from Antonio de Abellán y Carrasco, the alcalde mayor of the Cuatro Villas del Marquesado, to duplicate a map. The copy would take the place of the original map in support of a suit against Bartolomé Ruíz. In recognition of the map's unique pictorial content, the alcalde mayor mandated "que se trasunte por un maestro pintor" (that a master painter replicate it) and delegated this task to Zárate. Three weeks later, the painter turned up with officers from the Mixtec town to present the tattered original and its copy to the alcalde mayor. The intervening time between the map's commission and its formal introduction into the notarial record marks a significant moment not considered in the legal record: an intentional silence that favored the inspection and authentication of a map over the details of its production. And yet the reproduction had demanded the hand of an expert, someone well versed in the pictorial arts of an earlier period.

The map of Xoxocotlán copied by Zarate in 1686 (Figure 1.1a, Table 1.2) emphasized the town's natural boundaries to legitimize the claims against Ruíz. Oriented to the west (top of the map) toward the archeological site of Monte Albán's southern range, an important ritual center in Oaxaca's central valley, the map's upper portion includes a chain of stylized mountains that extend downward on the right-hand side. An ocelot (n. 1) sits atop the mountain at the top left while a stylized tree with red-feathered leaves stands on the right (n. 2). The ocelot suggests a symbolic relationship with the mountain reminiscent of the place-glyph used in earlier indigenous mapping to convey meaning, in this case describing Ocelotepeque (Ocelot Hill, or place of the ocelot: *ocelotl*=ocelot/*-peque*=hill). Mary Elizabeth Smith explains place-signs as logograms, "pictorial representations of a place-name in which the pictorial units are the equivalent of one or more words."[54] Indigenous painters used logographic expression in local maps throughout the sixteenth century, but this practice declined by the early seventeenth.

The moon in the map's top center (n. 3) suggests nightfall to indicate the cardinal direction west. The second moon on the farthest right (n. 4) appears to blend into the landscape, perhaps as an attempt to evoke *noo yoo*, literally "moon-faced," a reference to the flower that gave the town its first Mixtec name. After subduing the region in the late fifteenth century, the Nahuas rechristened the town Xoxocotlán, the "land of abundant sour fruits," because of the many plum trees in the region, a group of which defined the property under dispute. The presence of multiple names reveals a layer of ordering used to assign meaning to social and political space.[55]

In Zárate's copy, alphabetic glosses in Mixtec next to specific places (n. 9–21) inscribed the landscape to fit Mixtec needs, a practice that, as Barbara Mundy has noted, witnessed an attempt to control the blank spaces of a map but instead rendered them virtually unreadable to the Spanish audience.[56]

On the map's right-hand edge, an unnamed town represented by a church (n. 5) connects to another town (n. 7) by a southern road marked by footmarks, the pre-Colombian sign for travel, and hoof marks, a sixteenth-century device that signaled the arrival of horses and beasts of burden in Oaxaca.[57] A series of mojones, or boundary markers (n. 8a–c), define the town's borders along the road. A mojón with a cross on the top (n. 8b) suggests it represents the boundary described during the land survey conducted in 1643 when officers from Xoxocotlán, on arriving at the Royal Highway, petitioned the alcalde mayor to witness their placing of a cross on an ancient marker. Below this stretch of land lies the town of Xoxocotlán in the center of the manuscript symbolized by a church. Zárate inscribed it "*huee ñoho* Santa Cruz," the "sacred house of Santa Cruz," rather than Xoxocotlán. One may note the use of a Catholic theme, "The Holy Cross," a symbol that catered to Spanish sensibilities about religion and the state but also to indigenous peoples' incorporation of Catholicism in their daily lives. Leibsohn argues that the use of the church sign occupied a progressively privileged position on Indian maps, gradually replacing hill glyphs in the sixteenth century.[58] Churches—symbols laden with value across cultural spheres in the colonial world—allowed officials to identify towns on maps while drawing attention to indigenous spatial ordering.[59] It is no coincidence that Zárate and the painter before him situated the key town in the center of the map to emphasize its importance. J. B. Harley noted that such practices added "geopolitical force and meaning to representation" found on maps.[60] A partitioned area with a black and green border in the center-left portion of the map (n. 11) encases a series of boundaries, perhaps an attempt to indicate the old map's original purpose, as none of them appear to have any direct relationship with the Ruíz case. At the map's bottom center, a bright orange sun signals east.

TABLE 1.2. *Legend, map of Xoxocotlán (1686, no. 625, Tierras, vol. 129, exp. 4, f. 249. Archivo General de la Nación).*

1. Ocelotepeque [place of the ocelot]
2. Tree with red feather leaves
3. Moon (West)
4. Second moon; possible moon-faced hill
5. Villa of Oaxaca
6. Camino Real [Royal Highway]
7. Villa of Cuilapa
8a. Double-mound boundary marker
8b. Boundary marker with cross
8c. Boundary marker with cactus
8d. Estancia
9. *huee ñoho* Sta *crus* (*huee*=house) (*ñoho*=sacred) [sacred house of the Holy Cross]

10. *cuiti yuyucha noyoo* (*cuiti*=mound) (*yuyucha*=riverside, river mouth) (*noyoo*=moon-faced) [moon-face mound on the riverside]
11. *cuiti* S^n *Mi[gu]el* (*cuiti*=mound) [mound of San Miguel]
12. *ñooyud[z]ahui* (*ñoo*=place) (*yu*=stone) (*dzahui*=rain) [the place of stone rain]
13. *nodzahui coyho* (*no*=place) (*dzahui*=rain) (*coyho*=land that retains water, wet) [place where rainwater is collected]
14. *ñoho miniyu[yu]* (*ñuhu*=land) (*mini*=lake, wet, moisture) (*yu[yu?], yojo*=plain) [plain saturated with water]
15. *cu[?]a sie[?][ta]* [N/A]
16. *fran^co martin* [Francisco Martín]
17. *cuiti meeñoo* (*cuiti*=mound) (*mee*=in the middle) (*ñoo*=place, settlement) [mound in the center of the town]

The map's material condition played an important role in framing its message. Zárate used a large piece of coarse linen fabric (88cm × 79cm) and medium brown pigment for the background combining white, green, red, and violet colors to define mountains, streams, and buildings. His choice of materials reveals a distinct aspect of the map's message. As Harley has contended, "All maps employ the common devices of rhetoric such as invocations of authority . . . and appeals to a potential readership through the use of colors, decoration, typography, dedications, or written justifications of their method."[61] The 1686 map followed pictorial traditions that required the application of specialized knowledge for the selection and preparation of organic and inorganic materials to paint, a distinct aspect of indigenous cartography throughout Oaxaca and other parts of Mesoamerica. The use of cloth and its size evoke a genre of native pictorial manuscripts known as *lienzos*, painted genealogies and elite histories usually made on linen material typically produced during the second half of the sixteenth century.[62] Together, these elements gave the map a unique visual presence that intentionally summoned the past.

Indigenous maps did not strictly depend on spatial precision, relying often on the visual and symbolic elements that characterized their appearance. This rhetorical strategy appealed to an earlier period, a time immemorial when pictorial documents carried legal value in the Spanish courts, helping native towns and individuals secure grants of land and social privileges.[63] Yannakakis has observed that in the Zapotec sierra in northern Oaxaca, the importance of a native title "rested on its form—a title that straddled the eras of their 'gentility' and colonialism and that legitimized political power and landholding by virtue of both local lineage and royal authority—and not on its specific content."[64] In the case of the map of Xoxocotlán, the actual site of the dispute (a mere five acres) was not as relevant to the town as the fact that they controlled specific territorial boundaries tied to a long line of nobles predating the arrival of the Spaniards. By deploying the map, the town council attempted to reinforce this notion.

In a highly unusual act in the cartographic process, Domingo de Zárate inscribed two certifying texts at the bottom of each corner of the map. In the first (Figure 1.4) he stated the alcalde mayor approved the map on October 25, 1686; his rubric appeared below the inscription. The second gloss (Figure 1.5) reads: "By order of Captain Don Antonio Abellán . . . I copied this map based on the original given to me; [I made it] according to the traditions of my art of painting without damaging or diminishing a single thing."[65] Mundy has observed that

---

18. *ñoho chee ni sa noho cahua nduqun* (*ñuhu*=land) (*chee, nchee, ndaa*=flat, extended) (*ni, nee*=wholeness, complete) (*sa noho*=that which contains) (*cahua*=cliff, rock) (*nduq*=square) [completely flat land that contains the square rock]

19. cuiti coo caa (*cuiti*=mound) (*coo*=serpent, *caa*=metal/rattlesnake) [mound of the rattlesnake]

20. cuiti sacuaa (*cuiti*=mound) (*sacuaa*=deer) [mound of the deer]

21. This site most likely refers to Masatepeque, "deer hill" in Nahuatl; *no nicaa ydzu*, "where there was deer" in Mixtec according to Mary Elizabeth Smith, who notes a similar place-sign on the 1718 and 1778 maps of Xoxocotlán; *Picture Writing in Ancient Southern Mexico: Mixtec Place Signs and Maps*, 210.

22. En Veinte y cinco de Octubre de 1686 años se aprouó esta mapa p[r] el señor Alcalde m[or] y lo rubrique [rubrica]

23. Por orden del cap[tan] d[n] Antt[o] de Abellan Al[de] M[or] de las quatro Villas del Marquesado cupie [copie] esta Mapa segun su original que se me dio sin estrepar [estropear] ni disminuir cosa Alguna segun se acostumbra en mi arte de la pintura que ba sierto y berdadero como co[n]stara por el original qnda[concuerda?] con esta y en caso nesesario y antepongo el Juramento nesess[o] fh[o] en Antequera octubre 25 de 1686 años Dn Domingo de sarate

24. Sun (East)

25. Stream [red line]

1.4. *Certifying text I. Map of Santa Cruz Xoxocotlán (1686), no. 625, Tierras, vol. 129, exp. 4, f. 249. Archivo General de la Nación, Fondo Hermanos Mayo, concentrados, sobre 363.*

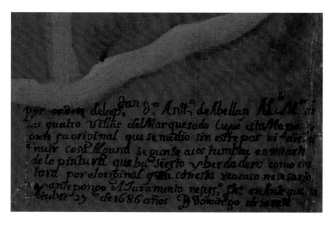

1.5. *Certifying text II. Map of Santa Cruz Xoxocotlán (1686), no. 625, Tierras, vol. 129, exp. 4, f. 249. Archivo General de la Nación, Fondo Hermanos Mayo, concentrados, sobre 363.*

indigenous painters rarely signed their maps, making Zárate's words all the more revealing.[66] For one thing, he understood the importance of his trade, *his* art of painting, a visual system with a distinct form and style that required the application of certain skills honed by masters in their craft. In another respect, Zárate's written glosses as well as Abellán's earlier commission bear witness to an exchange of services prompted by traditions tied to generations of conflict over land. At the end of the meeting, Medina, the scribe, recorded the following in a separate folio:

I certify under oath that the natives of the town of Xoxocotlán, subject to the villa of Cuilapa in this marquisate, presented two maps, one of them old, torn, and frayed with the passage of time, the other copied and produced according to and as the ancient one by Don Domingo de Zárate, cacique and a master of painting. [The map was] mandated and licensed by Captain Don Antonio de Abellán y Carrasco [to recognize] the borders and boundary markers of this entire jurisdiction. Having seen and compared one with the other, his lordship declared it true and faithfully copied and detailed, seemingly with the same boundary signs and expositions as the old one.[67]

The scribe's words accredited the relationship between the Indian master painter, the native town, and the Spanish official, in the process authenticating the map's contents and bringing the exchange of this service to an end.

The act of certification represents an important element of mapmaking in Oaxaca. Certification legitimized the use of native maps in a court of law. The lack of a proper certifying mark, usually in the form of a gloss and signature that verified the "true and faithful" depiction of a site, could render a map worthless from a legal standpoint. "What is crucial," notes Cummins of indigenous pictorial records in the sixteenth century, "is that a forum for the presentation of non-European evidence could be constructed so as to be judged as 'true.'"[68] The copied map's inspection in the late seventeenth century suggests a degree a familiarity between scribe, painter, and official and the use of pictorial documents recalling legal practices from a century earlier.[69] Admitting a map was an important part of the process, but it did not guarantee the owner a victory in litigation. Judges in Oaxaca during this later period "valued the written text above both orality and the image, especially where legal evidence was concerned."[70] In other respects, judges seemed to have grown so accustomed to native pictorial records that they could often identify titles of dubious origin.[71] For Xoxocotlán, the alcalde mayor's certification allowed the town to introduce the map into the proceedings.

THE COPIED MAPS OF XOXOCOTLÁN

The 1686 map of Xoxocotlán has enjoyed little of the attention directed at the more popular copied maps of Xoxocotlán made in 1718 (Figure 1.6) and 1771.[72] All three maps share some similarities, yet the traces of logographic writing and the representations of Monte Albán have drawn the attention of pre-Colombianists much more closely to the 1718 and 1771 models than to the 1686 copy, which has typically appeared as a footnote to the other two maps.[73] According to the two copied maps made in the eighteenth century, an earlier model made in 1660 defined the town's limits as a result of a survey ordered and approved by the alcalde mayor Francisco de Lagunas Portocarrero. The western mountains of Xoxocotlán, an area that straddled the ceremonial

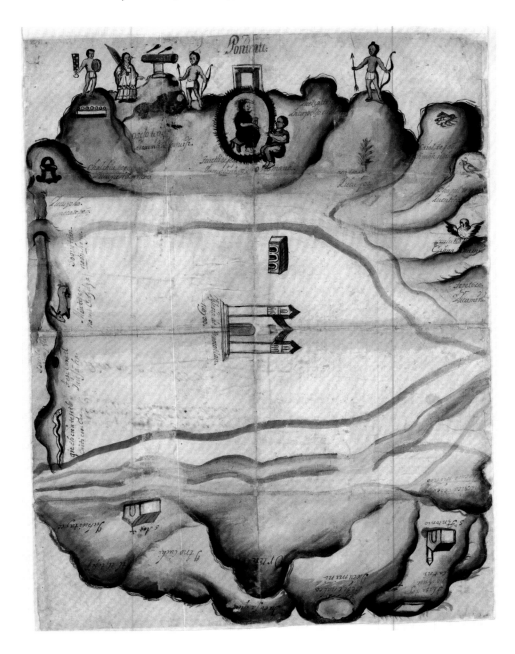

1.6. *Map of Xoxocotlán (1718 [1660]), no. 1176-OYB-7272-A. Mapoteca Orozco y Berra.*

site of Monte Albán and also appeared in the 1686 map, included a series of animals and plants as well as various military and ritual objects. The original painter used an adaptation of the place-glyph, a Mesoamerican convention that combined a hill symbol with an animal or thing to express the name of a town. Below each glyph, the painter or a scribe wrote both Nahua and Mixtec place-names for every locality.[74] Three warriors in loincloths—one holding a club and a shield, the other two holding a bow and arrow—share the space with three clothed individuals. The *teponaztle*, a ceremonial drum, and a noble woman wearing a skirt and blouse and holding a club sit atop the town of Ocelotepeque (place of the ocelot). After successfully identifying the town's mojones, the scribe returned the 1660 map to officials from Xoxocotlán.

The timing of this survey and the commission of the map came shortly after the 1659 amparo when Xoxocotlán litigated against Antonio Rendón. It seems likely that native officials feared another legal battle with Rendón or some other neighbor and decided to add a map to their titles to strengthen their position in any future entanglements. A 1718 copy of the map authenticated by a local scribe confirms Xoxocotlán used it after its original commission. The map inspection confirmed the copy faithfully resembled the model made in 1660. In 1771, the town commissioned another copy, this time based on the 1718 model. A comparison of the two reveals they differed in significant ways. For instance, the painter's choice of materials for the 1718 model included watercolors and European paper, whereas for the 1771 copy its painter opted for oil over a canvas sheet. The newer copy pictured more animals and flora, including an assortment of trees, shrubs, livestock, and a laborer caring for a herd on the upper right corner. The brushed quality of the 1771 version injects an element of European landscapes not noticeable in the earlier copy. While the written glosses on the 1718 map merely indicate place-names, the scribe's intervention in the 1771 copy focused on the map's surface, where a certifying text above the church of Xoxocotlán in the center, another to the right of it, and a large cartouche at the bottom of the page traced the map's lineage. These written elements tied each copy to its earlier model, confirming the relationship between town and land. The comparison of the two pieces suggests nuances existed between maps and their copies, variations that accounted for a painter's pictorial choices, a patron's needs, and an official's authority to legitimize documents.

CIRCULATION

The introduction of the map followed the Real Audiencia's decision in 1686 to grant Xoxocotlán an appeal on the verdict issued in 1682 in Bartolomé Ruíz's favor. An appeal meant mounting another full-scale inquiry, including land surveys, presentation of written evidence, and witness testimony. In preparation for the upcoming legal battle, two *regidores* (councilmen) from Xoxocotlán presented the map to facilitate an impending survey. They claimed the map described the town's territorial limits, its battered state impressing its age upon viewers and providing a unique memorial device to its holders. But the copy does not indicate with any precision the location of the disputed property. Instead, Domingo de Zárate, the map's painter, represented a visual order from a century earlier that described the town's spatial boundaries.

Indian maps aroused suspicion precisely because they interpreted the natural environment and its social relationships according to native traditions. In the case of Xoxocotlán, Ruíz's attorney questioned the officers' use of the map, stating:

> The reproduction of the map presented by the natives with the alcalde mayor's certification [and] its convenient comparison with the old painting . . . is useless. Without an accompanying title, the map does not give, nor can it give [its holders] legitimate right over land because it is an instrument that completely lacks the juridical authority to make it valid; it depends entirely on the will of those who make it and those who commission it.[75]

In fact, a decree issued by the Crown in 1643 validated the use of pictorial documents, at least theoretically, in New Spain.[76] Still, most officials could not make sense of an Indian map unless guided by a native painter who could explain its content. Yannakakis has argued that patrons of indigenous maps and manuscripts lost control of their reception "especially if the readers of the maps and texts did not share the cultural assumptions and codes that the maps and texts expressed."[77] Accepting an indigenous map into a legal proceeding allowed parties to make claims on land, but that did not guarantee the map a favorable reception, nor did all parties consider them appropriate forms of evidence. Despite the fact that Abellán y Carrasco, the alcalde mayor, certified the map and the copy's inspection, the attorney's comments challenged their authenticity.

After entering the public record, the 1686 map underwent further scrutiny in the hands of attorneys, magistrates, and other scribes who had access to it during Xoxocotlán's appeal. Juan López de Pareja, the town's attorney, introduced it as evidence in Mexico City in the fall of 1687. By the time Ruíz's lawyer petitioned the Audiencia in 1688 to drop the native's suit, he had also inspected the map, noting: "As a new copy it relies on the details of the ancient original that is not included [in the brief]. Even though [the original] could assist the natives [in their case], they refuse to exhibit it without a clear reason."[78] Authorities in Oaxaca mentioned the map in 1691 when it functioned as a guide during a *vista de ojos*, a boundary inspection, and a measurement of land in March of that year ordered by the Audiencia.[79] Weeks later, authorities questioned witnesses for the native town about their knowledge of the five acres. Their testimony foregrounds the map's role at the community level, where its introduction by Xoxocotlán's political officers and its use during the case by Spanish authorities served to reinvigorate community ties and spatial boundaries.

Witnesses responded to questions about the location of the five acres and about the parties involved in the dispute. During the interrogation, authorities referred all witnesses to the map and the legal documents the town had collected over time. Six of them, including eighty-year-old Juan Pérez, declared they had seen the map. Jacinto Gómez, a native from Atzompa who relocated to Xoxocotlán after marriage, and several others testified they had heard about the map. Two natives from neighboring San Pedro Apostol testified they knew "[Xoxocotlán] had a mapa/pintura and titles," both declaring they had "seen them and heard them read aloud, and they included the [disputed] piece of land."[80] The testimony of the last two witnesses suggests the map may have served as a tool used by prominent elders to orally recount the history of the town during ritual festivities and other important occasions.[81] But which map did witnesses reference—the original or the copy?

During the interrogation, witnesses would have had access only to the copy because of the frail state of the original, the reason given for commissioning the copy in the first place. The two Indians from San Pedro, however, surely referred to the old map in their testimony, especially since up to that point in time the copy itself circulated primarily within the region's legal channels. Others who had heard about the map confirmed its existence during the deposition. In both instances, the act of viewing the "true and faithful" copy established a symbolic link with the past, thereby setting a precedent that certified the town's response to spatial threats regardless of the outcome of the case. The interplay between witnesses, native officers, translators, and Spanish officials to define the map's use in a formal legal setting reveals the various stages of authentication—a joint effort between social actors with diverse, often conflicting interests.

WITHER THE PLUM TREES

On May 12, 1691, the alcalde mayor of the Cuatro Villas, Gerónimo Fernández Franco, ordered a measurement of the disputed five acres. He solicited persons knowledgeable in surveying, appointing two Spaniards with direct ties to the case. Juan de Almogabar and Joseph Rodríguez, the two men selected, had both testified a decade earlier during Xoxocotlán's first imbroglio with Bartolomé Ruíz. Even though Almogabar had appeared on behalf of the native town, he had seemed reluctant to support their claim, eliciting a warning from Xoxocotlán's attorney that the witness surely feared Ruíz. Joseph Rodríguez, a scribe and former alcalde mayor, had testified for the Spanish landholder, questioning the timing of the Indian town's suit. This obvious conflict of interest went unmentioned by Fernández Franco, the ranking official on the case. Two days later, at seven o'clock in the morning, Spanish and native authorities, Ruíz, the surveyors, a translator, and assorted witnesses met at the town's church to initiate the inspection. Generally, litigating parties avoided using formal surveyors because of their great expense, favoring "the documentary evidence by each interested party seeking legal title."[82] In this case, the pursuit of an accurate measurement of the land in question made it necessary to professionalize the survey. The alcalde mayor introduced a *cordel*, a rope that for the occasion measured 100 varas, assigning it to Almogabar and Rodríguez to mark distances; he mounted his horse and gave the order to begin the survey.

The group traveled west toward the old plum trees. When they arrived at the spot, the trees had withered. According to the scribe, the roots on the ground provided the only physical evidence of their existence: "We walked east to west nearly half a league from the town until we reached a boundary marker for a maize field [that had been] recently harvested [*está en rastrojo*, noted the scribe—"in stubble."]. Both the natives and Captain Bartolomé Ruíz said that that was the location of the plum trees mentioned in the royal dispatch; one could still find the trees' noticeable roots."[83] For Xoxocotlán, the remainder of the inspection seemed to reflect the loss of the trees. Almogabar and Rodríguez determined the distance between the town's last house, and the plum tree mojoneras measured 1,518 varas, well in excess of the *fundo legal* issued a few years earlier.[84] "From what has been seen and inspected," wrote the scribe, "the alcalde mayor finds that not only does the town possess the 600 varas mandated by the recent Royal decree [*real cédula*], but it exceeds [the mandate] by 918 and one half varas."[85] This revelation seemed to weigh heavily on the alcalde mayor more than any argument over an old boundary, triggering a question of necessity versus use. Tamar Herzog contends that, although these arguments seem to apply to all groups in Spanish America, in fact they represented "the most powerful and systematic instruments of native dispossession."[86] By the end of the inspection, the official declared Xoxocotlán's petition vague and unfounded, with so much access to land, that he couldn't

understand why the Indian town would wish to penetrate the five acres of land in dispute. One year later, the Real Audiencia ratified the five acres in favor of Ruíz, absolving the Spanish landholder from the accusations from the native town. The scribe who informed Xoxocotlán of the formal verdict noted that it did not challenge the decision.

CONCLUSION

In Oaxaca, an interest in the occupation of land for agricultural development and cattle ranching starting in the second half of the seventeenth century generated heavy competition for natural resources. To resolve conflicting interests, litigants were hard-pressed to trace and document the origins of their claims, a process that often included the presentation of a variety of written records, oral testimony, and maps. Entering into a legal dispute over land involved engaging the services of scribes, mapmakers, and lawyers to help navigate the parameters of a suit, aspects of which included topographical surveys, ritual boundary walks, and depositions used to establish possession and boundaries. These circumstances prompted the commission and use of Indian maps. As the case of Xoxocotlán established, natives demonstrated considerable shrewdness in navigating Spanish legal channels, though their efforts could sometimes go unrewarded. Despite the fact the Mixtecs from Xoxocotlán successfully used oral testimony between 1643 to 1649 to defend their land, changing perceptions of evidence worked against the town in the 1680s when written titles superseded other forms of records used to support a claim. Witnesses, especially elder Indian males, functioned as carriers of knowledge who played important roles in defining spatial boundaries. Spatial boundaries relied on written titles but also included the use of indigenous maps. By deploying a map, Xoxocotlán sought to establish a connection with the past to legitimate its use of land in the present. The copied map circulated across multiple settings, including town councils and the local and regional courts of Oaxaca and Mexico City, where it was scrutinized by a range of officials, legal professionals, and witnesses.

CHAPTER 2

PAINTERS

The painter from Tehuantepec—a mature man most likely of Zapotec origin—had made maps of this coastal region for Spanish authorities for at least a quarter of a century. In 1598, the alcalde mayor Gaspar de Vargas commissioned a map (Figure 2.1) from the painter for a livestock ranch that would inform the *merced*, or land grant petition, made by one Francisco de Figueroa.[1] After carefully surveying the landscape before him, the painter knew exactly what to do with his commission. To capture the two rivers that encased the requested parcel, important geographical features that bound the plot's location, he rotated the folio in a 90-degree angle, shifting the paper from a horizontal to a vertical position. He then aligned the two bodies of water that flowed from the west with the top of the map, its position reserved for the sun that included a written gloss, no doubt added by the scribe during the map's inspection, that read "*oriente*" (east). Below the sun, a striped rectangular device with an aperture in its bottom frame designates the requested site. The two small churches in the middle right and the center bottom represent the towns of Ixtepec and Zixitlán respectively,

helping officials to situate petitioned plots within the region's settled communities. After years of working with royal authorities, the painter understood that the maps supported petitions and that petitions followed a prescribed set of rules focused on determining geographic location. As the resident cartographic expert, the painter combined knowledge of local topography and politics along with an ability to produce colors and master a brush. These skills placed him in a unique position of power from which he could shape the region's spatial memories. The painter's choices speak subtly, but clearly, about cartographic priorities: orientation, petitioned site, surrounding towns, and major geographical markers mattered. More so, the case described above illustrates how painters adapted their skills over time to cater to multiple audiences.

Painters in New Spain represent an important, but understudied, social group that yielded considerable power over land-related matters. I argue that, from the late sixteenth century through the early eighteenth centuries, painters functioned as geographic interpreters, individuals who documented the natural and built

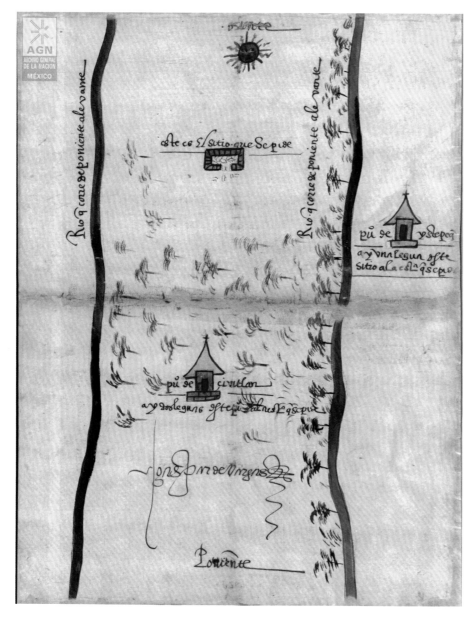

2.1. Map of Ystepeq and Zixitlan (1598), no. 2084, Tierras, vol. 2764, exp. 22, f. 302. Archivo General de la Nación, Fondo Hermanos Mayo, concentrados, sobre 363.

environment for multiple audiences and for a variety of reasons in a rapidly changing social setting beset by epidemics, spatial realignments, abuse of power, and dramatic cultural shifts. The maps they made speak of power shifts, conflicts, and negotiation, aspects of life vividly captured in a variety of cartographic symbols and drawings that repurposed traditional Mesoamerican imagery and elaborated new forms based on the introduction of European culture.

CRAFT ORIGINS

Painters, keen observers of social life, tapped into learning gained over centuries of interaction through trade, writing, warfare, and dynastic alliances across Mesoamerica. In the centuries leading up to the Spanish encounter in the early 1500s, artists from the central-west area of Puebla and the northeastern portion of Oaxaca known as the Mixteca enjoyed enviable reputations for making pottery, preparing pictorial manuscripts, and crafting religious iconography.[2] This "Mixteca-Puebla style," coined by the anthropologist George Vaillant in a series of influential essays written at the end of the 1930s, included a well-defined aggregation of deities, stylized picture-writing, and a common fifty-two-year calendar cycle. The geometric precision with which artists defined their lines, the standardization of signs, the use of vivid colors as decorative and symbolic components, and the exaggerated representation of figures likewise articulated important aspects of the style. Its influence extended beyond Mesoamerica as far north as the US Southwest and as far south as Nicaragua.

The work of missionary linguist-ethnographers, who documented the cultures of Mesoamerica in an effort to dismantle existing polytheistic ritual practices, provides tantalizing clues about the nature and scope of learning in precontact Oaxaca. The Dominican Juan de Córdova noted in his vocabulary of the Zapotec language various tiers of schools, including *yohotoatoceteni*, "schools where they teach," and *quechenoo quelahuecete*, "schools similar to Salamanca," the latter suggestive of the presence of institutions of higher learning. Likewise, Córdova pointed to *huelee*, or "masters who teach a variety of things," as well as "learned masters," *penihuechijñohuecocete*, and masters of an art or trade, *copeeche*, an activity that implied the passing of knowledge from an expert to a young novice.[3] In his *Vocabulario en lengua mixteca*, a dictionary intended for evangelization published in 1593, the Dominican Francisco de Alvarado observed similar patterns in the Mixtec language identifying schools (*huahi sadzaquaha*) and instructors (*yya yotasi tnuni huahi ñuhu*). The general Mixtec term for "master who teaches," *tay yodza ha ñaha*, differed from *ñahuisi*, "master of an art," a distinction found in Córdova's Zapotec language manual.[4] While this rich vocabulary reflects the Spanish compiler's own interests—tools used by clerics to break down the same indigenous cosmology native teachers had passed on for generations—it nonetheless allows us to consider the extent and importance of conveying ideas related to the transmission of knowledge.

After contact, cultural, social, and economic shifts brought on by Spanish colonization gradually transformed the use and production of pictorial manuscripts as alphabetic writing flooded notarial circuits, centers of learning, and government agencies. Across the Mixtec, Zapotec, and Nahua worlds, indigenous painter-scribes, learned not simply to write in Spanish but also to express their own language alphabetically.[5] Mixtecs identified a painter-scribe as *ñahuisi tacu*, "he whose craft is to write," while Zapotecs described such individuals as *huezee*; Nahuas in central Mexico used the term *tlacuilo*, "writer, painter." While never fully displacing pictorial activity, the adoption of alphabetic writing dramatically changed the social and political landscape, turning painting into an increasingly niche activity, a badge of honor for a select few with access to knowledge and sources. The Dominican Antonio de los Reyes observed, for instance, that Mixtecs distinguished between "the best scribe or painter," *huisicara*, from "the one who best applies color," *huisica nootacuta*.[6] References in Nahuatl, the lingua franca used throughout Mesoamerica, to a type of scriptorium known as *tlacuiloloyan*, "place to write," housed *tlacuiloca teachcauh*, "head painter-scribes" who oversaw the work of others as they made pictorial manuscripts, an act defined as *tlacuiloliztli*.[7] The compilers of the *Anales de Juan Bautista*, a record of events of the Valley of Mexico from the second half of the sixteenth century, identified at least two head painter-scribes, Francisco Xinmamal and Juan Icnotzin, among the thirty-six tlacuilo recorded in the city at the time.[8]

Migration histories that circulated during the late sixteenth and early seventeenth centuries accounted for the presence in central Mexico of powerful political dynasties from the Oaxaca region with superior skills in the pictorial arts. Fernando de Alva Ixtlilxochitl, the renowned *mestizo* historian descendent of the last rulers of Texcoco, noted that "two nations whom they called Tlailotlaques and Chimalpanecas who were also of the lineage of the Toltecs" originated in the Mixteca region. For Ixtlilxochitl, a distinguishing characteristic of this powerful dynasty centered on the ability of these groups to master pictorial writing and history more than any other tools of governance.[9] An accomplished historian in his own right, Ixtlilxochitl wrote his early-seventeenth-century *Historia Chichimeca*, an account of Mesoamerica up to the Spanish invasion of Tenochtitlan, based on native sources held in his family for generations, including the *Codex Xolotl*, an early colonial historical-genealogical manuscript made on native bark paper.[10] The ruling elite archived pictorial histories and genealogies, taking advantage of the visual sources to record their activities in trade, warfare, marriage alliances, and cartographic histories. A rich tradition of using older manuscripts as models carried into the colonial period, ensuring the circulation of visual records.

In his commentary on the 1686 map (Figure 1.1), Don Domingo's notion of membership in an ancient guild reminds us that generations of painters recognized their art as a unique instrument to capture information about elite genealogies and spatial relationships. Painters drew from a rich pictorial vocabulary from across Oaxaca and central Mexico, using their skills to produce a wide range of artifacts including religious paintings, murals, maps, tribute records, and historical accounts.[11] Because the audience and motivations shifted with time, so too did the symbols used to make the art of painting meaningful. In this sense, painters adjusted their tools, transforming and improvising new ways of conveying messages, especially when thinking about the native and Spanish audiences who typically played a part in commissioning and reviewing their work. In another sense, the art of painting symbolized a form of expression closely tied to indigenous identity and social memory. By 1686, when Domingo de Zárate made his statement about the art of painting, he did so purposefully to highlight the importance of pictorial activity in the negotiation of land and privileges not only through a pictorial record but also through a set of words written alphabetically on a map.

OBSERVERS

Footprints established an individual's presence in a specific geographical location, resulting in movement within that space. These traces also embodied a painter's scouting activities when surveying a region. The uniqueness of each footprint design provides an unofficial signature that helps to distinguish one painter from another: From the roughly outlined three-toed print of the painter from Aztatla, who in 1576 made a map for a livestock ranch in central Oaxaca, to the C-shaped impressions of the painter from Nochistlán (Figure 2.2), who surveyed the region to measure distances, feet tied painters to topographical activities designed to parse land.[12] But why could painters express spatial relationships to multiple audiences in the first place? How did painters contribute to developing new ways of understanding the physical landscape? How did knowledge of regional geography translate into power?

Mapmaking cut across generational divides. The eldest painters from the late sixteenth century included males born before contact. In their sixties and seventies by 1580, when a noticeable mapmaking pattern in the archive emerges, these men survived the dramatic political realignments that resulted from the Spanish conquest. A second group included those born in the 1520s and 1530s, the first generation raised under Iberian rule. These painters grew up with evangelization campaigns and labor drafts imposed by the new overlords while witnessing the reduction of their own power and authority. In their forties and fifties by 1580, these individuals maintained the reins of political and economic control in their communities by administering lands, labor, and tribute. A younger, third group, born between 1540 and 1560, lived through major spatial shifts brought about by the implementation of imperial policies and widespread disease.

Scant references to painters suggest indigenous men of *cacique* or *principal* status controlled the art of painting during the colonial period.[13] Wealth, a variable matter among caciques, created social differences between leading notables who often competed for land, labor, and privileges with each other and with Spaniards.[14] In central Mexico, the *encomienda* system contributed to a decline in the power of caciques, reducing their estates and draining them of laborers.[15] By contrast, during the early part of the century, swift negotiations between Spanish forces and the native elite, ensconced in such important centers of power as the Valley of Oaxaca and

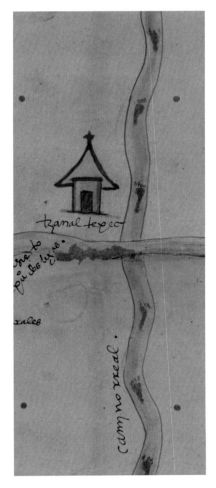

2.2. *Footprints: (a) Map of Tzanaltepec, Tonaltepec, and Oztutlan (1580), no. 1903, Tierras, vol. 2729, exp. 4, f. 107v y 108; (b) Map of Aztatla (1576), no. 1578, Tierras, vol. 2679, exp. 15, f. 15; (c) Map of Cuestlavaca (1582), no. 1609, Tierras, vol. 2682, exp. 9, f. 8. Archivo General de la Nación, Fondo Hermanos Mayo, concentrados, sobre 363.*

the Mixteca Alta, facilitated the retention of land and privileges for many nobles and towns while avoiding bloodshed on the scale of central Mexico. Complaints from caciques after the late seventeenth and eighteenth centuries about the commoner status of individuals in competing political factions signal the challenges aimed at caciques while foreshadowing the rhetoric they would use to defend traditional privileges and to discredit their opponents.[16] In the region of Tehuantepec along the Pacific Coast, Zapotec notables also retained entailed estates, mobilizing native labor for public works projects that allowed caciques to play key roles in local affairs.[17] Because of their leadership positions, caciques held interests in ranching, agriculture, trade, public affairs,

and scribe work while functioning as intermediaries between their communities and Spanish authorities; some also practiced the art of painting.

In the Mixteca Alta near Tepenene in the northwestern region of Oaxaca, the cacique Don Domingo de Mendoza used his skills in 1617 to make a map (Figure 2.3). Mendoza painted the map in order to petition an *estancia*, a site for ranching, for himself one league from Santo Domingo Tepenene, a subject town of the powerful Cuestlaguaca.[18] The map's two main features, a mountain in the form of an ancient temple on the upper left and a church traced with graph lines on the bottom right, reflect Mendoza's individual approach to pictorial representation. Mendoza presented the map to the

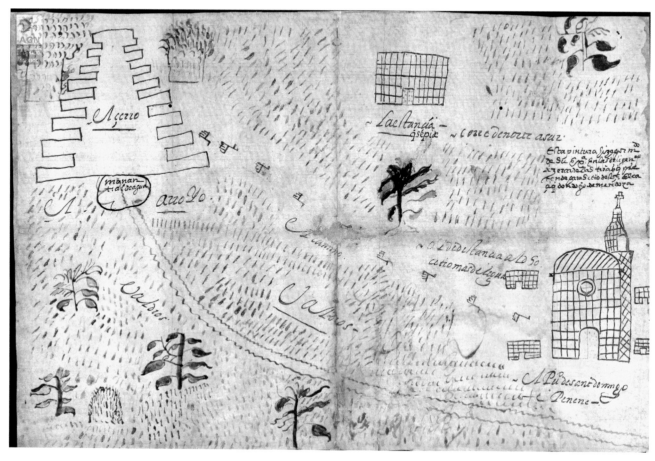

2.3. *Map of Santo Domingo Tepenene (1617), no. 2225, Tierras, vol. 2812, exp. 11, f. 312. Archivo General de la Nación, Fondo Hermanos Mayo, concentrados, sobre 363.*

alcalde mayor, who according to the scribe's inscription on the upper-right edge noted: "This map was made by order of his lordship for the proceedings related to the cattle site sought by Don Domingo de Mendoza."[19] In this instance, Mendoza served as both the painter of the map and its copatron, along with the alcalde mayor, applying his pictorial skills to negotiate a tract of land for himself.

Painters required cultural awareness to maneuver within Spanish bureaucratic channels and the structures of native town councils. Individuals operating between these two distinct milieus required fluency in languages and intercultural negotiation skills.[20] A painter's experience and cartographic output varied in accordance to

preparation, the strength or weakness of regional pictorial traditions, the presence of Spanish officials and settlers, and an individual's interests in local affairs. Alida Metcalf contends that, in sixteenth-century Brazil, differences in levels of participation characterized the role of intermediaries in their interaction with Portuguese explorers. Some functioned as "transactional go-betweens," that is to say those who facilitated communication between individuals and corporate entities, including "translators, negotiators, and cultural brokers." Others shaped through "writings, drawings, mapmaking, and the oral tradition . . . how Europeans and Native Americans viewed each other."[21] In Oaxaca, painters blurred the boundaries between these two groups.

Caciques gained experience to navigate the structures of imperial power, most notably the bureaucratic streets lined with alcaldes mayores and scribes who approved and certified everyday activities and documents, including the use of maps, by engaging with the Spanish officials for petitions and complaints, and to organize labor and tribute. Many natives practiced autodidactic learning to master elements of Spanish culture, especially in the manufacture of goods designed for local consumption.[22] It seems fitting that an element of this type of learning carried over into mapmaking. Combined with knowledge of the region's ecological environment, these skills allowed painters to interpret spatial relationships for their patrons, their communities, and themselves.

Mapmakers drew from a rich vocabulary that blended elements of indigenous picture-writing, Renaissance learning, and religious practice to give meaning to their maps. The application of pictorial devices used in Mesoamerican visual culture, the introduction of elements drawn from European history, the interpretation

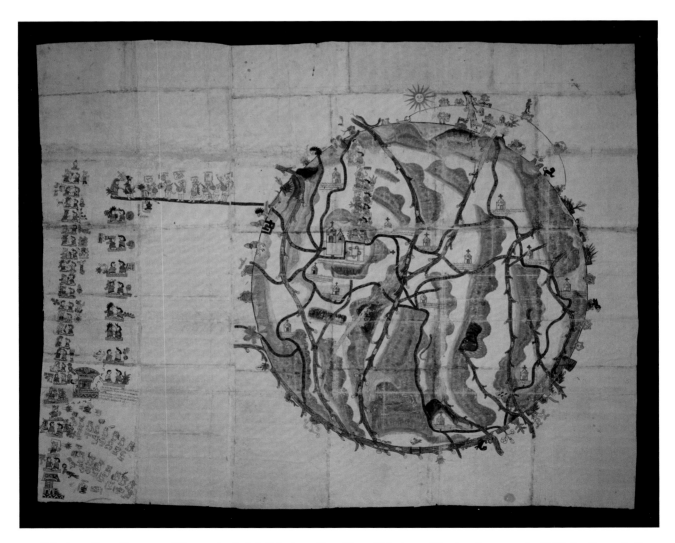

2.4. *Relaciones Geográficas map of Teozacoalco (1580). Relaciones Geográficas of Mexico and Guatemala, 1577–1585, Nettie Lee Benson Latin American Collection, University of Texas Libraries, University of Texas at Austin.*

of two- and three-dimensionality, access to pictorial documents, and the use of new media such as rag paper influenced the manner in which painters defined and portrayed spatial relationships in maps. At the individual level, each painter applied these elements to varying degrees and in distinct ways that reflected their personal choices as well as their exposure to different forms of learning. The map of Teozacoalco (Figure 2.4), made in the southeast reaches of the Mixteca region in 1580, represents historical lineages of rulers connected to the distribution of towns.[23] The painter displayed considerable skills rooted in Mesoamerican pictorial traditions in this well-known example made in response to the Relaciones Geográficas survey of lands, culture, and society. The use of ordered pairs (Figure 2.5), ascending from the bottom of the left-hand side of the map, accounted for generations of royal couples that made up Teozacoalco's political genealogy. The painter also utilized the A-O calendar device used to identify dates, architectural ornamentation symbolic of political authority, accouterments of power including headdresses and clothing, and feet to indicate travel.

Inside the map's globe on the right-hand side, the painter situated Teozacoalco, the *cabecera* (head town), in the central left surrounded by its thirteen estancias (dependencies). More than forty place-signs define the boundaries of this jurisdiction through the use of logographs—the images that expressed words or ideas. In logographic writing, painters used mountains, cacti, water, trees, plants, temples, people, weaponry, and other elements to represent words that assigned meaning to geographical markers and towns. The painter for the Teozacoalco map applied a Mixtec logograph of a man chiseling a stone temple (Figure 2.6) to describe *chiyo ca'nu*, or a "large/great altar."[24] The map's circular encasement also included the representation of rivers, animals, and three ruling couples directly linked to Teozacoalco.

The map's detail reflects an intimate knowledge of history and geography, mastery over various forms of visual representation, including logographic writing, and more technical matters associated with the production of the vibrant colors used to give meaning to its

2.5. *Ruling pair detail, Relaciones Geográficas map of Teozacoalco (1580). Relaciones Geográficas of Mexico and Guatemala, 1577–1585, Nettie Lee Benson Latin American Collection, University of Texas Libraries, University of Texas at Austin.*

2.6. *Great altar logograph, Relaciones Geográficas map of Teozacoalco (1580). Relaciones Geográficas of Mexico and Guatemala, 1577–1585, Nettie Lee Benson Latin American Collection, University of Texas Libraries, University of Texas at Austin.*

elements. Considering the use and application of these tools, one finds conceivable that an elder master individually made or oversaw the production of the Teozacoalco map. Hernando de Cervantes, the Spanish *corregidor* who petitioned the map, specifically sought the guidance of leading indigenous elders to respond to the questions in the Relaciones Geográficas questionnaire. Cervantes enlisted the help of Juan Ruíz Zuaso, the town's bilingual priest, to facilitate an interview between a group of Mixtec elder males and the Spanish corregidor. When preparing his responses on January 9, Cervantes credited his informants, noting: "We initiated a true and faithful report as best as we could infer from the [testimony of the] oldest natives from said town and from what one can visually survey."[25]

A thin line separated those trained under the supervision of the friars from the elder generation brought up under Mesoamerican customs, the former often viewing the latter with distrust for their adherence to Spanish customs. Although Spanish sources often clump *ancianos* (elders) and *naturales* (natives) together—as if these groups represented homogeneous entities that followed unified goals to acquire land, status, and privileges— interests often cut across generations, divided along Christian factions that supported missionary efforts versus traditionalist factions that sought to preserve native customs and rituals.[26] In the case of the Teozacoalco map, Cervantes's testimony seems simply to ratify what is visibly obvious: only someone deeply versed in the Mesoamerican pictorial tradition could have deployed the specialized tools used to make the map of Teozacoalco.

PRACTICE

Unlike painters in the Valley or the Mixteca, who made maps mostly to represent the interests of native *cabildos* and caciques, the painter of Tehuantepec described in this chapter's introductory vignette worked closely with Spanish patrons. From the early 1570s until the end of the century, royal officials sought his services to describe spatial relationships in Tehuantepec, and he generated over half a dozen maps of different parts of the region.[27] Most maps responded to the ranching boom that took place during the late sixteenth and early seventeenth

centuries, which redirected Zapotec, Zoque, and Huave land to Spaniards bold enough to negotiate the region's unique topography and extreme climate.[28] Zapotecs, based in part on the strength of their social hierarchy, maintained a tight hold on irrigated lands, developing a complex cropping system suited to the region's windy and arid weather.[29] The Huave took advantage of their geographical location on the coastal plain to retain lands but also to facilitate the trade of shrimp, fish, lime, and purple cloth in the region. Disease reduced the Zoque during the sixteenth century to a fraction of its precontact estimates, opening up land for Spanish ranching and transforming the local economy and culture.[30] The maps made by the painter of Tehuantepec document this period of Spanish expansion, one in which authorities sought to define spatial boundaries, in part, through visualization.

The earliest example of his work dates to 1573, when alcalde mayor Gaspar Maldonado commissioned a map (Figure 2.7) for a land grant northeast of Tehuantepec near Mistequilla and Comitlán.[31] To identify Tehuantepec, the seat of power in the region, the painter used its logographic place-name: a jaguar moving through a hill with a small Christian church at its foot. A distinctive house structure with a rectangular base and entrance covered by his trademark conical-shaped rooftop described a settlement in the center of the page. More than any other cartographic element, this motif defined the painter's signature style, a recurrent tool used to designate towns found on all of his maps. Likewise, his use of a rectangular horseshoe to designate livestock and cattle ranches also featured prominently in the painter's vocabulary. True to form, the painter had a distinctive way of drawing feet: shapely imprints clearly illustrated in early maps but that disappear over time from his later examples.

The use of such symbols calls attention to the visual qualities of land tenure—to what people saw. The introduction of agricultural infrastructure, including corrals, storage units, ranch houses, and fences, changed the physical landscape of central and southern Mexico, prompting the development of new ways of representing the mapped environment. Geographical elements

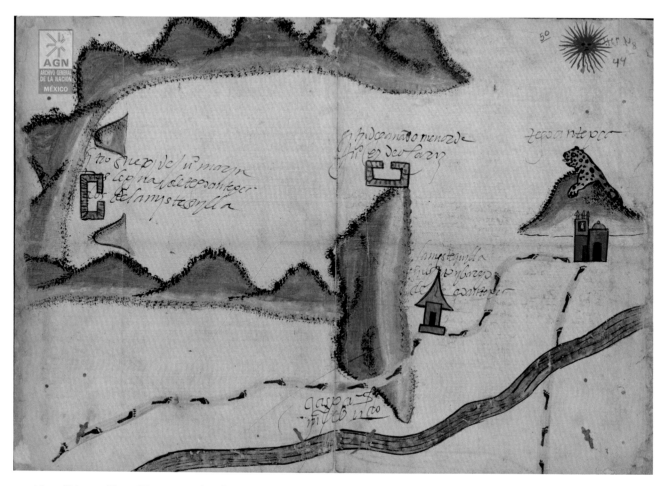

2.7. *Map of Mystequilla and Tegoantepec (1573), no. 2378, Tierras, vol. 3343, exp. 4, f. 43v and 44. Archivo General de la Nación, Fondo Hermanos Mayo, concentrados, sobre 363.*

such as mountains, rivers, lagoons, springs, trees, plants, animals, and rocks played prominent roles in defining boundaries, their representation on maps gradually changing to fit the needs of the patrons who commissioned the maps and the officials tasked with reviewing them. Painters borrowed freely from both ancient Mesoamerican logographic writing and from visual components such as heraldry, seals, religious iconography, paintings, printed matter, and architecture that accompanied Spanish colonization. Spaniards also introduced a host of animals that transformed the physical landscape of Mesoamerica. Horses and later oxen, swine, and sheep (Figure 2.8) left deep imprints on the American

terrain, eroding stretches of land used as pasture sites.[32] Native towns often complained to royal authorities of cattle invasions from neighboring estates and of ruined crops. By the second half of the sixteenth century, painters memorialized the Spanish presence in their maps with a simple but powerful gesture: they added hoofprints (Figure 2.9) to the roads where before only feet had traveled.

In another commission, the painter of Tehuantepec surveyed a much broader expanse of land. Juan de Torres de Lagunas, the region's alcalde mayor, requested a map (Figure 2.10) of the entire region from the painter in 1580 to complete a questionnaire on behalf of the

2.8. Animals, from upper left to lower right: (a) Horses, map of Aztatla (1576), no. 1578, Tierras, vol. 2679, exp. 15, f. 15; (b) Estancia with animal, map of San Juan Bautista, San Luys Tezontla, and Santa María Nochtongo (1579), no. 2052, Tierras, vol. 2762, exp. 10, f. 112; (c) Animal on the road, map of Santa Cruz Xoxocotlán (1686), no. 625, Tierras, vol. 129, exp. 4, f. 249; (d) Animals grazing, map of Santa María Guelaxé, San Gerónimo Tlacochaguaya, and Santa Cruz Papalutla (1778 [1690]), no. 0956, Tierras, vol. 1206, exp. 1, cuad. 8, f. 21; (e) Rancher on horseback, map of San Dionisio del Mar (1740), no. 0784, Tierras, vol. 584, exp. 1, cuad. 2, f. 55; (f) Cattle, map of San Dionisio del Mar (1740), no. 0784, Tierras, vol. 584, exp. 1, cuad. 2, f. 55. Archivo General de la Nación, Fondo Hermanos Mayo, concentrados, sobre 363.

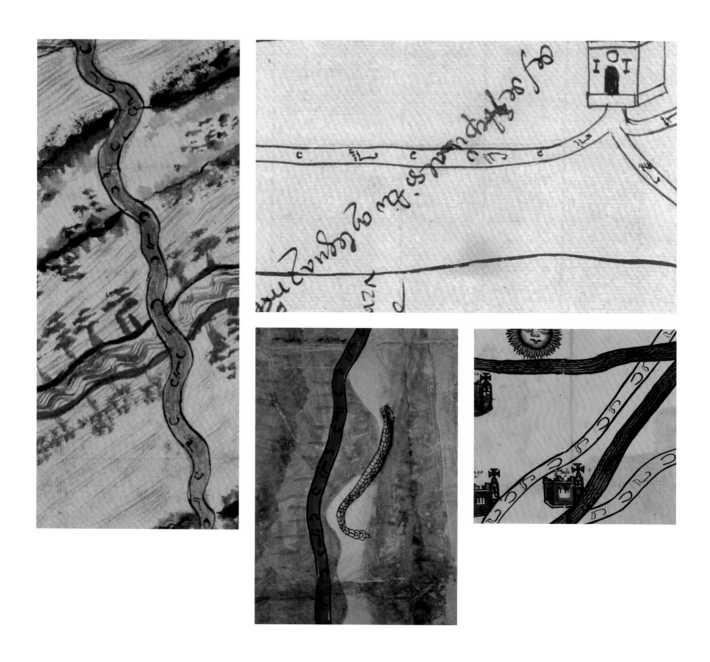

2.9. *Hoofprints interlaced with feet, from left to lower right : (a) Map of Tlaxiaco and Cuquila (1588), no. 1692.9, Tierras, vol. 2692, exp. 17, f. 8; (b) Map of Tepozcolula (1590), no. 1711, Tierras, vol. 2696, exp. 21, f. 8; (c) Relaciones Geográficas map of Teozacoalco (1580); (d) Map of Guaxilotitlan (1586), no. 1726, Tierras, vol. 2702, exp. 2, f. 10. Archivo General de la Nación, Fondo Hermanos Mayo, concentrados, sobre 363.*

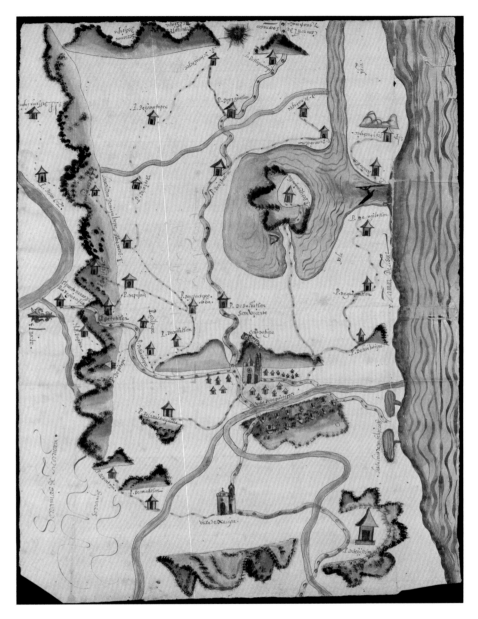

2.10. *Relaciones Geográficas map of Tehuantepec (1580). Relaciones Geográficas of Mexico and Guatemala, 1577–1585, Nettie Lee Benson Latin American Collection, University of Texas Libraries, University of Texas at Austin.*

King of Spain and his cosmographer to measure New World resources.[33] Oriented to the east, the map offered a detailed view of the area's aquatic condition, a complex system of waterways, lagoons, and rivers tied to the Pacific Ocean, which appeared on the right-hand side of the page, identified as "Mar del Sur" (The South Sea). The painter illustrated the towns and settlements with his distinctive rooftops, situating Tehuantepec in the center of the page, identified by the jaguar hill place-name identical to the one used in the 1573 land grant map. While the map from 1573 described the relationship between two ranching sites in proximity to one another, the Relacion Geográfica map provided an expansive view of the landscape, connecting roads and rivers to multiple settlements. In both of these maps, the painter applied a logograph to describe the place-name of Tehuantepec and the use of feet to denote a road or travel, elements drawn from the Mesoamerican pictorial catalog. The difference in maps recognizes the painter's versatility in representing specific and general aspects of the region as well as his disposition to generate unique maps tailored to the patron's needs.

Torres de Lagunas sought the painter's services a second time in 1580 to allocate a ranching site for the native town of Tzanaltepec on the eastern portion of Tehuantepec near Chiapas. This region suffered a steady

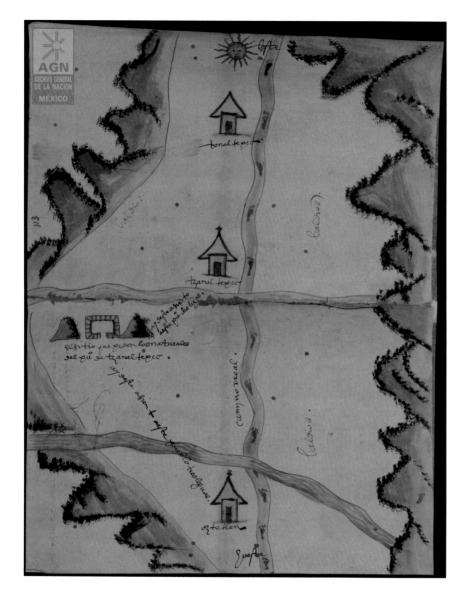

2.11. *Map of Tzanaltepec, Tonaltepec, and Oztutlan (1580), no. 1903, Tierras, vol. 2729, exp. 4, f. 107v and 108. Archivo General de la Nación, Fondo Hermanos Mayo, concentrados, sobre 363.*

population decline through the end of the sixteenth century and into the seventeenth, though these demographic changes did not deter Spanish ranchers from pursuing their objectives. The shortage of indigenous labor prompted Spaniards to import African slaves to support their economic activities, transforming Tzanaltepec into a predominantly black enclave by the 1670s.[34] On the Marqués's ranches in Tehuantepec, Africans and Afro-Mexicans held supervisory positions and occupied the

top ranching positions as *vaqueros*, or "cowhands."[35] Others ran packs of mules that transported such goods as the prized blue dye, *añil*, from Guatemala to Oaxaca, Mexico City, and Veracruz, a topic discussed in chapter 3.

For the commission, the painter of Tehuantepec made a map (Figure 2.11) that situated the site of land, marked with a rectangular structure near the center of the page, flanked by two small hills.[36] The three buildings with the conical top lined up along the vertical axis and the thick, mosslike outline along the edge of each mountain bear the painter's signature pictorial elements. A river that flows horizontally separates Tzanaltepec from the site by two leagues, while a major road marked by feet that runs east to west provides the map's vertical axis. The painter illustrated each of the three towns depicted in the map, with Tonaltepec at the top, Tzanaltepec in the center, and Oztotlán at the bottom, in his trademark style. From this point forward, however, the rest of the painter's cartographic output omits references of logographic writing. Considering the strong technique displayed in the Relación Geográfica map of 1580, one finds the absence of more elements from the Mesoamerican canon in the painter's later maps in some ways surprising. Did the painter, for instance, have to include a logogram for a Spanish audience? He seemed to think he did not. One assumes the change took place as a result of the artist's willingness to adapt his pictorial skills to fit the audiences' needs, coupled with the expectations of the patron for the finished product.

In the two maps (Figures 2.12 and 2.13) made for the alcalde mayor Hernando de Vargas in 1585 and 1586, the painter outlined major geographical features of the coastal town of Tlapanaltepeque, including treeless plains, mountains, streams, roads, and the Pacific Ocean at the bottom of the page.[37] The use of a rectangular

2.12. *Map of Tlapanaltepeque (1585), no. 2391, Tierras, vol. 3343, exp. 20, f. 8. Archivo General de la Nación, Fondo Hermanos Mayo, concentrados, sobre 363.*

structure with a triangular rooftop signaled the location of Tlapanaltepeque, from where officials measured distances to the desired sites of land. Neither of the maps included any traces of logographic writing, though hoofprints continued to designate roads; yet even this most visible element disappeared from the painter's later maps (Figure 2.1). Over time, the painter developed a simple but effective formula: a few well-placed structures and lines combined with a discrete amount of color, which allowed officials to easily identify petitioned sites, ranches, and towns within the region. Armed with pictorial skill and geographical knowledge, the mapmaker contracted his

services to at least five different alcaldes mayores who sought maps over a period of twenty-five years.[38]

MISSIONARY INFLUENCE

The arrival of European missionaries in the sixteenth century profoundly reshaped indigenous society in Mesoamerica. Early evangelists guided by providential design and a millenarian impulse to save the world set out to reinvent native society according to Christian principles.[39] Throughout the Viceroyalty of New Spain, orders of Franciscans, Dominicans, Augustinians, Jesuits, and Mercederians systematically dismantled

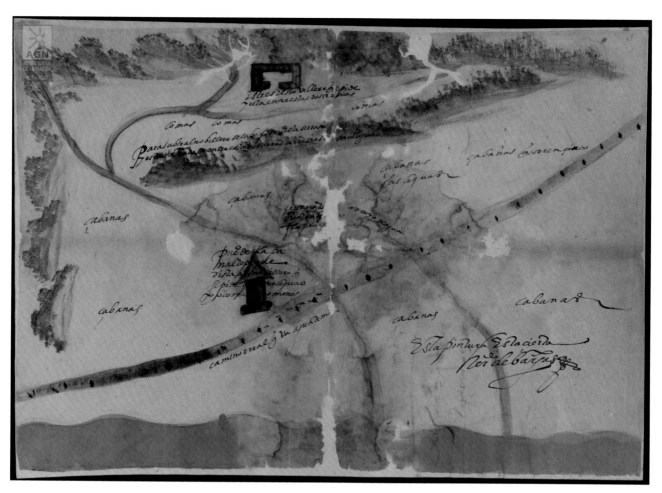

2.13. *Map of Tlapa[na]ltepeque (1586), no. 1965, Tierras, vol. 2737, exp. 25, f. 29. Archivo General de la Nación, Fondo Hermanos Mayo, concentrados, sobre 363.*

traditional religious practices by destroying pagan temples, criminalizing native priests, and demonizing Indian deities.[40] As part of their strategy, Christian clerics placed the children of the most powerful indigenous leaders under their care to educate them as faithful Catholics. This strategy served the double purpose of driving a wedge between the old customs and the new. Missionaries encouraged their students to keep a vigilant eye on rituals that smacked of idolatry, even if that meant denouncing their parents and elders.[41] In Yanhuitlán in the 1540s, generational conflicts divided the region when those who had grown up under the care of the Dominicans accused a group of powerful caciques of reverting to the old ways.[42] The vocational and spiritual education of children allowed clerics to promote their interests at the local level.

In some cases, young males attended institutions outside of Oaxaca. Francisco de Salinas, a Cuicatec lord from the western part of the region, studied at the renowned Colegio de Santa Cruz in Tlatelolco, a Franciscan school established initially to prepare indigenous youths for the priesthood. At Santa Cruz, pupils learned European philosophy and religion and to read and write in Latin and Spanish.[43] Alphabetic writing allowed Nahua, Mixtec, Maya, and Zapotec students from across the realm to write in their own languages, reshaping modes of communication that had traditionally relied on pictorial expression and oral history.[44] After completing his studies at Tlatelolco, the Cuicatec lord returned home, where in 1580 he joined a delegation of elders for a meeting with the region's district officer. During their encounter, the elders responded to questions in the Relaciones Geográficas about political history, trade and commerce, geography, and cultural practices.[45] Salinas's indigenous background and his European training placed him in a unique position to communicate, in written and verbal form, with both his Cuicatec peers and the Spanish officials.

Missionary orders used prints as well as canvas and mural paintings to explain religious doctrine. In the seventeenth century, the Dominican Francisco de Burgoa recalled the early efforts of such individuals as Gonzalo de Lucero, whom he identified as the first Dominican to preach in Oaxaca. Burgoa glorified Lucero's work, noting: "He walked barefoot through the unconverted towns of the region, to preach to them in the Mexican language that he knew well and was the one spoken within the towns subjected to the Ministers of Emperor Moctezuma. This servant of God took with him some rolled canvases with paintings of the principle mysteries of our Holy Faith."[46] Often, Indians produced the canvas paintings and other visual sources used for indoctrination.[47] The conversion crusade undertaken by the missionary orders in New Spain amounted to what Serge Gruzinski refers to as a "war of images," a campaign waged through the displacement of pre-Colombian visual culture, particularly that of a religious nature, replacing it with Christian imagery.[48] Indeed, Spaniards assaulted the New World with a visual canon that also included everyday items, like clothing, and such military objects as artillery, steel swords, helmets, armor, and insignias. Crosses, rosaries, paintings, and prints gave way to the construction of massive Christian temples designed to awe and inspire, the materials used to build them drawn from the ruins of destroyed ancient ritual centers that honored the gods.[49] By the latter part of the sixteenth century, residents and travelers could spot Dominican churches across Oaxaca from leagues away.[50] Images, reasoned religious authorities who set policy during the Third Mexican Provincial Council, facilitated the task of reshaping native understanding of the cosmos.[51]

Objects produced in the Iberian world did not fit neatly into conventional modes of description bound to medieval, Renaissance, and Mesoamerican ideals or to pre- and postcontact dichotomies centered on loss and acculturation. Postmodern lenses have likewise failed to sufficiently explain the fluency (cultural and otherwise) that, as Alessandra Russo has recently argued, allowed indigenous artists to perfect "the 'dominant' culture to the point of being able to both be at ease with it and to thwart it."[52] Russo applies the notion of the untranslatable, a concept that for her embodies "the concrete difficulties and infinite possibilities at play during passages from one artistic world to another, analysis of the choices made, the inevitable losses and the unsuspected inventions at work between forms." Case in point: about

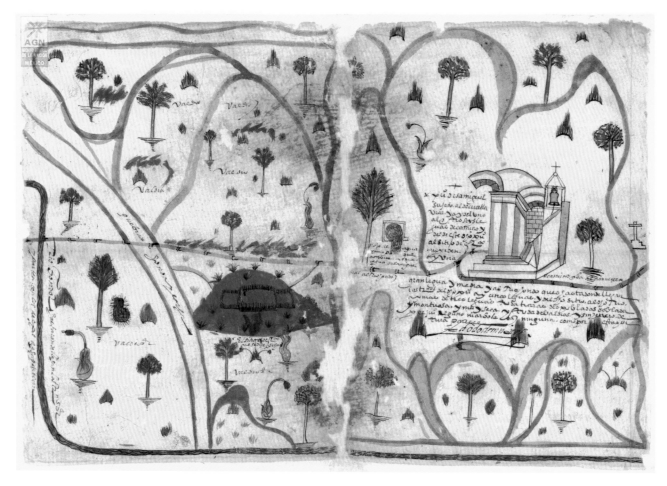

2.14. *Map of San Miguel Cuestlavaca (1582), no. 1609, Tierras, vol. 2682, exp. 9, f. 8. Archivo General de la Nación, Fondo Hermanos Mayo, concentrados, sobre 363.*

eighteen leagues north of Teozacoalco in the highland region of the Mixteca Alta, a painter from the Cuestlaguaca region made a map (Figure 2.14) in 1582 to petition a site of land for a livestock ranch run by the town of San Miguel.[53] Painted on paper with a combination of green and yellow, the painter's rendition presented his own particular vision of a landscape described by the region's corregidor as "unpopulated, broken, mountainous, and dry terrain." Alternating feet marked the presence of New Spain's major artery, the Royal Highway, a road that passed through San Miguel, moving toward the livestock ranch that sat on the side of a

small hill. The church on the right (Figure 2.15), a symbol that represented the town of San Miguel, reflected the painter's application of depth and space, the use of three-dimensionality no doubt a response to the movement of European prints to the Americas. Engravings and other printed images of religious scenes, such as Albrecht Dürer's *The Holy Family with Two Angels* (Figure 2.16), circulated across New Spain, inside and outside of convent walls, and were used by clerics to teach aspects of the Catholic faith.[54] In both the map and the print, an emphasis on the vaulted features of the church allowed each artist to project a sense of depth through

2.15. *Church, map of San Miguel Cuestlavaca (1582), no. 1609, Tierras, vol. 2682, exp. 9, f. 8. Archivo General de la Nación, Fondo Hermanos Mayo, concentrados, sobre 363.*

loopholes, ambiguities, silences, and lapses available to them."[56] The system of castes in colonial society reduced all relationships of power to the simple fact that, regardless of social status, Spaniards enjoyed mastery over the colonial world.[57] The unequal standing of natives when confronted with Spaniards, even for the most powerful caciques and noblemen, served as a motivating factor to develop new tools to express spatial relationships.

Churches, the most important buildings in colonial society, symbolized townships and represented the most recognizable cartographic element on any given map, a practice tied to churches' role in daily life as the centers of power and social interaction across cities, villas, and towns in New Spain. The relationship between the painter, the map's patron, and the authorizing official who inspected it led to a systematization of its use that

perspectival drawing and shading. Although one may find it difficult to determine whether the painter of Cuestlaguaca viewed Dürer's print of the Holy Family, his use of three-dimensionality had roots in the circulation of religious imagery made in Europe. Ultimately, the painter blended stylistic elements that defied pictorial genres and simple categorization.

Late-sixteenth-century mapmaking witnessed a defining moment when painters experimented with new techniques, shifting back and forth from conceptual to perceptual interpretations of the natural environment. Typically associated with European image-making, perceptual illustrations present elements of three-dimensionality and an illusion of spatial depth, whereas conceptual ones appear in two-dimensional, flat spaces.[55] The maps do not suggest an abandonment or immediate replacement of one style over another but rather the disposition of painters to try out new ideas. Faced with multiple Spanish and indigenous audiences, a painter's need to convey a message required, in James Scott's words, "an experimental spirit and a capacity to test and exploit all

2.16. *Albrecht Dürer, The Holy Family with Two Angels, c. 1503. The Metropolitan Museum of Art.*

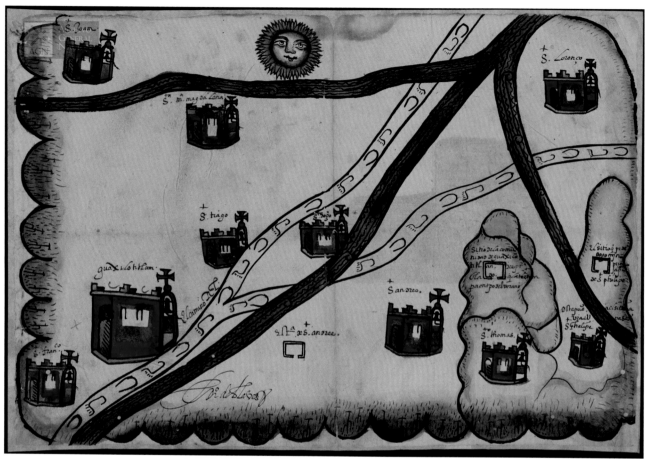

2.17. *Map of Guaxilotitlan (1586), no. 1726, Tierras, vol. 2702, exp. 2, f. 10. Archivo General de la Nación, Fondo Hermanos Mayo, concentrados, sobre 363.*

various audiences could easily interpret. This simple premise allowed painters to communicate spatial relationships while developing their own pictorial voice: as long as painters clearly depicted churches, they could apply different styles and techniques. After all, the idea of the church served as a systematized element of map-making; its representation could, and did, take on a variety of forms. The painter of the map of Guaxilotitlán (Figure 2.17), a former Zapotec ritual center northwest of Antequera in the Valley of Oaxaca, made a painting in 1586 for Domingo Martín, an Indian notable from the subject town of San Felipe, to petition a site for a livestock ranch.[58] Mountains frame the map's base and its left edge while two roads emerge from the top-right

corner, merging into a single artery toward the bottom-left portion of the page; footprints and hoof marks indicate travel. The painter used a dark green shade to color a river with two tributaries that cut across the region. Along with the roads and mountains, the painter's style reflected native pictorial traditions, yet the most noticeable items on the map include the ten churches of various sizes scattered across the page. Colored in deep crimson with gold and black outlines, the churches represent Guaxilotitlán and the surrounding towns. The fact that the painter chose to depict local settlements with a church instead of the more traditional mountain/hill place-sign (*teptl*) reflects the transformation of indigenous pictorial expression.

In Cuestlaguaca, painters such as Domingo de Mendoza used maps to support their negotiations with royal officials. One map made in 1590 (Figure 2.18) describes the site for a *caballería*, a measure of land of about 105 acres, near Tepenene petitioned by Francisco de Mendoza, another cacique from the region.[59] The painter represented the town with a small church in the center-left portion of the map, where feet connected Tepenene with Concepción and with the cabecera Cuestlaguaca three leagues away. The two serpents facing away from each other below a large church represent the place-name for Cuestlaguaca: "in the plain of snakes." An arm extends from a teptl place-sign to indicate the town of Tepenene. Mary Elizabeth Smith suggests that the separation of the church from the place-sign may reference the site

of the town before the Spanish *congregaciones* (resettlements) of the sixteenth century.[60] Within indigenous settlements, control of mapmaking remained largely in the hands of a select few (typically caciques who made and stored maps and pictorial documents). Considering the location where this map and the 1617 map of Tepenene (Figure 2.3) circulated, one can plausibly speculate that Francisco and Domingo de Mendoza had a familial bond. If so, the former almost certainly transferred knowledge of the art of painting to the latter.

A decade later, another map (Figure 2.19) that recorded the petition of Don Juan de Salazar for a livestock ranch near Tepenene reflected certain similarities to the 1590 map.[61] On February 20, 1600, Salazar met in Tepenene with Felipe de Echagoyan, the alcalde mayor

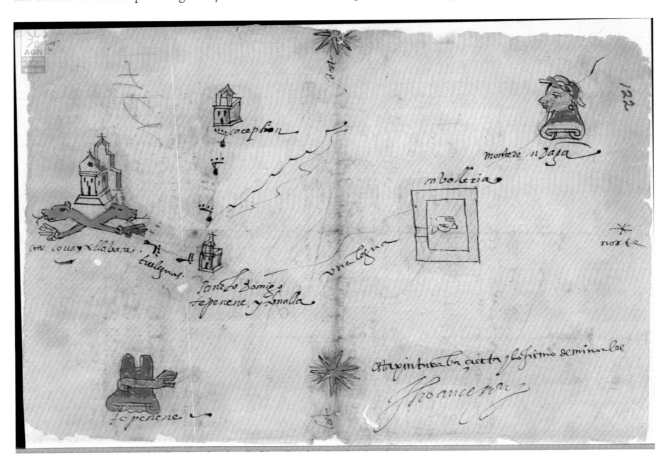

2.18. *Map of Santo Domingo Tepenene and Couayxtlabaca (1590), no. 1904, Tierras, vol. 2729, exp. 5, f. 117. Archivo General de la Nación, Fondo Hermanos Mayo, concentrados, sobre 363.*

of Yanhuitlán, to review the map. Oriented east, the map's painter incorporated traditional Mesoamerican iconography, including a river along the center of the page with sixteen houses on either side, a road with feet to indicate travel that reaches the desired site, and the teptl hill, which indicates the site of the livestock ranch where the alcalde mayor inscribed the caption "*aquí el sitio*," or "the site [is] here." In the center of the page, a church in three-quarter view represents the town of Tepenene, while a sun at the top of the page signals east. A recent study by Eleanor Wake suggests that the sun, more than a commonly used cartographic device that symbolized the eastward orientation, formed part of an assortment of astral bodies including moons, stars, and planets (Figure 2.20) that "emphasized the antiquity and inalienability of indigenous land."[62] Wake's insightful approach ties native spatial routines, most notably ritual boundary-walking, to celestial observation, aspects of which some painters incorporated into their maps. She concludes that the "maps thus explain an Indian vision and ordering of geography that was unlikely to have been comprehensible to European eyes, in matters of orientation or anything else."[63] Wake's analysis sets astronomical observation at the center of the mapmaking process, helping to articulate a more precise vision of painterly activity. The celestial objects on the 1600 map

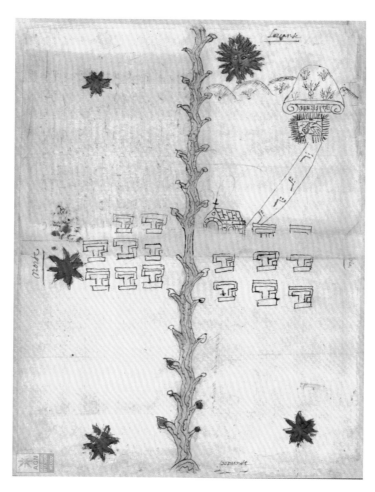

2.19. *Map of Tepenene (1600), no. 1812, Tierras, vol. 2719, exp. 23, f. 9. Archivo General de la Nación, Fondo Hermanos Mayo, concentrados, sobre 363.*

2.20. *Celestial bodies: (a) Sun, map of Tzanaltepec, Tonaltepec, and Oztutlan (1580), no. 1903, Tierras, vol. 2729, exp. 4, f. 107v y 108; (b) Sun, map of Guaxilotitlan (1586), no. 1726, Tierras, vol. 2702, exp. 2, f. 10; (c) Sun, map of Tlaxiaco and Cuquila (1588), no. 1692.9, Tierras, vol. 2692, exp. 17, f. 8; (d) Star, map of Santo Domingo Tepenene and Couayxtlabaca (1590), no. 1904, Tierras, vol. 2729, exp. 5, f. 117; (e) Moon, map of Tepozcolula (1590), no. 1711, Tierras, vol. 2696, exp. 21, f. 8; (f) Moon, map of Tlaxiaco, Cuquila, and Mistepeque (1595), no. 1614, Tierras, vol. 2682, exp. 17, f. 18. Archivo General de la Nación, Fondo Hermanos Mayo, concentrados, sobre 363.*

of Tepenene (Figure 2.19), most notably depictions of the stars, share a striking resemblance to the ones on the map painted in Tepenene in 1590 (Figure 2.18). Both maps include stars that share an outline contoured with medium lines filled in with flat washes of color. Though other elements, including the use of the teptl hill, differ from one another, the styling used to illustrate the objects in the sky suggests familiarity with local visual practices and an adherence to the pliable nature of pictorial record-making.

The circulation of maps and other pictorial records foregrounded the elaboration of new maps. Cartographic activity of the late seventeenth and eighteenth centuries in many ways emulated the "mapping tradition" of the late sixteenth century through the copying of maps.[64] The reproduction of pictorial manuscripts represented a primary means of transmitting spatial knowledge in Mesoamerica, the maps of the late sixteenth century themselves inspired by earlier models tempered through decades of cultural exchange with Europeans. The practice of reproduction presupposes a reliance on older documents that contextualizes the circulation of maps across time.

When Domingo de Zárate described himself as a master who practiced the art of painting in 1686, he unintentionally opened a curtain that had veiled the continued practice of pictorial record-making in Oaxaca. How did knowledge of mapmaking circulate during this later period after the demise of the first few generations of painters? What changes did painters introduce into the mapmaking process, and what do these shifts tell us about land tenure, local politics, and privilege? Extant evidence suggests elders bore the burden of transferring their knowledge to younger generations by using pictorial records as didactic devices. When identifying the painting used to legitimize the petition made by the Juárez de Zárate brothers in 1690, Julián de Santiago, a seventy-year-old former political officer from Santa Catarina Ixtepeji, confirmed the map belonged to the Juárez family. He told authorities his knowledge stemmed from an oral exchange with seniors in his youth, with the scribe noting: "The elders have suggested it and explained it to him."[65] Sixty-year-old Lucas de Santiago declared, "I know the map in which the origin and descent of those named in this petition is the true and ancient one. . . . I have heard it said by others, older and more ancient than me."[66] Pictorial knowledge relied in large part on oral exchanges between junior members of a town and the elders who taught them about their community's culture and history. The testimony of the two men suggests spaces existed where individuals discussed and learned about the use and manufacture of pictorial manuscripts and maps. These individuals gained not only specific tools designed to provide a valuable service but also access to knowledge they could use to reaffirm social status within elite circles of caciques and principales who led town affairs.

In some instances, elders used maps as mnemonic devices to recite the history of their communities, transmitting in the process important spatial and geographical knowledge used to establish autonomy. Lucas de los Santos testified in 1691 on behalf of the Mixtecs of Xoxocotlán about their ancient map (Figure 1.1) and the land titles in their possession. The town used the map in the late 1680s and early 1690s to litigate against a Spaniard over five acres of land. During an interrogation to establish the map's authenticity, de los Santos declared he had seen the map and had witnessed the town's elders reading it aloud. Likewise, thirty-eight-year-old Joseph

de Santiago testified he knew the map and had also heard elders reading from it. Similar practices took place in other regions of Oaxaca, where "logographic descriptions punctuated pictorial boundary maps, evoking boundary and place names for a prominent community elder who, through oral exegesis, could interpret the visual representation and publicly rehearse the community's history and the identity of its founding ancestors during important days of the ritual calendar."[67] Orality and visuality played central components of indigenous learning, contributing to the production of maps in the region.

Making claims about authorship and ties to the art of indigenous painting for maps made during the eighteenth century is a tricky endeavor. The iconography, precision, and style of the sixteenth century disappeared by the eighteenth century, leaving in its place an uneven output of maps characterized by exaggerated, but not always well-defined, proportions, an occasional return to large surfaces on cloth, and a shift toward naturalist landscapes. The map of San Andrés Tlacozahuala prepared in 1704 (Figure 2.21) located lands that would serve as capital for the establishment of a *capellanía*, a pious work endowed to generate funds in support of the celebration of Masses for the salvation of a person's soul.[68] The painter identified the two selected plots in the center-right portion of the map by their Mixtec place-names (Yodzosica and Yuchadzinchaco), the latter coupled with a rectangular surface. The placement of stylized mountains along the edges of the page and the network of roads and rivers that connect the powerful seat of Yanhuitlán to smaller towns such as San Andrés and San Francisco on the upper portion of the map recall the scale and styling of maps from an earlier generation. Upon closer inspection, however, differences in the pictorial elements of the map reflect the changes that transformed the art of painting. The painter of the map of San Andrés Tlacozahuala, for instance, omitted any traces of logographic writing used in the past to help connect place-names to the natural, physical, or animal elements that gave the toponyms meaning in the first place. Likewise, feet and animal prints—those ubiquitous symbols of movement, boundaries, and authority—also disappeared from the cartographic vocabulary of later painters. How, then, is it possible to discern an author's social background when some of the most important elements of indigenous mapmaking disappeared?

The path, to be sure, is thorny and uncertain. And yet a few key social and pictorial markers indicate that natives continued to make maps despite transformations that often left them unrecognizable from the cartographic productions of the late sixteenth century. At no other time in history had indigenous landholders come under such threat as they did starting in the late 1600s. Litigants turned to multiple forms of evidence, including maps, genealogical histories, and tribute records, to establish control over land. For individuals such as Domingo de Zárate, practicing the art of painting functioned as a badge of prestige: membership in a select club that for generations had interpreted spatial relationships for multiple audiences with an interest in land and spatial division. The painter of the map of San Andrés Sinaxtla (Figure 2.22), made in 1704, likewise applied circularity to organize a series of boundary markers represented by teptl signs in black and red ink.[69] In addition, he introduced elements seldom, if ever, seen in earlier cartographic activities. Drawing from alphabetic writing, the painter of the map of Sinaxtla glossed his own sites by identifying place-names in Mixtec, reminiscent of the way Domingo de Zárate approached the making of his copied map of Xoxocotlán. Only cardinal

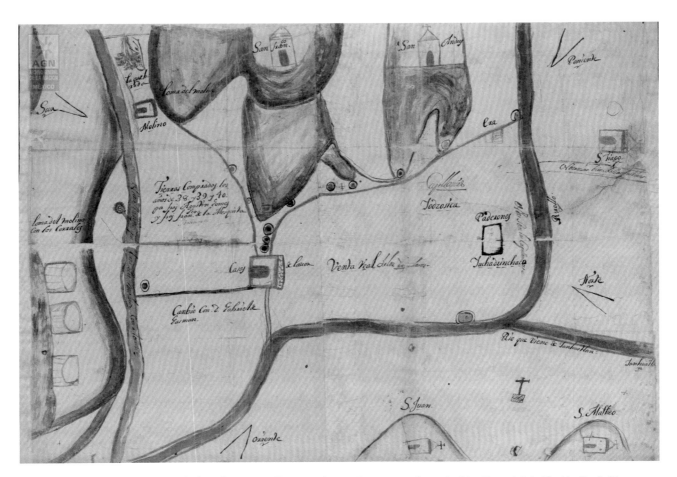

2.21. *Map of San Andrés Tlacozahuala (1704), no. 0658, Tierras, vol. 220, 1ª pte., exp. 1, f. 277. Archivo General de la Nación, Fondo Hermanos Mayo, concentrados, sobre 363.*

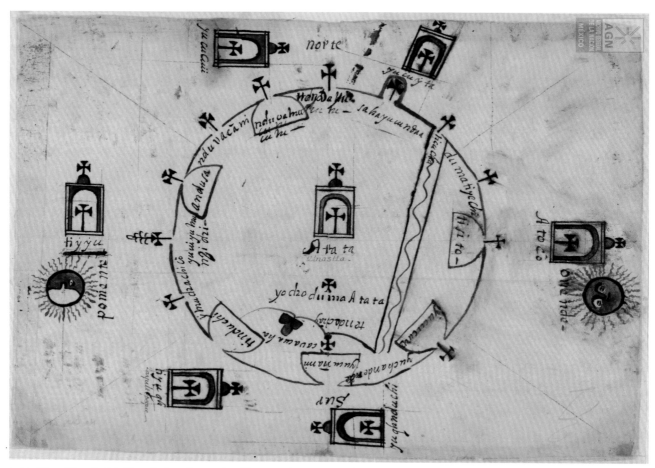

2.22. *Map of San Andrés Sinaxtla (1714), no. 0670, Tierras, vol. 308, exp. 4, f. 29. Archivo General de la Nación, Fondo Hermanos Mayo, concentrados, sobre 363.*

directions—north and south on the top and bottom, and east and west represented by the sun and a red moon on the right and left—appeared in Spanish. Faint lines in the background indicate the painter traced a grid before he committed any pictorial elements to the map. Two diagonal lines divide the folio into four parts, while several shorter lines helped the painter trace the elements of the map; native artists from the sixteenth century did not apply this technique.

Over time, modern archival science has impacted interpretations of the purposefulness of the painter's method by extracting maps from their original positions in the documentary record, which in turn has affected

the way catalogers filed them along with other maps that shared similar characteristics. At the AGN, the map of Sinaxtla has traditionally appeared in a vertical position in printed and digital catalogs, a schema that for no apparent reason privileges the west end of the map. For their part, modern scholars have taken at face value the categorization deployed in cataloging without noticing that the intended way to read the map is to rotate it clockwise ninety degrees. Doing this allows the viewer to gain a clearer understanding of the painter's intentions. Notice, for instance, that in this position the centrality of "A[s]tata" (Zinastla) jumps out at the viewer, the textual elements coming clearly into focus. The difference in the color of the two glosses reflects the difference in materials used by the painter, who made the map and labeled its elements in Mixtec with a deep black carbon substance, and a Spanish official, who authenticated the map by identifying the town with its Nahuatl place-name by using an iron-based mixture that has faded over time. After adding the place-names within the map's central circular area, the painter moved in a counterclockwise position to incorporate churches and celestial bodies across the edges of the map, applying a black outline filled in with red in the archways and black in the crosses. Despite the classificatory scheme imposed on the map, perhaps as a result of the original scribe's filing of the record with the written documentation, these elements offer a narrative of adaptation and change that nonetheless reflects clear indigenous artistry.

One cannot say the same about the map of San Pablo Mitla (Figure 2.23) made in 1730.[70] Deployed to mitigate a dispute over two tracts of land between the natives of San Pablo Mitla and the Dominican friars of Etla in Oaxaca's central valley, the map reflects a unique aesthetic that blends conceptual and perceptual visions of local geography. Drawing with charcoal on four folios bound together by adhesive to generate a larger mapping surface, the painter illustrated the mountains on the upper portion of the map and the town of Mitla on the far right. The presence of a key on the bottom left, a feature not usually found on sixteenth-century indigenous maps, signals the intervention of three individuals: the painter, a judge, and the scribe, who together compared the map with the region under consideration. Shading allowed the artist to suggest three-dimensional volume that signals a greater affinity toward a perceptual interpretation of the landscape, but boundary markers

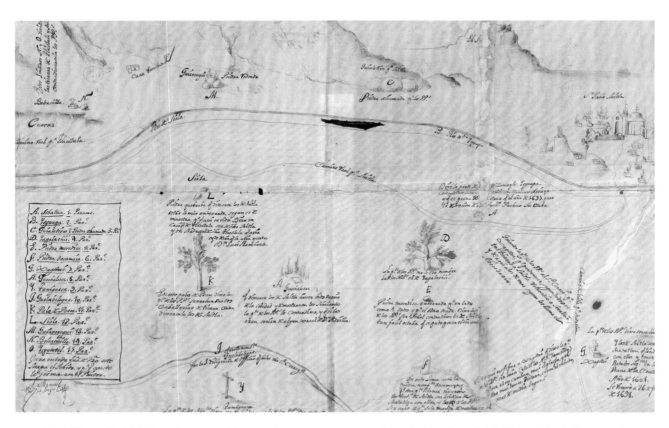

2.23. *Map of San Pablo Mitla (1730), no. 0719, Tierras, vol. 489. 1a. parte, exp. 1, f. 271. Archivo General de la Nación, Fondo Hermanos Mayo, concentrados, sobre 363.*

used to define the spatial relationships between Mitla and its neighbors appear on the map more as conceptual features of the landscape. The large size and positioning of crosses, small groups of stones or single rocks, trees, hills, and even a pedestal leave little doubt as to which elements of the map carried more value, though they do not reveal details about the map's author.

The map of San Pablo Mitla possesses qualities utilized by eighteenth-century surveyors in their own maps. Cartographic technology centered on European ideals of accuracy and science had coexisted alongside indigenous mapmaking since the early colonial period.[71] Surveying—a principal element to define spatial boundaries—combined Euclidian geometry with specialized knowledge about Spanish law and imperial policy. Where the surveyor's trusty tools—"a pocket clock, a compass, a pen, a bottle of ink, white paper, a rule, a square, a cordel, and a subdivided two-vara wooden staff"—sought to ensure precision, surveying suffered tremendously throughout the colonial period from errors made as a result of measuring devices, lack of formal training among the surveyors, and faulty techniques used to field-measure.[72] The extent and geographic diversity of the empire, coupled with changing agrarian policies, limited consistency in weights and measures.[73] These two factors contributed to regional variances used

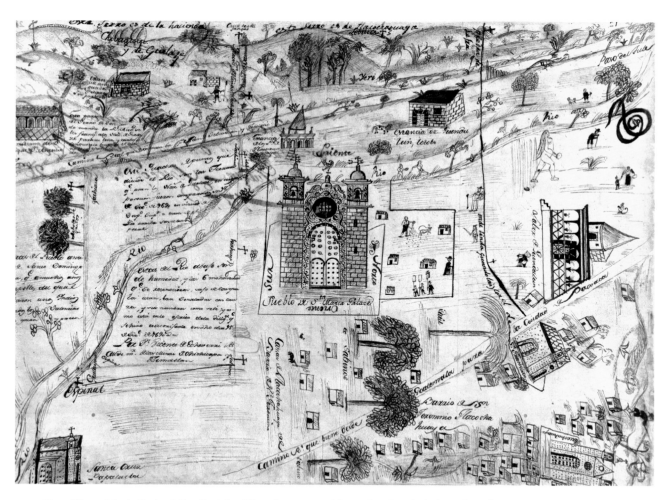

2.24. *Map of Santa María Guelaxé, San Gerónimo Tlacochaguaya, and Santa Cruz Papalutla (1778 [1690]), no. 0956, Tierras, vol. 1206, exp. 1, cuad. 8, f. 21. Archivo General de la Nación, Fondo Hermanos Mayo, concentrados, sobre 363.*

to account for units of land. By the eighteenth century, a lack of understanding of the frames of reference used to prepare geographical sources thwarted Bourbon efforts to engage in a systematic study of the empire's extent. As a result, during the latter part of the century, authorities deployed a series of measures, including scientific expeditions to the Americas, geodesic mapping, and engineering projects along the frontier in order to redress the imbalance.[74] Maps played a central role in these efforts.

Reproduction—the request by a patron or official to copy an old map, usually for the purpose of providing evidence in a legal proceeding—likewise complicates ideas about authorship. Consider the map of Santa María Guelaxé (Figure 2.24), a Zapotec town southeast of Antequera.[75] Made in 1778 by an unknown painter, the map followed an earlier cartograph originally commissioned in 1690 to protect the boundaries of the Zapotec settlement. The extant version of the map supported Guelaxé's petition for access to coal and wood on a southwestern boundary that neighbored with a nearby ranch, and it possessed many of the attributes of native mapmaking. An ornate and carefully detailed church in the center of the page draws the viewer's gaze. Around the church, men engage in agricultural activities on town lands while women collect water by the river west of the main church. Elsewhere, a man sleeps with his head on his knees and a bag strapped to his back while an Indian in a *tilma*, a tunic with a strap over the shoulder typically worn by the male indigenous nobility, stands with a spear in his hand facing the church (Figure 2.25). His much larger counterpart, an unclothed woman with dark, waist-length hair, walks commandingly over the landscape, her impressive figure twice as large as any other human figure in the map. This unique picture of everyday life reflects labor patterns and economic activities as well as attitudes toward authority, in this case directed at the church in the form of two natives subverting traditional social roles. While the original map of Guelaxé sought to define all town boundaries, the copy's primary function rested on defending a single *mojón*. The choice of cartographic symbols to represent human settlements allowed the painter of the 1690 model to appeal to Spanish sensibilities surrounding religion and authority, but for all

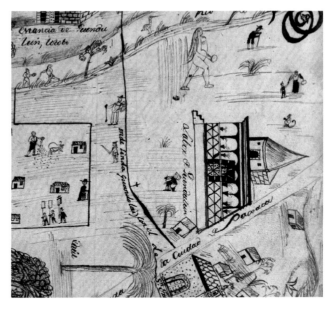

2.25. *Detail, map of Santa María Guelaxé, San Gerónimo Tlacochaguaya, and Santa Cruz Papalutla (1778 [1690]), no. 0956, Tierras, vol. 1206, exp. 1, cuad. 8, f. 21. Archivo General de la Nación, Fondo Hermanos Mayo, concentrados, sobre 363.*

we know, a determined Spanish scribe, a curious alcalde mayor, or a commissioned mestizo artist could have just as easily copied the 1778 map.

CONCLUSION

The history of indigenous painters is one of transformation and adaptation as much as it is a study of custom and tradition. One can clearly discern that the trail they charted on the historical landscape combined pictorial skill, geographic knowledge, and legal savvy with a measure of common sense, self-interest, and determination thrown in for good measure. In the contested social climate of the viceroyalty, painters shaped the way people envisioned space, especially territorial boundaries, in an effort to retain legal rights to property. They made their maps purposefully to serve their clients and, in some cases, their own interests as people bought, sold, leased, and petitioned land. Painters drew from shared cultural experience, fluency in languages, and an understanding of the way the political environment under Spanish rule sought to redistribute power and authority.

CHAPTER 3

MATERIALS

It is the painter's craft to know how to use colors, and
draw and give meaning to images with carbon, and to
properly combine colors for grinding and mixing.

BERNARDINO DE SAHAGÚN,
HISTORIA GENERAL DE LAS COSAS DE NUEVA ESPAÑA

Deep in the woods of the mountains in western Oaxaca, a group of Mixtec priests searched carefully for a particular species of pine tree used to make ink. They followed the orders of a man known as Don Francisco, a native lord from the important head town of Yanhuitlán in the Mixteca Alta who had instructed them to seek wood for a ritual of spiritual conversion. Don Francisco, like many other indigenous leaders throughout the Americas, received the sacrament of baptism into the Catholic faith sometime prior to 1545 as a result of Dominican incursions in the region that helped convert large numbers of natives. But despite their strong efforts, evangelicals' zeal never fully eradicated old rituals and beliefs, especially in the most trying of times. A devastating drought had forced Francisco and his followers to consider what their abandonment of the old deities in favor of the Christian god had done to alter their relationship with the natural world. The *cacique* concluded that the failure to venerate the old deities influenced the traumatic events they faced, and he would stand by his decision to convert to Christianity no longer. His actions, dangerous as they were under the watchful eye of religious authorities highly critical of apostates, required offerings to an unspecified deity in order to make amends. Ink stood at the center of this clandestine ritual.

When the men in the forest finally located the necessary wood, they burned it in order to turn it into charcoal, which they dutifully presented to Don Francisco. Don Francisco then ground the charred wood in a vessel, where he mixed it with liquid and a bonding agent before applying it to his bare flesh. "I am no longer a Christian," he proudly exclaimed, "I have returned to what I used to be."[1] Don Francisco observed the ancient customs by piercing his ears to offer his own blood to the gods while those present in the covert ceremony perfumed him with copal, an aromatic tree resin they burned during the ritual.[2] To conclude the transformation, the cacique sacrificed a handful of quails as a token of his faith. The preceding account, told by an Indian slave identified simply as "Juan" before an Inquisition tribunal in 1545, vividly captures the ideological conflicts faced by those who bridged the pre-Hispanic and colonial periods when forced to negotiate droughts, disease, and punishment.

For Don Francisco, the pressure of a drought pushed him to revert to the ancient practices through an elaborate cleansing ritual. *Nduta tnoo*, or "black water," the conventional term for ink in Mixtec, played a central role in that transformation. It should come as little surprise to find priests making ink, for this group controlled the pictorial writing that facilitated the diffusion of beliefs and practices across Mesoamerica.[3]

In addition to exposing the limited success of European efforts to eradicate indigenous religious practices, the incident represents one of several paths available to examine the way painters experimented with plants, minerals, and insects to produce permanent dyes, pigments, paper, and ink. As the epigraph at the beginning of this chapter suggests, materials mattered.[4] The choice of materials used to make maps, I propose, opens a window onto a laboratory of botanical knowledge rarely taken into account in discussions of early modern science. From the use of the *tzacutli* root, an antilaxative that could also serve as a bonding agent applied to pigments, to the ritual use of *ocote* ink, the black substance made of pine adopted by priests in religious ceremonies and by painters in pictorial writing, mapmaking helps situate indigenous knowledge within frameworks of scientific practice. In Oaxaca and other parts of New Spain, painters experimented with tree bark, flowers, fruit, and leaves as they negotiated dispossession of lands, healing of bodies, commerce, trade, and access to food. Seldom have we asked about this knowledge or about the exchange networks that helped it thrive.

This chapter takes place amid fierce negotiations among Europeans, Indians, and mixed-raced peoples in New Spain over the power to control the secrets of nature. Guided by equal measures of curiosity, ambition, and profit, Spaniards sought to capture, dissect, and learn from an indigenous botanical knowledge they often feared, in part, because of its association with esoteric practices and magical healing.[5] The same expertise that fueled the detailed reports penned by men such as Bernardino de Sahagún and Francisco Hernández continued to serve painters who made maps.[6] In the pre-Colombian period, temples, schools of learning, botanical gardens, and individual estates allowed specialists

to experiment with the properties of plants, but these institutions deteriorated rapidly after contact.[7] Under Spanish rule, indigenous healers carried on specific botanical knowledge, securing medicinal remedies for Indians, Spaniards, and Africans afflicted with disease.[8] Likewise, agricultural merchants supplied a wide array of goods in local markets that ranged from spices and vegetables to beautifying products, simultaneously forming an integral part of the transatlantic trade centered on dyes and pigments. Each of these points of contact—securing medicinal remedies, selling beautifying products, making pigments—represent specific spaces where discrete groups of people engaged with generations of scientific experimentation. Just as in other parts of the early modern world, practical experience tied to commerce, commodities, and health fed scientific practice.[9]

INK

A pictorial analysis of the maps used in this study yields important clues about a painter's technical skills. They achieved a diverse chromatic range through the mixture of plants, minerals, roots, insects, fluids, and fruit that constituted the adhesives, ink, and colorants used to make maps. Each map included two to three colors with green, brown, and yellow appearing most commonly followed by red, blue, and black. Color in pictorial manuscripts of the pre-Colombian period had a close association with ritual and politics, though the practice of assigning meaning to it did not always carry over to the second half of the sixteenth century, when painters tailored maps to appeal to scribes and royal officials more interested in establishing locations and boundaries.[10] Some painters such as the artist from Cuquila described below relied on monochromatism, or the use of one color to illustrate maps, a practice known among the Mixtec as *dzo eeni nuu tacu* (painting of a single color).[11] The use of this convention tied into pictorial traditions that extended beyond the realm of the Mixtec in Oaxaca into central Mexico where, twenty years earlier, Alonso de Molina, an influential Franciscan grammarian, had also observed similar practices.[12] Terms such as these convey the significance that materials and color played in the art of painting to carry messages.

Like many other colorants and dyes used in the art of painting during the contact period, ink brought together generations of experimentation and design that allowed painters to produce maps and other pictorial records. In the Mixteca alone, painters used various techniques and materials to produce ink. Some favored the use of *tetlilli*, or "black stone," a dark soil native to the region, while others relied on the more popular *ocotlilli*, a carbon-based ink made from the aromatic pine known as *ócotl* reminiscent of the kind prepared by Don Francisco and the priests.[13] The latter blend caught the attention of sixteenth-century commentators including Francisco Hernández, the royal physician and naturalist, and Bernardino de Sahagún, the Franciscan missionary and ethnographer.

Both men relied on indigenous informants to learn about the intimate relationship individuals in Mesoamerica enjoyed with the natural world. Focused principally on the medicinal properties and commercial appeal of New Spain's botanical environment, Hernández spent seven years, from 1570 to 1577, in New Spain cataloging native plants and their uses. While there, he sought the help of indigenous physicians and botanical specialists to learn about "the secrets of nature," but these specialists only grudgingly turned over samples and regularly lied or misdirected him about the qualities of plants.[14] "I will not talk about the perverse Indian guides," he wrote in "An Epistle to Arias Montano" in 1580:

> Nor will I speak of all their fraudulence, or terrible lies, which caught me off guard more than once; how they played tricks on me, which I took care to avoid with all the tact at my disposal; and how often did I get the properties and even the names of the plants wrong because I depended on false information from an interpreter.[15]

The secrets of nature would not yield easily to Hernández's imperial gaze. In the poem, the physician complained of "the ingenuity of the Indians in the wild, who could not be persuaded to reveal a single secret of nature," forcing him to test the remedies he learned about on himself at great risk to his life.[16] Yet he depended on them for knowledge and guidance, as well as to help illustrate his work.

To assist in the cataloging of plants, Hernández drafted native painters, whom he tasked with illustrating the most noteworthy examples of a corpus of more than three thousand botanical specimens in addition to dozens of insects, reptiles, and minerals.[17] He bitterly complained about them too:

> I cannot begin to count the mistakes of the artists who . . . were to illustrate my work, and yet were the greatest part of my care, so that nothing, from the point of view of a fat thumb, would be different from what was being copied, but rather all would be as it was in reality.[18]

This comment is telling in important ways. It situates a ready pool of native artists willing to cooperate with Hernández to carry out his mission to depict botanical specimens as close to reality as possible. Regardless of the tension between himself and his informants and contributors, the physician managed to capture considerable insight into the practice of transforming raw elements into colorants. He observed, for example, the manner in which painters in the Mixteca prepared ocotlilli, noting they cut the wood into chips, which they burned, producing thick black smoke captured in clay jars until it condensed. The painters would then scrape the soot from the inside of the jars, forming small round balls that according to Hernández could be purchased at local markets for individual use.[19] Sahagún's masterful multivolume history of Nahua culture and society, a work banned by authorities in Spain after its completion in 1577, reported that painters in central Mexico prepared a similar blend as the one described by Hernández. The Franciscan called it "wood-smoked ink" (*tinta del humo de teas*), praising the black substance for its qualities and high demand. Sahagún identified the specialized jars to prepare and distill the mixture as *tlicomalli*, noting the substance was "worth the cost of many inks."[20] For generations, ocotlilli ink and its variants served as an essential component of Mesoamerican ritual practices as well as pictorial writing and mapmaking.

3.1. *Map of Mistepec, Chicaguastla, and Coquila (1595), no. 0867, Tierras, vol. 876, exp. 1, f. 122. Archivo General de la Nación, Fondo Hermanos Mayo, concentrados, sobre 363.*

In the 1590s, the painter of ribbed mountains, a moniker tied to his use of ribs or nubs to emphasize a hill's unbroken terrain, applied these principles to make ink for his maps. Active in and around the region of Tlaxiaco, one of the most populated settlements in the northwestern jurisdiction of Teposcolula, he put his skill on display in 1595 to paint a map (Figure 3.1) on behalf Don José de Castañeda, a Mixtec lord who petitioned for a livestock ranch from Spanish authorities.[21] Don José required the map to demonstrate to authorities the plot's location, a task the painter pursued by anchoring the map's vanishing point (*punto de fuga*), the small head town of Cuquila, at the bottom center of the page.[22] From this point, a curved line moves upward across the page, followed by a set of footprints that split into a *Y*, leading travelers to the town of Chicahuaxtla in the upper left and to Mixtepec on the right. The large oval in the center of the page identified the petitioned site.

While it is reasonable to speculate that the painter used a wood-smoked ink of the ocotlilli variety, the reality is that a number of other mixtures, each with its own unique formula, circulated across central and southern New Spain. Some painters transformed *tlaliyac*, a mineral extracted from the earth either as clods with bits of silver and gold particles or as black stones, into ink. Sahagún and Hernández both observed that, in the Morelos region northwest of Oaxaca, a place traditionally recognized for its exceptional pre-Colombian botanical garden, painters made "very good ink" with *nacazcolotl*, a fruit in the shape of "twisted ears" from the *huanacaxtle* tree.[23] Commonly known as "elephant-ear tree," huanacaxtle thrived in tropical climates across the Americas, including Oaxaca. Hernández commented the fruit was "very astringent and somewhat dry," qualities associated with yellow bile that regulated warm diseases, anger, and depression.[24] When observing the properties of plants, Hernández applied a framework based on the four humors Europeans believed inhabited the body as liquids: blood, phlegm, black bile, and yellow bile. Native physicians did not share the Hippocratic reference, drawing instead on knowledge from ritual practices and magic to inform healing, botany, and scientific learning.[25] These folk healers held unique positions in the social hierarchy of New Spain because they offered viable options for treating illness in a space where professionally trained practitioners were scarce.[26]

The clash of ideologies notwithstanding, knowledge about plants moved within discrete groups across the viceroyalty. Sahagún learned about nacazcolotl to make ink under the worst of circumstances, roughly the same year the devastating *cocoliztli* epidemic swept over the Valley of Mexico in 1576. As the Franciscan and his team of painters and informants worked diligently on the final stages of the *Historia general*, the rising death toll left chaos in its wake. Sahagún noted with despair that, after thirty years free of epidemics, he found himself in the midst of "a great and universal pestilence" that claimed dozens of lives on a daily basis. Likewise, Hernández continued to work on his botanical compendium when conscripted by royal mandate to enter the fray in the fight against the deadly disease, an endeavor

he launched into by conducting autopsies on stricken bodies and learning about the remedies used by native healers.[27] This dark and difficult period witnessed continued communication between the two Spaniards and the indigenous physicians, botanical merchants, and painters who tapped into their respective pools of knowledge to discuss some of the properties associated with plants and minerals.

Two decades later, the painter of ribbed mountains again applied his skill to prepare another batch of ocotlilli for a map (Figure 3.2) he presented in 1599 to the Spanish scribe Alonso de Morán.[28] Annotations on the map, certifying elements added by officials of the Crown to render records legible, suggest the map functioned to determine the number of tributaries in Cuquila and its small subject town one league to the south. Two structures—a temple and a church framed in the upper central portion of the page—define the map's point of origin, a place from where a network of roads followed by a series of three-toed footprints spread to other parts of the region. The arteries connect Cuquila to Tlaxiaco, an important center of power in the northwest Mixteca, as well as to Ocotepec in the south and to Chicahuaxtla in the southwest. The inverted bell-shaped hill enclosing an ocelot, an element tied to Cuquila's place-name, bear the signature ribbing that characterized the painter's work. Church, temple, and hill include a black and white decorative frieze running along the bottom of each structure consistent with pre-Colombian and early colonial pictorial writing.[29] Likewise, the painter detailed a band of small cylinders below the church's bell used to convey political and religious authority, an element drawn from Mixtec architectural design.[30] Two rivers that flow diagonally across the page in parallel lines encase all three elements.

The painter's signature black ink draws attention to methodology, consistency, and experimentation, elements that defined the production of pigments and colorants. Ursula Klein and Emma Spary observe that

---

(OPPOSITE PAGE) 3.2. *Map of Coquila (1599), no. 2463, Tierras, vol. 3556, exp. 6, f. 175. Archivo General de la Nación, Fondo Hermanos Mayo, concentrados, sobre 363.*

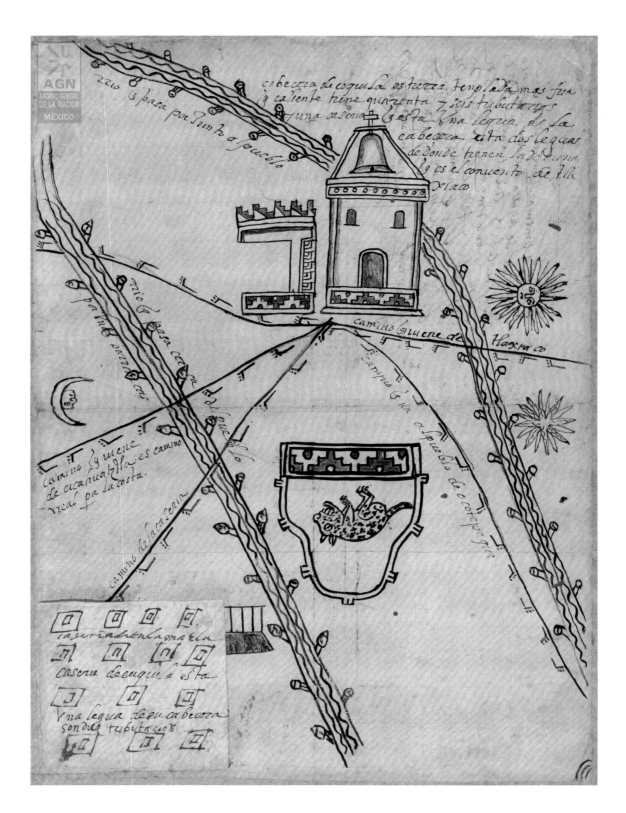

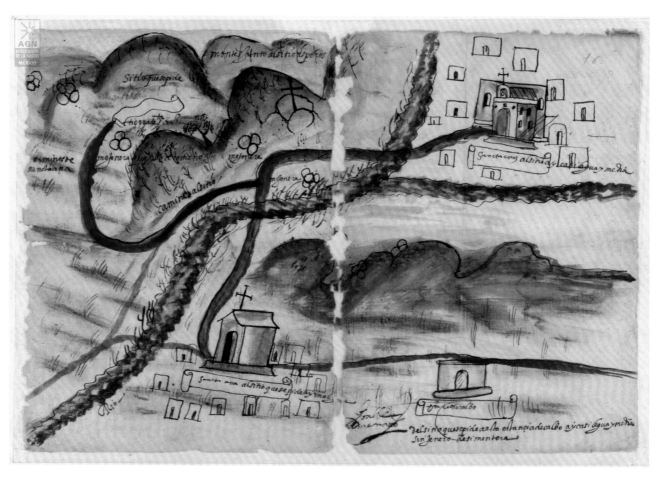

3.3. *Map of Santa Ana and Santa Cruz (1591), no. 0581, Tierras, vol. 56, exp. 5, f. 16. Archivo General de la Nación, Fondo Hermanos Mayo, concentrados, sobre 363.*

the skills required to consistently mix materials demonstrates dexterity in this activity, one resulting from observation, practice, and "artisanal innovation."[31] These same qualities allowed Purepecha painters in the modern state of Michoacán to transform the bark of the *huitzquahuitl*, a large tree of reddish wood native to the region, into ink. According to Sahagún, they would split the bark into pieces, grind it, and place it in water until it turned deep crimson. From this mixture, painters could obtain a bright red dye by combining organic materials and a stone known as a *tlaxocotl*, or they could obtain ink by mixing tlaliyac soil and other unspecified elements.[32] Tlaxocotl, described in Spanish as *piedra alumbre*

(alum stone), existed in great quantities and functioned as a mordent in the mixture of colorants.[33] A variant of huitzquahuitl ink known as *huitztecolayotl* incorporated brazilwood, a species of tree native to South America but also found in Oaxaca and Morelos. Painters boiled the red dye from the brazilwood with tlaliyac until the substance thickened and the black liquid cooled.[34] The Dominican friar Francisco Ximénez commented in his *Historia natural del reino de Guatemala* (1722) about a rich black soil used in the Maya region to make black ink. "God has even blessed these parts with black inks," he said, "both to dye and also to write. In that mountain range of Zacapulas, next to the town of Cuzal, there is a mineral in the form of black soil that just by crumbling it in water produces the blackest ink to write."[35] The rich array of organic and inorganic ingredients incorporated into the production of colorants and dyes speaks to the sophisticated relationship between natives, plants, and minerals.

The variety and composition of inks is often clearly visible when examining indigenous maps. The thin black lines used to define the visual elements in the 1591 map of Santa Ana and Santa Cruz in southeast Oaxaca (Figure 3.3) reflect a luster not visible in the more opaque and matted finish achieved by the painter of ribbed mountains.[36] Originally prepared to petition a site of land marked by an empty banner, the painter applied yellow and charcoal to give the mountains a moss green effect that contrasts sharply with the stylized renderings of the master from Cuquila. The painter made these colors drawing from the same botanical knowledge that guided the fabrication of ink. The black outline from the painter's ink contrasts sharply with the iron-gall ink used by the scribe to inspect the map. Scribes and officials used their own blends of ink to authenticate maps. Like painters in the New World, Spaniards involved in the notarial arts required a basic understanding of the material composition of their most precious commodity, a concoction that mixed wine, acid, and gum.

RECIPES FROM THE OLD WORLD

Written commentary on the front and back of the 1599 map of Cuquila (Figure 3.2), which identified roads and rivers, described local climate, measured distances between places, and counted the number of tributaries, points to the presence of multiple hands involved in the inspection of records across the span of maps' lives.[37] The practice of authentication, an exercise between painters, scribes, and regional judges to identify and annotate the contents of a map analyzed in chapter 4, gave authorities the opportunity to review and to ask a painter questions in order to validate it according to legal protocols. The patch of paper (Figure 3.4) on the map's bottom-left corner, for instance, covered the original illustration used by the painter, a dual church-temple motif, for a *casería*, a settlement of houses sometimes used to accommodate

workers on an estate.[38] During the inspection or sometime shortly after, the scribe placed the patch over the original illustration, preferring to visualize the *casería* with small houses spread out evenly, conforming to royal directives for the settlement of villages and towns. Spaniards commonly used the solution known as iron-gall ink, a mixture of tannins, sulfates, and gum from the Old World, to write the alphabetic glosses that accompanied a map's pictorial elements. Iron-gall ink played a crucial role in the making of maps, allowing scribes and officials to codify and make them legible for others and in preparation for their transition into one of various archives where maps and documents rested for future reference. Scribes visually transformed maps with the ink they used, a substance that supported the task of authentication but that also contributed to a map's unique material condition.

Spaniards had their own traditions for making ink that tapped into centuries of practical learning and experimentation.[39] In the peninsula, carbon-based and other unknown mixtures circulated with the popular iron-gall inks. Late medieval and early modern Iberian

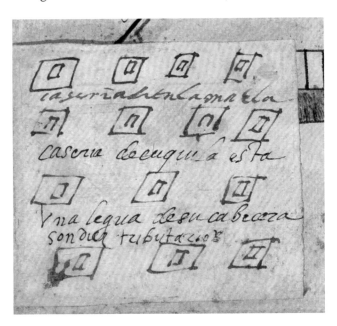

3.4. *Paper patch, map of Coquila (1599), no. 2463, Tierras, vol. 3556, exp. 6, f. 175. Archivo General de la Nación, Fondo Hermanos Mayo, concentrados, sobre 363.*

formulas for ink suggest the majority of users prepared the iron-gall variety. Privileged knowledge available to a few select individuals often circulated in manuscript form mostly through the writings of notaries and scribes who scribbled mixtures in loose notes or who annotated recipes on the margins of a page.[40] In print format, ink recipes appeared primarily in treatises on calligraphy and orthography such as Andrés Flórez's *Doctrina christiana del ermitaño y el niño* (1546), a variation of a common recipe used throughout the Hispanic world:

> Good ink is made from white wine and the common type from water; it is better if it is puddle water. Add an ounce of mashed nutgalls to a pint of water and boil until a third is dissolved. Strain, mix an ounce of copperas [ferrous sulfate] or better yet vitriol, and add a quarter ounce of Arabic gum, stir well and move in strained lukewarm water. Repeat as necessary.[41]

The acidic quality of tannins, usually obtained from tree galls, produced a dark substance when mixed with iron salts and diluted in water or wine; gum acted as a binding agent for the mixture. Individuals obtained various lusters and shades of ink depending on the ingredients that also include onions, pomegranates, and liquor. Diego Bueno, for example, added sugar and six ounces of brandy to his mixture of galls, vitriol, and gum.[42] Variations of Flórez's and Beuno's formula circulated throughout Europe and the Hispanic world.

Others took advantage of the Atlantic trade to experiment with new ingredients. Nicolás Monardes wrote in his *Historia medicinal de las cosas que traen de nuestras Indias*, a compendium of curative plants from America published in Seville in 1574, about a rich soil from the New World used to make ink. "Of the black [soil]," he declared, "I can say someone sent me a small sample from which to make ink. When diluted in water or wine, you can make fine ink to write well, and it has a blue hue which makes it more pleasant to the eye."[43] An accomplished physician, Monardes never actually traveled to the Indies, relying instead on the extensive network of merchants, sailors, explorers, and family members who did make the journey.[44] These groups travelled across the Atlantic and introduced into Europe a wealth of New World plants and minerals that individuals such as Monardes could then acquire. The studies prepared by commentators such as Hernández, Sahagún, and Ximénez indeed confirm a variety of soil types, including tlaliyac, which fit Monardes's description. More important, this instance reveals another important point of contact where indigenous knowledge about the natural world reached beyond its traditional domain, informing the experiments of a curious doctor an ocean away.

Differences in preparation characterized the making of ink in the Iberian world. In his *Arte sutilísima*, printed in 1553, Juan de Icíar instructed readers to place a solution of three ounces of crushed galls into half a pitcher of rainwater under the sun for a period of two days, after which one should add two ounces of vitriol and set to rest for another two days.[45] Ignacio Pérez used the same ingredients but mixed galls, vitriol, and gum each in separate vessels with water and wine, letting them sit for a period of six days, stirring four to five times a day. He instructed users to "place a large cauldron over a good flame" and to then "deposit the jar with the galls and let it boil for an hour," a process that should be repeated for the contents of the other two containers.[46] Differences depended less on the ingredients used to make the composition than on the method of preparation.

Despite the variances, ink formulas highlight the properties individuals valued in the liquid substance, qualities such as tone and durability that made it stand out. To add luster, Icíar recommended boiling his solution moderately while adding pomegranate peels.[47] For writing on paper, José de Casanova in his *Primera parte del arte de escribir* (1560) recommended using water ("it is looser, [and] it has less body and strength") but for parchment he suggested wine. "It is imperative it be wine," he declared, "for the black is better, it settles and endures more." After describing the mixture of ink prepared over a two-week period without the use of fire, Casanova remarked, "I have acquired experience with many recipes that circulate in written form and I have found none that produce better results than this one."[48] In some instances, individuals even valued ink for its medicinal properties, which helped to alleviate certain ailments of the skin. The sixteenth-century Spanish physician and pharmacologist Andrés Laguna provided a basic recipe for making the liquid substance, noting: "Writing ink heals puss-filled sores and burn wounds over which you must apply thick coats with water until the sores granulate."[49] Laguna tied his remedy to ancient knowledge associated with Pliny and Dioscorides, both of whom had discussed the medicinal properties of the prized black substance.[50]

The advent of the printing press called for inks of different viscosities that would function with typeset, woodblocks, and copper plates as opposed to quills and other devices used to write by hand. Joseph Moxon, an English printer and mapmaker who lived in the seventeenth century, praised Dutch ink, a substance that circulated in Spain, for its varnish and described the method used to make it.[51] Moxon's recipe repeatedly cautioned those attempting to execute it about the dangers involved, "for the process of making ink being as well laborious to the body, as noisome ungrateful to the sense, and by several odd accidents dangerous of Firing the Place it is made in."[52] The author's detailed description exposes the dangers of tampering with materials, echoing Adrian Johns's assessment that, outside of the unpleasant work involved in making ink, it also "imputed a certain grappling with nature's powers and propensities."[53]

Printers in Spain used similar technology to produce inks of various kinds. An inventory of books, machinery, and other artifacts, including metal type for printing presses, boards, vellum, and paper made in 1557 for a shop in Burgos, reveals some of the instruments required to make ink and other materials. Among the thousands of books held in stock, 15,827 in all, Juan de Junta's bookstore also included two cauldrons, one made of bell-metal, the other made of copper, a large stone to grind vermillion for red ink, two inkwells, a special copper cask to make varnish, and a mortar and stone set to crush various materials.[54] Bookshops in Spain engaged in wholesale distribution and bookmaking, also functioning as retail centers for more mundane articles such as paper, parchment, and ink.[55] Evidence from other parts of Europe points to the high demand for ink supplied by individuals such as Junta. In London, the stationer Robert Pask aggressively promoted a blend of black ink made from unspecified materials he sold as "hard balls," a package reminiscent of the ones sold in the markets of Mexico City to produce the same substance. In a printed announcement from the 1670s, he advertised that his product guaranteed users a stain-free experience, noting: "You may wear them about you, without any damage to the ink or your linen." Pask catered to government officials, lawyers, poets and playwrights, and his fellow merchants of the city's Royal Exchange who consumed vast quantities of the liquid substance. To use the ink, one simply "cut a little of it into fair water, or any wine (except red)."[56]

Though we must be careful not to draw too many conclusions from this seventeenth-century English example, the advertisement corresponds to a pan-European identity that spread rapidly after Guttenberg but never fully abandoned handwritten manuscripts of various kinds. Pask, as Juan de Junta did in Spain, provided specialized services and products to his diverse clients, some of whom facilitated the administration of the realm or enlightened its thriving literary scene.[57] Participants in London's manuscript culture, just as those in Seville, Madrid, Mexico City, and Lima, expected their tools to possess certain attributes and to function in specific ways. Not surprisingly, a concern over cost, quality, and ease of use anchors Pask's message. But the advert reveals that more than affordability and practicality guided the product's marketing. It speaks to Pask's expertise, his choice of materials, and his method of preparation founded on experimentation, a process that allowed him to make claims about his ink's quality and endurance in the first place. As Klein and Spary have noted, "The production and manipulation of materials required both high levels of technical competence and familiarity with systematic experiential knowledge."[58]

Many of the printed recipes for ink (including those by Casanova, Pérez, and Icíar) circulated in New Spain during the colonial period, where scribes used variants of these mixtures to write documents and, on occasion, to make their own maps.[59] In 1583, the Spanish scribe Juan de Aragón sketched a map of Teotitlán in the southwestern region of the Valley of Oaxaca (Figure 3.5) for a

3.5. *Map of Teutitlán (1583), no. 0560, Tierras, vol. 35, exp. 7, f. 11. Archivo General de la Nación, Fondo Hermanos Mayo, concentrados, sobre 363.*

3.6. *Ink detail, map of Teutitlán (1583), no. 0560, Tierras, vol. 35, exp. 7, f. 11. Archivo General de la Nación, Fondo Hermanos Mayo, concentrados, sobre 363.*

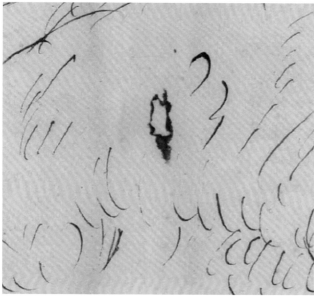

survey to allocate land.[60] Aragón mapped a largely isolated part of the region surrounded by mountain ridges in the north and plains and heavily forested mountains in the east. The scribe surveyed the area from a southwestern point near Teotitlán's *estancia* on the bottom-left corner, fanning the region's geographical features across the page and creating a useful blank space in the center on which to later inscribe the map. "And this is the true painting," certified Aragón with a flourish of his pen. The scribe used a variety of iron-gall ink to draw the map's components, including the road to Tlacolula that ends at an estancia held by Teotitlán on the left edge, as well as to annotate unused territory with the word *baldíos*, or "empty lots." One can glean his choice of

substance in the two holes along the map's central axis (Figure 3.6) where blots of ink concentrated, burning through the paper over time, a product of iron-gall ink's corrosive effect.

Indigenous *pintores* incorporated European ink into their own inventory of materials. In 1617, Don Domingo de Mendoza, a native cacique from Tepenene in the Mixteca Alta, drafted a map (Figure 3.7) to petition Spanish authorities for a livestock ranch a little over a league away from the main town.[61] Mendoza used a palate of three different colorants to define a triad of trees with vibrant red blossoms and another trio with yellow flowers. In the two most inconspicuous elements on the map—the mountain in the shape of an ancient temple

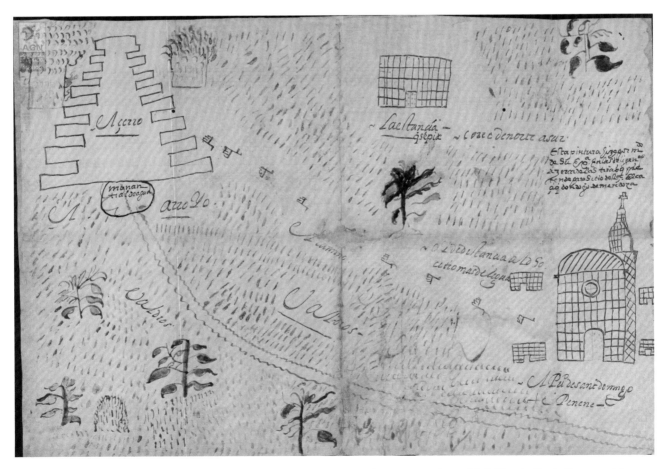

3.7. Map of Santo Domingo Tepenene (1617), no. 2225, Tierras, vol. 2812, exp. 11, f. 312. Archivo General de la Nación, Fondo Hermanos Mayo, concentrados, sobre 363.

3.8. *Verso, map of Santo Domingo Tepenene (1617), no. 2225, Tierras, vol. 2812, exp. 11, f. 312. Archivo General de la Nación, Fondo Hermanos Mayo, concentrados, sobre 363.*

on the upper-left corner connected by a trail of feet to the church on the bottom right—he did not incorporate color but instead drew with iron-gall ink. Notice the effects of the substance on the page when the map is turned over (Figure 3.8). The lines of the pyramid-shaped mountain, visible at the map's upper right, have seeped through the page, leaving noticeable traces comparable to the scribe's certification on the left-hand edge. The map's material condition suggests indigenous painters learned to use Old World substances, which they combined with their own blends in order to represent spatial relationships and the natural environment.

PAPER

The painter of turquoise landscapes collected nearly two-dozen blank folios of European origin (Figure 2.4), the type of standardized paper that notaries and clerics used to keep track of the comings and goings of natives and settlers. He gradually assembled each individual folio, and when the occasion demanded, he cut and altered the size of other sheets of paper to give shape to the rather large rectangular surface he would use to make a map of the region. At an impressive 176cm × 138cm, the map of Teozacoalco is perhaps the best-known example of the pinturas made for the Relaciones Geográficas, and certainly one of the largest indigenous maps produced during the early colonial period on European paper.[62] The painter tied Mixtec dynastic couples—that is to say ordered pairs of male and female rulers aligned on the left-hand side moving upward from the map's bottom—to land and political power. This process allowed him to express significant historical episodes and to interlace place-names and boundaries along a circular landscape on the right-hand side. In the twentieth century, the map gained notoriety for facilitating the decipherment of several precontact pictorial manuscripts made in Oaxaca, including the Vindobonensis, Nuttall, Bodley, and Selden. The renowned Mexican archeologist Alfonso Caso wrote famously that the Teozacoalco map was "a key, a true Rosetta Stone for the final interpretation of the Mixtec codices," a characterization that has defined this record ever since.[63] During the second half of the twentieth century, studies of the map illustrated continuities and changes in Mesoamerican writing systems and pictorial techniques, especially as scholars of colonial Mexico turned increasingly to the analyses of indigenous-made sources after the 1980s. Less frequently observed are the map's considerable proportions, an aspect that contributes to its message of authority and hints at its complex material condition.

Any viewer can clearly notice the outlines (Figure 3.9) where the papers were joined with glue, a patchwork of nearly two dozen folios that remain fully cemented to each other just as they were over four centuries ago. These points of conversion represent a space that captures acts of collecting, organizing, and visual design as well as those associated with plants and experimentation

3.9. *Paper detail, Relaciones Geográficas map of Teozacoalco (1580). Relaciones Geográficas of Mexico and Guatemala, 1577–1585, Nettie Lee Benson Latin American Collection, University of Texas Libraries, University of Texas at Austin.*

necessary to produce a bonding agent. Pintores applied adhesives made from plants, copal, and rubber to join things. The pseudobulbs of the tzacutli plant (storage organs that grow between the stem and two lymph nodes typical among orchids) served to prepare a resistant and durable solution. Tzacutli functioned both as a binding agent when mixing it with other natural elements to make colors, as well as a glue.[64] Hernández noted that tzacutli was valued for its "white, fibrous" roots, which possessed strong adhesive qualities.[65] "The root is cold, humid, and viscose," he noted; "you prepare with it excellent, tenacious glue that Indians, especially pintores, use so that the colors adhere firmly [to paper] and the figures won't fade easily." The physician noted painters cut the parts into small pieces and dried them in the sun, grinding the dried parts into powder and then mixing them with cold water.[66] Because of its powerful adhesive properties, tzacutli also served medicinal purposes; healers used it to treat patients with dysentery and other maladies associated with laxity.

The painter of turquoise landscapes fulfilled a commission entrusted to him by the elders of Teozacoalco, a powerful Mixtec kingdom in central Oaxaca subdued by Spanish-led forces by the 1520s.[67] The elders' petition responded to a request from Hernando de Cervantes, the region's corregidor, who himself carried out instructions from the King's royal cosmographer to answer a survey of natural resources, culture, and history known collectively as the Relaciones Geográficas. The questionnaire's tenth question called for officials to prepare a map that illustrated a town's layout, including streets, important buildings, churches, and monasteries. Although a dutiful servant of the King, Cervantes, like many of his counterparts across the viceroyalty, had no intention of making the map himself, so he enlisted the help of capable indigenous painters recognized for their prodigious skills.[68] Spanish settlement in the region brought with it dramatic religious, judicial, and political changes that modified the balance of power, turning labor, material goods, and financial resources away from ñuu interests into royal coffers. With the map, the elders of Teozacoalco intended to make a bold statement about land and political power.

Although painters and artisans never fully abandoned native papermaking activities in New Spain, their adoption of European paper allowed them to converse with authorities on the standard medium of the empire. This bureaucratization of the mapmaking enterprise included a measure of practicality and access, yet the use of paper could also take unexpected political turns. In the case of the Teozacoalco map, the presence of European paper to make the map is less surprising than the fact the painter used so much of it. One can only imagine the reaction of Cervantes and the Spanish priest who met with the elders on January 9, 1580, when the painter unfolded the rather large map in their presence. Cervantes had redacted the detailed instructions he had received from Spain to the Indians, but there had been no discussion about size, quantity of paper, color, or projection. The large surface reflected a creative way to incorporate new materials into an evolving pictorial genre that attempted to express spatial and political relationships.

From the sixteenth century to the early eighteenth, indigenous pintores used a variety of mediums on which to map, adapting to changes in technology as well as access to goods that resulted from Spanish colonization. Following the life of this processed material brings to mind Ulinka Rublack's assessment that transforming "material required a high degree of knowledge about developing craft techniques, a fascination with the transformation of textures, and a willingness to participate in their further development through experimentation."[69] Rublack proposes that studies of matter divorced from the more typical analyses of consumption patterns shed light on other areas of inquiry such as ecological management, craft innovation, and the specialized language employed to discuss materials.[70] To make paper, craftspeople in Mesoamerica drew from the botanical and the animal worlds, practices later recorded by European missionaries. Francisco de Burgoa, an early commentator of the cultural and natural history of Oaxaca, observed in his *Geográfica descripción* (1674) that indigenous painters made their records "on paper from the bark of trees and [on] tanned leather."[71] A distinguished member of the Order of Preachers prone to hyperbole and hagiography, Burgoa nonetheless had deep roots in his native Oaxaca, learning Mixtec and Zapotec to facilitate his evangelical efforts. The Dominican tapped into a stream of ethnographic work prepared by his predecessors in the region over the course of the previous century and a half, drawing heavily from the work of Francisco de Alvarado, another American-born Spaniard and fellow Dominican who in the late 1500s compiled an impressive vocabulary of the Mixtec language.[72] In cataloging the language, Alvarado captured details of the relationship between materials and technology. Terms such as *dzoo ñee ñuhu*, or "paper on which the ancients wrote," establish specific parameters of knowledge centered on literacy, tradition, and craft skills, but they also signal shifts in time that can often transform material processes.[73]

Burgoa's description points to the use of paper made from the bark of the ficus tree described by Sahagún as *amacuauitl*, more commonly known as *amatl*. When he described papermaking in central Mexico, Sahagún observed, "There are in this land some trees they call amacuauitl. Their bark is smooth and their leaves very green. They are about the size of peach trees. They make paper from the bark, and when it [the tree] is old, they cut it, and it sprouts anew."[74] Hernández described the process of preparing the bark in the following terms:

[They] only cut the tree's thick branches, leaving the shoots. They are soaked in water and left to steep in the rivers or streams overnight. The next day, the bark is stripped off, and, after removing the outside cuticle, it is extended by pounding it with a flat rock which is cut with certain grooves supported by an unpolished willow rod folded in a circle in the form of a handle. The flexible wood yields; it is then cut into pieces that when pounded once again with a flatter stone, easily join together and are [then] smoothed. Lastly, they are divided in sheets of two *palmos* in length and approximately a palmo and a half in width, [a size] that imitates our thickest and most common paper, but these are smaller and whiter though much inferior to our smoothest paper.[75]

These fascinating instructions detail important themes that marked the history of paper in the Americas. Quality from the Spanish perspective, for instance, rested with an even surface unencumbered by irregularities, according to Hernández. Paper is a tactile material handled extensively by one's hands that witnessed users folding, tearing, flipping, crumpling, and cutting it depending on what the occasion demanded. The act of writing required intimate contact with the surface as people regularly brushed up against it with every stroke of the pen. But variability on the market on either side of the Atlantic suggested that not all paper was created equal. In central Mexico, observed Sahagún, native paper vendors "pounded it" if using local materials, but they also offered a range of paper from Castille, "white, or strong, thin, thick, and long, or thick, poorly made, granular, rotten, off white, or brownish-gray."[76]

Few maps and pictorial documents made on indigenous paper survive from Oaxaca. The Codex of Tecomastlabaca (Tecomaxtlahuaca) in the Mixteca Baja, a tribute register commissioned in 1578 by the local cacique, Don Francisco de Arellano, represents one of the few surviving examples of papermaking technology in the region.[77] Arellano deployed the pictorial record to contest Spanish policy that sought to count servants in indigenous households as independent tributaries responsible to the Crown, not to the caciques as practice had dictated until the 1560s.[78] Although the exact composition of the paper is unknown, the painter prepared a long strip that measured nearly five feet in length on which he recorded six generations of ruling couples and the services and in-kind tribute they had enjoyed.

Materials used to make indigenous paper varied according to the availability of certain plants, a situation usually conditioned by a region's climate and geography. Ficus and mulberry trees, for example, flourished in tropical and warmer climates while maguey thrived in temperate and cold ones.[79] Maguey, a multipurpose plant used to build fences and roofs, for firewood, plates, and rope, for medicinal practices, and to draw thread for shoemaking and fabrics, also supported papermaking.[80] Barbara Mundy asserts that works on paper during the pre-Hispanic period carried value beyond their symbols, qualities potentially associated with the regenerative properties of the ficus tree. "Paper," she observes, "was not an inert material, a blank surface on which to write, but a substance with properties of its own."[81] According to Hernández, paper informed various aspects of ritual life, including "wrapping and [is] very adequate and useful among these western Indians to celebrate the feasts of the gods, to prepare sacred garments, and to adorn funerals."[82] In Tehuantepec, Zapotec tribute records made on maguey paper during the sixteenth century included bundles of paper for ceremonial use collected by Nahua authorities, an act reminiscent of payments registered in central Mexico, including the nearly half a million sheets of paper recorded as tribute in the *Codex Mendoza*.[83] Toponyms such as Amatitlán in the Mixteca, "the place of paper trees," describe a relationship between the sacred material and the ficus, though the Nahua place-name may have reflected the priorities and knowledge of the Aztecs who controlled the area prior to contact rather than that of Mixtecs who may have described their place-name according to a very different reading of the natural landscape.[84]

Ritual aspects attributed to paper are hard to track after contact when religious campaigns of evangelization seared through cities and countryside, stamping out old practices. What is clear is that while the production of paper decreased dramatically it never fully disappeared. Any traces of the old religion and its ritual consumption of paper gradually melded with Christian beliefs or disappeared into the backdrops of peoples' private lives, transforming the use and meaning of the sacred material. On occasion, authorities stumbled upon the intimate spaces where locals continued to employ native paper to nourish the gods in special celebrations. During the idolatry campaigns of the late seventeenth century in the Villa Alta region of Oaxaca's northern sierra, officials sounded the alarm when they caught a woman "wrapping together with great diligence and hiding some papers of *yaguichi* [Zapotec: *yaga*="tree"; *guichi*="paper"], instrument of their pagan idolatry, and also a bundle of feathers, all of the said wrappings seemingly very blood-stained and newly made."[85] The incident exposed the covert practices of a large number of people who continued to venerate the old deities, in part by making native paper to capture and protect sacrificial offerings that replenished the ties between the sacred and the profane.

What exactly did the woman try to conceal? Clearly, religious and secular authorities recognized the feathers and blood as dead giveaways for native rituals, and yet they only singled out paper as an "instrument" of idolatry. Papermaking formed part of a set of practices intentionally hidden from authorities because the use of paper contributed to illicit rituals that could lead to severe punishment, if not death. But paper also represented proprietary attitudes associated with trade secrets available to only a select few. Pamela Long's work on craft knowledge in Europe from late antiquity to the Renaissance has demonstrated that concepts such as intellectual property took shape in the Middle Ages "centuries before the emergence of the modern legal terminology that describes it."[86] Long observes a tension between "open" traditions of knowledge exchange found in treatises and manuals of the mechanical arts, versus the covert practices of the craft guilds who jealously guarded their secrets. Similarly, in the New World, botanical knowledge about plants and the technology used to transform materials such as bark into paper represented a collection of skills traditionally confined to

specialists, not the population at large. As noted in the previous section of this chapter, when Spaniards such as Hernández poked their noses into indigenous spaces of knowledge, natives chose what information to share.

In some regions of Mexico, clandestine papermaking activities carried into modern times, offering a whisper of longstanding processes traditionally shrouded in secrecy. Ethnographic evidence points to pockets in Veracruz, and along the border between Hidalgo and Puebla, where ritual specialists have traditionally made *amate* paper based on the old techniques.[87] Magical healers among the Otomí in San Pablito prepare paper to support rituals associated with fertility, health, and divination.[88] Observers of the Otomí since the twentieth century have recounted ceremonies where specialists use and cut various colors of amate paper into anthropomorphic shapes (Figure 3.10) that represent spirit deities. These figurines serve as a receptacle for the sacrificial offerings made by the ritual specialist, who "may kill a chicken and sprinkle its blood over the paper figurines laying on their paper beds while praying and chanting."[89] As the evidence from Villa Alta described above suggests, this sort of secret knowledge has been highly contested since the colonial period. Hans Lenz, a successful Mexican papermaker of German ancestry, dedicated much of his scholarly interests to studying the social, economic, and environmental history of paper in his native country. During the summer of 1943, Lenz corresponded with two of his contacts in Ixhuatlán de Madero, a Nahua town in northern Veracruz near Chicontepec, anxious to learn about the fate of paper he had recently commissioned for his research. On a previous occasion, Lenz had acquired paper from a local *curandera*, a ritual healer, who along with her husband presided over the health and spiritual matters of a village called Naranjo Dulce, but the amount they supplied during his visit did not suffice—Lenz wanted a larger sample.

The Mexican papermaker commissioned a local agent from Ixhuatlán to return to Naranjo Dulce to purchase additional samples. When the agent made contact with the curandera and her husband, they informed him that word had spread across the village of their recent dealings with Lenz, angering the townspeople, who threatened

3.10. *Otomí* amate *paper figurines. From author's personal collection.*

Animals, too, could be used to make paper. Surviving pre-Colombian and early colonial codices, including the Fejérváry-Mayer, Bodley, and Selden, attest to the skills displayed by artisans in Oaxaca to prepare deerskin for writing.[91] Painter-scribes sowed the material "together as a screenfold manuscript, so that each strip could be folded back upon the next and viewed individually."[92] The finely crafted tanned leather pages of the Codex Colombino, a twelfth-century pictorial manuscript that celebrated the accomplishments of the Mixtec lord Eight Deer, reveals one way in which painter-scribes shaped *ñee cuisi* [*ñee*=hide; *cuisi*=paper], or "parchment," for bookmaking.[93] Screenfold books narrated historical events, political genealogies, ritual practices, and other aspects of life before the conquest. Language often accounted for distinctions based on the materials used for such purposes. A difference among Mixtecs existed, for instance, between paper made out of animal skin, "sacred vellum" (*ñee ñuhu*), and the one made out of natural materials, "sacred paper" (*tutu ñuhu*), distinctions that further suggest matter defined certain rituals.[94] Terms such as *quitimani*, "animal hide," and *quitichibi*, "animal hide without hair," similarly locate tanning processes among Zapotecs who also made material distinctions.[95] Tanners in central Mexico, noted Sahagún, used the thick bark of oak trees to tan, but he did not provide a detailed explanation of its use; perhaps it served as a dye, or it could very well have functioned as a makeshift brush to remove hair from the animal pelt.[96]

Native communities and individuals preserved maps and other pictorial manuscripts, some on ancient hide, during the colonial period that circulated during ritual festivities or to support legal disputes traditionally tied to land-related matters. Sahagún recounted that in 1570 two trustworthy clerics in Oaxaca "viewed some very ancient paintings, illustrated on deerskin, which narrated many things that alluded to the preaching of the Gospel."[97] Despite linking the indigenous past to Christianity, a subject that lay and religious intellectuals often grappled with during the course of the colonial period, Sahagún's interest in native technology and learning guided his explorations of indigenous societies of Mesoamerica.[98] As late as the eighteenth century, caciques

their lives should they sell any more. For villagers, the couple's power rested, in part, on their ability to mediate the relationship between fertility deities, bountiful harvests, and land—essential elements of sustained growth and stability. It infuriated townspeople that the couple would consider turning over such a valuable resource, an act that appeared to give away the village's patrimony.[90] The alcalde of Ixhuatlán de Madero later told Lenz that a retinue of eight men armed with knives and guns apprehended his agent, who barely escaped with his life after a deadly shootout that claimed the life of at least five people, including Lenz's suppliers. In the end, the samples of paper did, in fact, reach Lenz in Mexico City, but they came at a great cost. Paper, for some, mattered a great deal.

from Tututepec along Oaxaca's Pacific coastline safe-guarded the twelfth-century Codex Colombino, using it in the early 1700s to support a dispute with neighboring San Miguel Sola.[99] The introduction of European paper in the sixteenth century reduced the use of deerskin for painting, contributing to the transformation of indigenous manuscript traditions. In spite of these changes, the Codices Porfirio Díaz, Baranda, and Dehesa attest to the continued fabrication of deerskin to support manuscripts as late as the seventeenth century.[100]

RAGS, RECYCLING, AND POWER

By the final decades of the sixteenth century, the most popular medium to make a map was the European rag paper favored by Spanish scribes in Europe and America. From the late Middle Ages through the end of the early modern period, old rags served as the main ingredient to make this type of material. In the thirteenth century, papermakers in Spain and Italy developed specialized machines powered by hydraulic mills that converted cloth into pulp. The most sought-after type of paper in New Spain was the *superior de Cataluña*, Catalan paper prized for its consistency and smooth surface, though high demand in both Spain and New Spain required the importation of Dutch, French, and Italian paper as well.[101] In a sample of five dozen indigenous maps from the Oaxaca region, painters overwhelmingly used paper over cloth. The *reçute* or *in plano* size (32cm × 44cm), a standard paper cut used by scribal, legal, and religious networks, circulated widely in New Spain.[102] The use of European paper in native mapmaking—specifically the reçute size—reflects a shift tied closely to the region's demand for written manuscripts used to petition and defend land during the late sixteenth century, a subject analyzed in chapter 4 and the epilogue.

European paper acquired a major role during the early Spanish settlement of Oaxaca as a tool on which to inscribe authority and goods: scribes and officials allocated natural resources, organized labor drafts, indoctrinated, made appointments to royal posts, recorded tribute, and bestowed and certified property on paper. "Paper," notes José Piedra, "is far from being simply a static or passive surface that serves to display words

and worth."[103] Paper functioned as an object used to empower its holder, signifying an act of validation and accomplishment. Various efforts to secure a steady supply of paper in central Mexico in the years following the fall of Tenochtitlán call attention to the medium's importance in establishing colonial rule. Individuals such as Juan de Zumárraga, the first bishop of Mexico, petitioned King Charles V in 1534 not only for the authorization of a printing press but also for a paper mill. By 1538, Zumárraga thanked the King for authorizing the press but noted, somewhat demoralized: "Due to the lack of paper, little progress [has been made] in terms of printing making it difficult [to publish] the works that are ready here [in New Spain] and others that soon will be ready to go to press."[104]

The continual shortage of paper led entrepreneurs such as Hernán Sánchez de Muñoz and Juan Cornejo to propose establishing a mill in Mexico City that would take advantage of local materials. The Crown jealously guarded the right to award licenses to individuals seeking to establish paper mills in the New World, relying instead on the hundred or so papermakers in Spain under royal sanction.[105] After reviewing the proposal in 1575, Philip II granted the two men a patent to produce paper over the next twenty years, noting: "We have been made aware that you have found in New Spain certain material from which to make paper in abundance and that you have made experiments to confirm [the project's viability]."[106] Perhaps the two men came into contact with one of the amate papermaking regions in central Mexico and thought they could replicate the process or conscript local populations for this purpose. Although the historical record does not reflect the outcome of the venture, the example reminds us of the high premium individuals placed on paper and the lengths they went to supply the much-needed material to its users. In Oaxaca, Burgoa commented on the good quality of the paper used to write an indigenous handheld book about traditional culture, "*un libro de mano escrito en buen papel*," an ironic statement considering the book caused a stir among Spanish clerics who could never identify its "secret" author. Shortly after clerics confiscated the book it disappeared from a church, where it rested in a safe

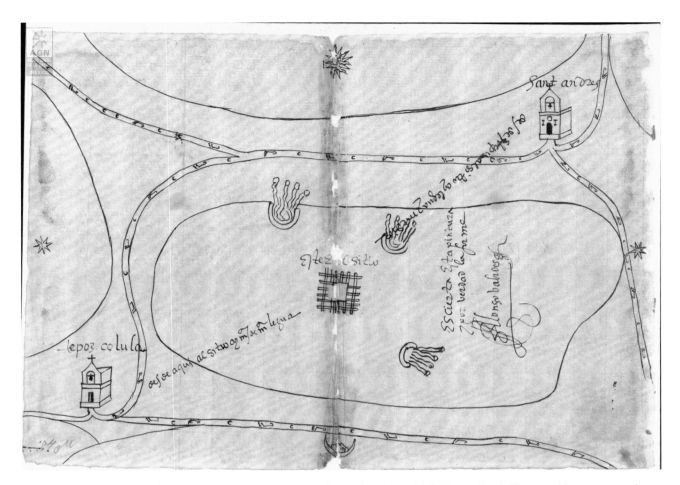

3.11. *Map of Tepozcolula (1590), no. 1711, Tierras, vol. 2696, exp. 21, f. 8. Archivo General de la Nación, Fondo Hermanos Mayo, concentrados, sobre 363.*

with two locks. Burgoa commented simply, "It vanished as if it were made of smoke."[107]

The reçute folio partially defined the packaging of native maps, which when folded in half fit neatly into a scribe's file. Notice the crease mark along the center of the folio in the map of Teposcolula (Figure 3.11) made in 1590, a drawing used to petition a site of land, represented by a grid, in the center of the page.[108] Grids tied land settlement to policies of urban design pushed by authorities in Spain to organize space in the Indies, and they often showed up in native maps across New Spain.[109] The deterioration along the folio's central axis speaks to the ease with which notaries tucked maps into

a sequence of numbered folios that formed each docket in the Spanish Empire's vast sea of paper. It is only in modern times that archivists uprooted maps from their original positions in their respective cases, a product of modern "archival logics," or organizing principles, that allowed people to put records to use.[110] Divorced from boundary surveys, the testimony of witnesses, and other quotidian activities associated with land tenure, maps have lost a large portion of their notarial identity.

In the modern archive, maps form part of specialized cartographic collections assembled based on the interests of users and institutions. Archivists traditionally organize collections by time frame and regions of the world that align closely to contemporary political boundaries and cultural similarities. One need only peruse the organizational scheme of *The History of Cartography* series, a multivolume study of encyclopedic proportions that examines mapmaking across time and space, to see these ideas in motion.[111] So-called traditional mapmaking practices of America, Africa, the Pacific, and Southeast Asia are distinct from cartography in the European Renaissance, Antiquity, and the Middle Ages. Maps made by indigenous people form part of a subcategory defined by ethnic and technological differences separate from European cartography of the same period. The fact these maps circulated in manuscript form tucked away inside official dockets limited their visibility across the Hispanic world to the circuits where judges, notaries, caciques, and translators transacted business on a daily basis: individual towns across the Viceroyalty of New Spain connected to the Audiencia in Mexico City by a stream of paper.

Map archiving in the years following the original commission followed a set of priorities tied intimately to land and to notarial traditions tasked with documenting peoples' actions. "Notaries' workshops," observes Kathryn Burns, "were the gateway through which others made their entry into the records, the courts, [and] the archives."[112] When originally submitted to authorities,

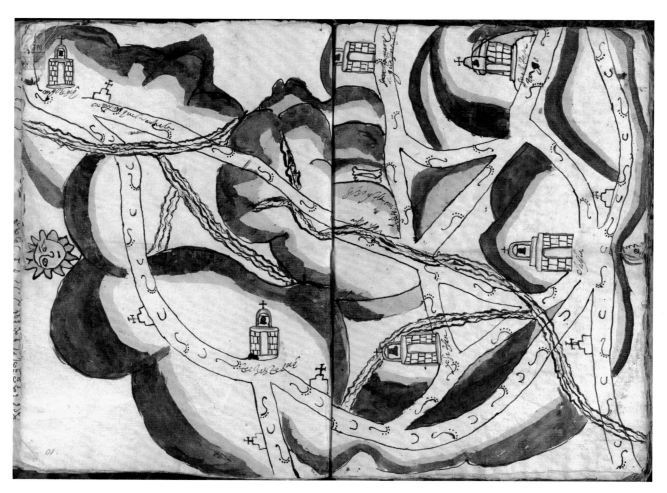

3.12. *Map of Myltepec (1617), no. 1776, Tierras, vol. 2711, exp. 7, fs. 9v. y 10. Archivo General de la Nación, Fondo Hermanos Mayo, concentrados, sobre 363.*

maps formed part of a docket of related papers. Visual and alphabetic manuscripts "functioned as both a measuring stick of cultural hierarchy in a colonial world and as a vehicle for incorporating native peoples into the colonial project," observe Joanne Rappaport and Tom Cummins.[113] The map of Miltepec (Figure 3.12) is one of a handful of surviving examples still bound to its original docket, illustrating where and how scribes incorporated maps into the documentary record, sowing them into a collection of dockets that made up a *legajo*, or "bundle."[114]

In Oaxaca, paper could also be obtained in one of the region's major markets, weekly affairs that brought together a rich tapestry of goods for local and regional consumption. In the Valley, the Villa of Oaxaca hosted a weekly market, as did Mitla, Chilateca, Ocotolán, and Ayoquesco.[115] The market of Suchitepec in the Mixteca supplied residents from Yanhuitlán, and other markets, including "the great market center" of Miahuatlán, supplied a predominant Zapotec population in south-central Oaxaca.[116] Merchants of various kinds carried paper in their inventories. In addition to a wide array of imported fabrics, including damask, silk, taffeta, camlet, felt, ribbed silk (*capichola*), Brabant linen, printed and semifine cotton, as well as local silk from the Mixteca, Captain Martín de Arce stocked twenty-two reams (*resmas*) of paper in his cloth shop in Antequera in 1684.[117] A resma consisted of twenty *manos*, or "quires," each made up of twenty-five folios.

Paper shortages at different moments in time across the viceroyalty's three-hundred-year history drove early modern recycling efforts that sought to provide relief to paper consumers in need of the material. Antonio de Robles described in vivid detail in his *Diary of Notable Accounts* a tumultuous season in 1677 during which the cost of paper reached unprecedented heights. In August, he noted one resma cost fifteen pesos and a mano cost six reales. A few days later, a mano reached one peso.[118] In early December, word spread that 700 resmas from Guatemala purchased at fifteen pesos each, the going retail price, would soon reach Mexico City. When the paper finally arrived at the end of the month, merchants doubled the price. "The cost of paper," Robles noted somberly, "has gone up so high that a ream costs thirty

pesos, a quire costs two pesos, and a folio one *real*." These conditions prompted consumers to take apart old books to sell the paper, especially in light of the fact the publishing industry, in Robles's estimation, suffered greatly because the dearth of paper prevented it from publishing any works. "The presses are not operating," he told his readers.[119]

Bookmakers had recycled paper since the Middle Ages when illuminated manuscripts filled the bookshelves of Europe's courts and monasteries, a practice that carried into the print era.[120] A copy of Diego Antonio Francés de Urrutigoyti's *Forum conscientiae sive pastorale internum* (1651), a religious treaty on private morality that circulated in Oaxaca, bears scars of the effects of paper shortages.[121] Printed originally in Zaragoza, Spain, the book's boards reveal pastedowns of recycled paper (Figure 3.13) designed to cover the folded vellum that enveloped the front and back covers. In this specific instance, the sheet of recycled paper documented demographic information tied to couples and their offspring: "Victoriano Caballero of twenty years of age, married to Sipriana Hernández Guzmán of eighteen years, with a son, Juan, three years," "Thomas de Chávez of forty-five years of age, married to María Hernández of thirty-six years of age with four children, Juana, twelve, Ventura,

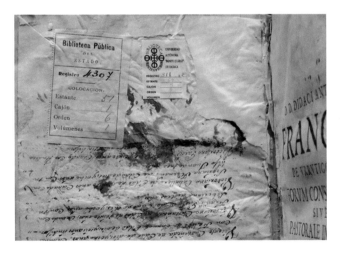

3.13. *Recycled paper pastedown in Diego Antonio Francés de Urrutigoyti,* Forum conscientiae sive pastorale internum ad Ioannem de Palafox et Mendoza *(Zaragoza, 1651). Biblioteca Francisco de Burgoa.*

nine, Atanacia, five, and Juan, three years old," and so on. The editors of a recent collection of essays on the lives of used things argue recycling did not constitute "marginal, disconnected phenomena" but rather "related practices of reuse, salvaging, and transformation" that represent a "fundamentally relevant process to understand" the early modern era. By examining the care and daily management of objects, they argue, we can more effectively consider the life of things over their long histories.[122]

Paper fueled the empire. Without it, the scribal cogs that fed the leviathan grinded to a halt, unable to track, count, divide, judge, or correspond with and for others. Paper's ubiquitous role in everyday civil transactions, reports, sales, criminal investigations, and land grants supported settlement and American expansion. Provincial bureaucrats and the scribes carried their tools during visits to towns to survey land that generated maps. The overwhelming use of European paper to map signals an important technological shift born out of convenience. Despite this change, painters looked to surfaces other than rag-based paper when it came time to make a map, a move tied directly to styling and message.

TRACKING THE MAP OF OUR LADY OF THE ROSARY

Other pictorial traditions in Oaxaca, most notably sixteenth-century manuscripts made on large cloth surfaces known as *lienzos*, described genealogical information as well as geographical markers and place-names associated with indigenous settlements.[123] Mixtecs identified surfaces used to make these large pictorials as *dzoo cuisi* (cloth; paper) and *dzoo yadzi* (cloth; maguey fiber) based on material distinctions that hinted at the varied uses of agave in certain pockets of the viceroyalty.[124] Over time, mapmakers often chose to paint maps on these larger cloth surfaces and paper composites in the style of the map of Teozacoalco, but unlike the lienzo tradition from the sixteenth century they rarely represented genealogies and pictorial histories.[125] Instead, the materiality of the large cloth surfaces in tandem with the creative application of color through a continued manipulation of the natural world functioned as message carriers for both officials and townspeople who understood them as

indicators of a distinctly local, and fiercely indigenous, art of painting.

Sometime in the middle of the eighteenth century, the painter of circular landscapes prepared the map of Our Lady of the Rosary (Figure 3.14), the patroness of the Mixtec town of Santa María Atzompa in the Valley of Oaxaca, with these goals in mind.[126] He used a large linen surface (roughly 120cm × 61cm) to depict a series of boundaries associated with land administered by the town's religious confraternity (*cofradía*). The map hints at indigenous craftsmanship but enjoys a very different pictorial aesthetic compared to maps made in the sixteenth century and early seventeenth. No footprints dot *this* landscape. Instead, carefully detailed churches and buildings that applied three-dimensionality helped situate a series of *mojoneras* (boundary markers) in a circular pattern around the edges of the cloth. The map's top-left corner reveals the painter's strategy of representation, one that relied on the use of colors to rank social and political relationships repeated in other parts of the map. The space includes the town of Atzompa (Figure 3.15), which sits on a hill just below a bright red sun. The painter used shading and crosshatching to generate tonal effects that give the church and the two adjoining buildings, the *casa real*, or "noble house," and the *casa cural*, or "curate's home," a sense of depth. Throughout the map, the painter illustrated important buildings in blue to mark their distinction from the brown community dwellings situated on the hills below. This positioning on the canvas served as an indication of their importance in the local structures of power, reinforcing a difference in status.

The visual schema described above defined other components of the map. The painter used it to ascribe meaning to an agricultural and cattle ranch designated as "Father Crespo's hacienda" and to locate the town of San Lorenzo, where a church and a noble home sit side by side. The absence of a curate's house in San Lorenzo may point to the fact that the community did not have a resident priest, a marker of distinction at the regional level, as clerics enhanced a town's status.[127] While it is tempting to establish a deeper significance between color, ritual, and authority, the diversity in mapmaking

3.14. *Map of Nuestra Madre del Rosario (c. 1750s). Formerly part of the collection of historic records from the Municipality of Santa María Atzompa, Oaxaca. This map disappeared in 2008.*

3.15. *Atzompa, map of Nuestra Madre del Rosario (c. 1750s). Formerly part of the collection of historic records from the Municipality of Santa María Atzompa, Oaxaca. This map disappeared in 2008.*

during this period renders this subject a highly speculative venture. To be sure, certain colors (including white, black, and red) held ritual meaning in Mesoamerican society, but their use on indigenous maps did not necessarily translate into standard cartographic practice.[128] Although each map includes its own visual schematic organized around a set of principles defined by the painter's skill, access to materials played an important role in a map's aesthetic.

Certain colorants circulated more widely in Oaxaca during the eighteenth century. Conservation specialists have identified indigo (*añil* in Spanish), a coveted blue dye that fed European textile markets in the eighteenth century, on native maps from the late sixteenth century as well as other pictorial records produced by indigenous painters.[129] The production of añil in the viceroyalty enjoyed some prosperity from the 1580s to the 1620s but declined in the seventeenth century due to protectionist policies in favor of pastel production from Europe. During the second half of the eighteenth century, the period when the map of Our Lady of the Rosary was made, vast sums of capital from peninsular and Creole Spaniards in New Spain financed profitable dye operations in Mexico and Guatemala.[130] Harvesting the crop brought together petty merchants, entrepreneurs, investors who financed and operated farms, Indian and low-wage workers who provided labor, Spanish officials who inspected and approved shipments, and ground and maritime transportation services that moved the product from one destination to another.

Indigofera plants, the genus from which people extracted indigo dye, grew abundantly in New Spain. Although major indigo production for overseas trade originated in Central America in regions such as Santiago de Guatemala, Tegucigalpa, Honduras, San Salvador, and San Vicente, areas in Mesoamerica including Michoacán, Jalisco, Guerrero, Morelos, Puebla, Colima, Chiapas, and Tabasco also produced the blue dye. In Oaxaca, indigo trees and shrubs thrived in places such as Huajuapan, Nochixtlán, and Teposcolula in the Mixteca, Nejaja in the eastern part of the state, Miahuatlán in the south-central region, Mitla, Antequera and the Cuatro Villas in the Central Valley, and Tehuantepec along the coast. These regions witnessed the propagation of a variety of species including *Indigofera suffruticosa*, *Indigofera cuernavacana rose*, and *Indigofera thibudiana*.[131]

The plant's leaves served as the main component to make the blue dye. Hernández noted that *xiuhquilitlpitzahoac*, a plant with long cylindrical stems (about "the width of [your] little finger," he said) and small red-and-white flowers produced the leaves known as *xiuhquilitl* used to make the blue colorant *tlacehuilli* or *mohuitli*. He instructed users how to prepare:

> Cut the leaves into pieces and add to a kettle or cauldron of boiled water removed from the fire and lukewarm, or better (according to specialists) cold and without placing it over the flames. Stir it forcibly with a wooden shovel, and drain the dye-water slowly into a clay vessel or jar allowing the liquid to pour through some holes it has at a certain position to let the material from the leaves sit. This residue is the colorant. Dry it in the sun, strain into a hemp bag and then form into small disks, which harden when placed on plates over hot coals; and finally, store and use them during the year.[132]

One of the many indigenous artists who illustrated the Florentine Codex prepared a drawing detailing the life of the plant found in its natural state until it reached the hands of a painter as a finished product (Figure 3.16).[133] Nearly two centuries later, one of the variants of the blue colorant found its way into the hands of the painter of circular landscapes who used it to make the map of Our Lady of the Rosary. While Sahagún emphasized xiuquilitl's qualities, noting "this indigo color produces a gleaming dark blue dye, it is a valued commodity," not all species of indigofera produced the same vibrant tones.[134] Hernández described *xiuhquilitlpatlahoac*, a broad-leaved variety of indigo (*añil latifolio*), instructing readers to use the same method described above "except," he pointed out, "this plant is inferior which is why I say nothing about its cultivation."[135] On a commercial level, nearly two dozen varieties of indigo dye circulated within New Spain's networks, including the prized *tinta flor* (flower ink), *sobresaliente* (outstanding), a medium-grade dye,

3.16. *Xiuhquilitl*, Florentine Codex, *Book XI. Biblioteca Medicea Laurenziana.*

tlamama, "to carry"), small two-wheeled vehicles known in Spanish as *carretas* and large mule-drawn carts for hauling large loads (*carros*) shared these arteries with people riding on horses and mules as well as assorted foot travelers.[138] A network of roadside inns, or *ventas*, along key points on the major roads provided shelter and sustenance for travelers and their often-numerous animal companions.[139]

Pictorial depictions of roads allowed pintores to situate the viewer geographically within a region where proximity to a major highway enhanced a town's power. In the map of Our Lady of the Rosary, roads function to define spatial relationships on a regional scale. El Camino Real (the Royal Highway) starts from the town of San Lorenzo Cacaotepec in the bottom-right corner and divides the map into two distinct sections. El Camino de Etla, another major artery in the region, cuts across to the top of the map and effectively creates a third space anchored by the Cerro de Apastle to the right and the Cerro Calichoso to the left. The presence of these two roads constitutes what Alessandra Russo calls *desdoblamiento*, a technique used by early colonial artists to create a balance of elements by placing them on the margins of the map.[140] Notice how the Royal Highway connects both the town of Atzompa on the top left and the town of San Lorenzo on the bottom right. At the same time, the Cerro de Apastle and the Loma de Torcas become anchors on the top right and bottom left respectively. Roads stitch together towns and mountains, providing a visual balance to the representation of space.

Indigo merchants relied as much on muleteers to safely transport large shipments of indigo across dangerous terrain, as royal officials in Mexico City depended on mail carriers to deliver important papers across a web of regional outposts. Sylvia Sellers-García argues that Spanish officials viewed space as a product of routes and time: "Distances," she notes, "were understood as time-space intervals connecting hierarchically organized places."[141] Along the way, from one place to another, coveted materials had a tendency to attract unwanted attention. Consider the testimony of Juan de la Cruz, a forty-year-old *mulato* from Tehuantepec, a coastal town in southwestern Oaxaca along the Pacific and, it seems,

and the less refined *corte* (cut). Besides its diversity of plants, Oaxaca also benefited from its geographic location along the Royal Highway that connected Central America—the richest indigo production zone in Spanish America—to the heart of the viceroyalty. An important commodity for the European export market, añil usually traveled north from Guatemala, where more than a hundred harvesters from Central America specialized in processing the blue colorant.[136] Processed indigo regularly flowed to Antequera, the Spanish seat of power in Oaxaca where officials and merchants inspected and acquired it through various means on its way to Mexico City and beyond.

Roads and trails—the same routes typically described on local maps—allowed individuals to move goods from one location to another. Roads represent significant features of indigenous maps that connected major population centers across the region through a web of narrow pathways, major highways, and regional thoroughfares in constant use by people and animals.[137] Pack-animal carriers, porters known as *tameme* (from the Nahuatl:

a harbor for muleteers constantly on the move. De la Cruz operated a train of forty mules with his brothers Bartolomé and Thomas. People knew him as "el perdido" ("the Lost One"), a moniker that hints at brushes with the law and incorrigible behavior. On January 6, 1756, Juan agreed to transport a hundred *zurrones* (leather pouches) of indigo dye of various kinds from Guatemala City to Antequera in the Valley of Oaxaca, a 450-mile journey across a series of treacherous mountain ranges. When they finally reached their destination on February 1, 1757, the scribe in Antequera who received the shipment confirmed the quantity but noted a discrepancy in weight: "[The] hundred bags appear to be the same ones recorded in the shipping order dated January 6, 1756 . . . in terms of quantity, but not because of their weight, due to the error you can perceive from the assigned weight."[142] Two days later, the intended recipient of the shipment, Don Francisco Joseph Moreno, a merchant from Antequera, complained to authorities about the missing colorant and accused de la Cruz and his brothers of failing to deliver the entire load.

Authorities caught up with de la Cruz on February 5, sequestering his pack to serve as collateral against his debt to the merchant from Oaxaca. In prison, he told authorities that during the journey from Guatemala, somewhere between Tamazola and a place known as La Punta, his two brothers and a third individual identified as Manuel de Obregón opened the leather pouches full of indigo with the intent to sell portions of its contents. A number of people gathered for the opening of the pouches, including Joseph Torres, a man he described as a "white highland mulato" (*mulato blanco arribeño*), who subsequently fled to Guatemala, and another person from Tehuantepec known as Juan de los Santos, who authorities imprisoned shortly after the theft. Juan told officials that "an Indian named Alejo with a cross-eye from the town of Tonalá" made off with a good portion of the ink and that a resident from Ciudad Real named Bartolo Amola, and the Spanish vagabond Pedro Ponce from Chiapa, purchased the rest. Juan claimed he sat at the head of the pack train and therefore failed to see the exchange that took place; not until they reached Tehuantepec did he learn from his brother what had happened.

It is uncertain how much blue dye the Indian, the merchant, and the vagabond purchased or why they acquired it in the first place, but it is clear that a black market existed for the prized colorant. Perhaps these interlopers functioned as retailers for local consumption, or maybe they dyed fabrics; some may even have used it to make and even annotate maps of indigenous origin.

The legend (Figure 3.17) starting on the upper-right side of the map of Our Lady of the Rosary represents an unusual, but not altogether strange, element of native mapmaking in the eighteenth century. For one thing, legends, short annotations detailing the elements of visual records by assigning them numbers or letters, did not usually form part of the components of an Indian map. Influenced by European systems of ordering applied in maps and illustrations, native painters introduced

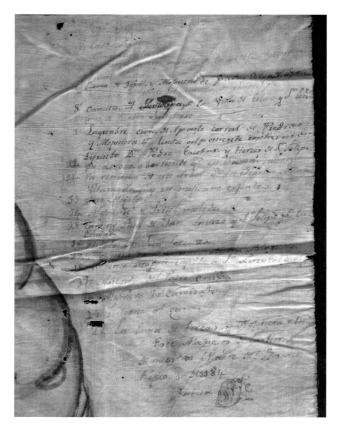

3.17. *Legend, map of Nuestra Madre del Rosario (c. 1750s). Formerly part of the collection of historic records from the Municipality of Santa María Atzompa, Oaxaca. This map disappeared in 2008.*

legends during the eighteenth century to identify mountains, rivers, plants, rocks, dwellings, ranches, and other manmade structures as well as social and political relationships between a region's inhabitants. The use of text functioned to validate a map's pictorial elements in order to establish spatial relationships. Interestingly, the use of red and blue colorants not only illustrated the pictorial elements of the map but also functioned as ink to write the key—a rare occurrence considering most alphabetic text found on maps came from the hands of Spanish officials that favored the iron-gall variety.

CONCLUSION

The historiographical narrative of maps has traditionally focused on the analysis of pictorial illustrations and the meaning of lines and symbols used to express place, geography, and objects. But the narrative that has resulted from this line of inquiry traditionally centers on the way painters incorporated or rejected Western ideas and culture, as well as on how they gradually lost or preserved Mesoamerican pictorial strategies over time. Inevitably, a history of displacement emerges at the end of the sixteenth century that sees indigenous mapping and pictorial activity enter into full decline, reappearing on occasion (generally without much success) in a cheap version of its former self to help mitigate encroachment. This chapter has instead presented an alternative model centered on uncovering the diverse bodies of knowledge associated with the material condition of maps. By peering into the maps' deepest fibers and thinking about their material composition, I propose we are able to present a panoramic view of mapmaking centered on experimentation, transfer of knowledge, and the ability to adapt to the introduction of new ingredients and ways of knowing. The combination of these activities shaped the form and function of maps, and as we will see in chapter 4, it was an aspect that notaries and officials attempted to standardize and authenticate on a regular basis.

CHAPTER 4

AUTHENTICATION

Legal writing sustained the idea of empire.

ROBERTO GONZÁLEZ ECHEVARRÍA, *MYTH AND ARCHIVE*

No one knows how long Gonzalo Messia de Magaña had to wait for his map (Figure 3.12); perhaps it was not long at all.[1] As *corregidor* of Huajuapan in the Mixteca Baja—a hot, dry, and weather-beaten region in the northwest—he received notification from the viceroy in late January 1617 about the petition of a royal grant of land (*merced*) by the political officers of Miltepec to add to their corporate holdings. The instructions laid out a series of steps to authorize the grant of land: a statement of the site's purpose, notifications to neighboring towns and settlements, identification of existing or potential conflicts, the recording of witness testimony, and a physical visit to the land in question. In preparation for the inspection, the instructions also requested Messia "make a map of it [the site known locally as Ytlaumitepec] with clear annotations so that it is legible."[2] The map's primary intent informed imperial aspirations focused on describing the distance and relationship between the major settlements and the petitioned site of land. The viceroy requested a *traslado*, an authorized copy of the proceedings, to inform the viceregal archive in Mexico City once the town received

possession of the site; he reminded the corregidor of the four-month waiting period to allow for any possible complaints to surface. Maps made in Oaxaca had circulated for decades within local and regional bureaucratic offices in the hands of scribes, alcaldes mayores, corregidores, native officers, *caciques*, and lawyers who used them to inform petitions of various kinds associated with land and its division.

Messia de Magaña visited Miltepec on Saturday, May 13, to follow up on Miltepec's petition. In order to perform his duties, he needed the support of a scribe to record and keep track of petitions, testimonies, and other public acts associated with the granting of the merced, but none was available. To resolve this issue, Messia appointed a scribe and recruited a Spaniard fluent in Mixtec and Nahuatl to serve as translator. The following day, the three men waited for announcements at the end of Sunday Mass to notify those present of the petition of land and the scheduled site visit. When the corregidor, his support staff, and four witnesses arrived on May 17 to make the inspection, a large crowd awaited him. Representatives from the neighboring towns of Ixtlán, Suchitepec, Tequixtepec, and Huajuapan accompanied the officers and commoners from Miltepec on the inspection. This public act, an important element of defining spatial relationships in Oaxaca, allowed neighbors from the region to safeguard their boundaries, to limit aggressive expansion, and to record and preserve the event for posterity.

When the group reached Ytlaumitepec, they surveyed the site. According to the scribe's account, the corregidor "called for the painter Domingo Hernández, to make a map and description of the site, indicating the place where the community of Miltepec has petitioned the merced; said map should be clear in every aspect including its annotations and neighboring towns."[3] In the next sentence, the scribe confirmed that, in fact, "said map was made in the presence of the corregidor who ordered it be given its proper place in the proceedings."[4] On paper, the scribe moved from the act of calling the painter and commissioning the map to signing and filing it in one fell swoop, the two moments flowing seamlessly into one another without any gaps in time. In reality, the space that separated them included a series of calculated steps that formed part of the negotiation of spatial relationships in Oaxaca. The simple act of calling the pintor during the *vista de ojos*, a commonly used term to refer to site inspections, had required planning, most likely a discussion between the corregidor and town officers facilitated by the translator days earlier to assure the presence of a painter. According to the scribe's account, the painter made the map during the inspection, which meant he visited the site carrying such tools as brushes, pigments to make colors, and paper. The corregidor and those present then waited for the painter to finish his rendition, a striking green and yellow maze of roads, stylized mountains, and churches that brought together the region's geographical elements in visual form. Once it dried, the corregidor had the opportunity to inspect the map and make clear annotations to identify towns, roads, and natural features.

One of the most important aspects of indigenous cartography concerns the practice of authentication, a multifaceted process to annotate and legitimize the contents of a map. Regularly extending over several months in two or more cities, authentication involved painters, scribes, officials, lawyers, and litigants at different points in time examining maps but also offering critiques about their use or their content. During authentication, officials had the opportunity to review a *pintura* and to ask the painter questions about its elements in order to validate it according to legal protocols. Scribes and officials actively engaged in the mapmaking process, leaving written traces of their actions on the surface of every map they inspected. Their writing recognized towns and place-signs, and it appeared next to rivers, trees, rocks, buildings, and crosses. Officials aired potential conflicts, measured distances, suggested pathways, and in some instances added pictorial elements in their efforts to make sense of the maps and their coded messages. Regional bureaucrats would include maps in the briefs they sent to the Audiencia, the highest judicial body located in Mexico City, where they would undergo another round of evaluation at the hands of judges, scribes, and attorneys before being archived or returned to their place of origin.

Fraught with tension due to differences embedded into the Spanish legal system that favored the European minority, authentication made maps legible by relying on written formulas designed to shape and classify individuals and their activities. Indeed, as González Echevarría observes in this chapter's epigraph, legal writing supported the notion of empire. But just how did legal writing and notarial culture account for the presence of maps and pictorial records? Traditional narratives of Amerindian cartography have, in their efforts to unpack indigenous agency, created a perception that maps somehow served marginal roles in litigation and that they represented an inferior—and often misunderstood—form of evidence. Why, then, did scribes and officials commission and use indigenous maps in the first place? To what extent did they understand the maps they viewed? If disapproval or distrust of pictorial documents existed, as some evidence suggests, why did officials continue to inspect and accept maps well into the eighteenth century?

In the pages that follow, an exploration of the various dimensions of authentication brings to light the complex interplay between Spanish and indigenous actors in response to the use of maps. My analysis gives special attention to the certifying and descriptive glosses found on a majority of maps made from the late sixteenth through the early eighteenth centuries by the scribes and officials who inspected them. Painters controlled geographic and pictorial knowledge as well as the tools needed to make maps, but scribes and officials helped define a map's content to fit Spanish legal principles. Drawing from recent scholarship that centers on the intersection between manuscript studies and legal culture, I argue that conferring sameness to maps represented an official's most important task, an activity designed to render documents legible to a broad bureaucratic audience. The quest for sameness reveals itself in the repetitive nature of the written commentary, short passages focused on the identification of places, distance, and geography, usually culminating with an *X*-marks-the-spot moment in the form of the conventional gloss "here is the site."[5]

By reviewing and annotating, officials at the local level tried their best to account for the diversity of maps and other pictorial records submitted by indigenous towns to litigate claims and petitions. Sameness represented a pivotal tool used to facilitate communication between officials by reducing signs and pictorial representation to alphabetic expression, an imperfect process burdened by the mediation of translators and the inconvenience of cultural dissimilarities. Once the iron-gall ink touched the surface of a map, an official's annotations legitimized its presence in the imperial record, thereby helping users—present and future—to more effectively articulate their claims to land and other privileges. The process forced scribes and Spanish officials to learn about the elements of each map they reviewed, as well as about the painter's intentions when they surveyed boundaries and the geographic elements that defined them. Authentication depended on a strong measure of common sense to articulate and emphasize the requirements imposed by the Crown. As authentication was a changing concept responsive to shifts in power relationships and issues of representation and rights, common sense facilitated this delicate aspect of an official's duties.[6] "This is true and faithful," they certified on countless occasions after

reviewing a map, branding it with their signatures in an act of possession that sought to convey authority and truth in the state's eyes.

The intervention of a number of social actors during and after the initial review helped to define the role of the map in any given case. For painters, certification served as a forum to verbally explain, either through an interpreter or on their own, the content of their maps. Their input helped to negotiate the allocation of land, the fixing of boundaries, the confirmation of property holdings, and encroachment. Authentication represented a pivotal moment for painters to direct a map's message because, once it entered New Spain's bureaucratic channels, they lost a substantial measure of control over it.[7] Authorities accepted pictorial records as a matter of rule, even if, as we will learn below, they had doubts about their provenance or content. Although the submission of maps represented a successful first hurdle for litigants and petitioners, the process shifted to the capital of the viceroyalty, where authorities, lawyers, scribes, and native representatives provided commentary when necessary. Following the maps' submission, a majority of them associated with land grant petitions during the late sixteenth century often received immediate stamps of approval by officials, necessary tools to fulfill government stipulations used to access land. In contrast, major pushback from competing landholders and their representatives in the late seventeenth and eighteenth centuries generated fierce critiques from litigants who recognized the threat of maps as evidence. In this case, the burden of authentication fell squarely on litigants and their attorneys more than on the provincial bureaucrats who admitted them into the record.

MAPS, MANUSCRIPTS, AND NOTARIAL CULTURE

During the second half of the sixteenth century, attempts to administer New World domains generated surveys, expeditions, and laws that led to spatial realignments, measurements of ecology and culture, and record-keeping practices designed to capture accounts of state. Philip's 1568 *junta magna*, a summit of high-ranking civil and ecclesiastic officials, addressed issues related to missionary practices, tribute collection, fiscal responsibility, labor assignments, land allocation, and illegal trade.[8] These efforts contributed directly to the region's mapping impulse, an activity tied squarely not only to land, politics, and resources but also to ritual and culture. While the trend in studies of mapped environments moves toward a decentralization of maps from the state, this chapter highlights the way state efforts to measure, allocate, and distribute land relied heavily on native geographic knowledge.[9] According to Daniel Lord Smail, "It has become de rigueur to speak of state interest in and control over early modern developments in mapping," themes that subordinate cartographic practices to the whims of rulers and their trusted advisers.[10] But what of indigenous maps that, while responding to imperial rule, did so from distinctly local perspectives and with uniquely local goals in mind? As this chapter demonstrates, the authentication of maps marks a critical, but often overlooked, site of knowledge that generated new ways to think about, rationalize, and acquire land through a mutual language of spatial representation with a distinct indigenous character.

Used to accompany suits and petitions of various kinds, maps circulated widely within the channels of New Spain's institutional bureaucracy. The use of language and writing to structure Spanish imperial administration in the viceroyalty generated a steady production of handwritten manuscripts detailing the activities of officials, explorers, clerics, merchants, lawyers, and others involved in colonization.[11] At the local and regional levels, scribes generated thousands of pages each year when individuals needed to address authorities in writing for formal transactions that required a record. Along with corregidores, *gobernadores* (governors), and alcaldes mayores—provincial bureaucrats who administered justice and collected taxes at the regional level—scribes participated closely in the commission and authentication of indigenous maps. These groups gradually developed an understanding of visual representation, assimilating and codifying it into an evolving imperial archive that had to account for the unique pictorial dimensions associated with manuscripts of indigenous origin in New Spain.[12]

The culture of manuscripts that grounded the administration of empire during the colonial period has garnered critical attention from scholars across methodological fields. For the literary critic Ángel Rama, the "lettered city," an elaborate bureaucracy designed and directed by *letrados*—the individuals trained in law and liberal arts supported by the work of scribes and regional officials—played an instrumental role in shaping imperial design. In Rama's estimation, this "priestly caste" exercised power by controlling writing and the empire's medium of communication in Spanish American cities.[13] Joanne Rappaport and Tom Cummins, an anthropologist and an art historian respectively, have pushed Rama's idea of the lettered city further by articulating a much broader space of literacy that emerged from the interaction of European and New World traditions.[14] They argue that orality, a common denominator of both cultures, mediated alphabetic and visual literacy in the northern Andes. These forms, inextricably bound to each other, allowed imperial authorities to move their agenda forward and gave natives opportunities to articulate their complaints, petitions, and desires.

These studies offer attractive frameworks to consider the circulation of manuscripts, especially indigenous maps. At the local level, scribes, provincial bureaucrats, and translators came into first contact with maps. Toward the end of the sixteenth century, imperial authorities adopted a policy of selling public offices in the New World, including *escribanías* (scribal appointments) and *alcaldías mayores* (regional judgeships), to generate income for the royal coffers. Royal scribes had the ability to perform their duties in any town or city of the realm, whereas public scribes could work only in one place. The requirements for holding a scribal appointment depended on knowledge of the written word and on individual qualities of honor valued in the Hispanic world, including *vecindad* (civic privileges and duties) and an Old Christian background.[15] In practice, authorities in America regularly appointed scribes who did not always meet the Crown's standards. A stream of reprimands from Spain between 1564 and 1669 accused the viceroys of failing to scrutinize the selection of scribes, a practice "resulting in notable errors and invalidating testimonies, investigations, and examinations."[16]

In New Spain, regional officials such as Gonzalo Messia de Magaña, the corregidor of Huajuapan described at the start of the chapter, sometimes appointed scribes in remote regions of the empire not necessarily based on qualifications but in order to meet a region's demand. Since these officers covered various towns and settlements, securing allies through scribal appointments—lucrative endeavors in and of themselves—facilitated the duties of public administration and could, perhaps, open opportunities down the line.

The methods of examination, authentication, and archiving that took place after maps were introduced into the Spanish courts depended on established notarial procedures, as well as on the unseen social forces with which officials and notaries contended on a case by case basis. Kathryn Burns's *Into the Archive*, a compelling historical account of notaries and their clients in the Andes, provides a stimulating analysis of notarial culture and the way it shaped legal documents such as petitions, wills, complaints, land titles, and appointments. Burns argues that the deconstruction of the notarial record and the archives built from it allow us to better understand the tension between legal writing and individual agency in the colonial world. Records, she says, represent "a space where negotiations once took place, around the notarial template, leaving traces of understandings that often belie the wording of the text."[17] Notarial practices that sought to systematize the production of records contributed directly to the proliferation, and protection, of maps and titles. The scattering of important documents among family, local, and regional archives attests to the value placed by individuals on record-keeping and also to the practice of copying, which facilitated the production of legal papers, both of which carried notarial fees.[18] These efforts contributed to the circulation of scribal manuscripts within a culture of handwritten documents that defined the Iberian world. Scribes, of course, played prominent roles in a society that generated massive amounts of documentation, recording the public actions individuals wanted preserved according to prescribed legal formulas. Patrons, posits Burns, sought their services precisely because in matters of law their word was truth.[19]

Instructional manuals that circulated in the New World allowed scribes to select from a range of templates to articulate sales, mortgages, wills, leases, licenses, and other contracts.[20] These state-sanctioned guides to learning the notarial arts did not, unfortunately, include how-to sections on pictorial records from faraway places. Instead, scribes and officials applied notarial techniques for the authentication of maps that focused on identifying towns, roads, boundary markers, unused lands, distance, and rivers. Their annotations allowed the Crown a measure of control over an impossibly complex spatial patchwork largely accessible only through native intermediaries who supplied geographic knowledge, historical memory, diplomatic support, and translation services. The authentication of maps, a process intimately tied to surveying and site visits, forced scribes and officials to depend heavily on painters and other informants to point out relevant details of the landscape. Their actions responded to directions such as those that informed the *merced* petitions and called for clearly depicted maps.

For all its color and unique design, the map (Figure 4.1) inspected by the scribe Pedro Valadés in 1609 for a livestock ranch near Juxtlahuaca in western Oaxaca followed one simple rule: to describe the relationship between major settlements and the petitioned site.[21] The town appeared on the left side of the map, represented by a church within a circular enclosure of mountains. Valadés wrote "Justlaguaca" underneath it. He also identified the road with footsteps that moved away from the town and guided the viewer to the petitioned site known as Ixcotepec. Valadés's annotations reflect the manner in which officials prioritized and ordered space, an itinerant practice dependent on movement—walking and riding—tied to land, surveys, and boundary-making.[22] On the back (Figure 4.2), the scribe authorized the inspection by noting, "The map and description, with the bearings it contains, was mandated by the alcalde mayor who signed it himself along with said scribe."[23] Signatures afforded the bearers of maps juridical authority that embodied and invoked the signatory who attested to its contents. Signing implied such acts as viewing, reading, writing, categorizing, and discussion, all of which helped define the contents of a map.

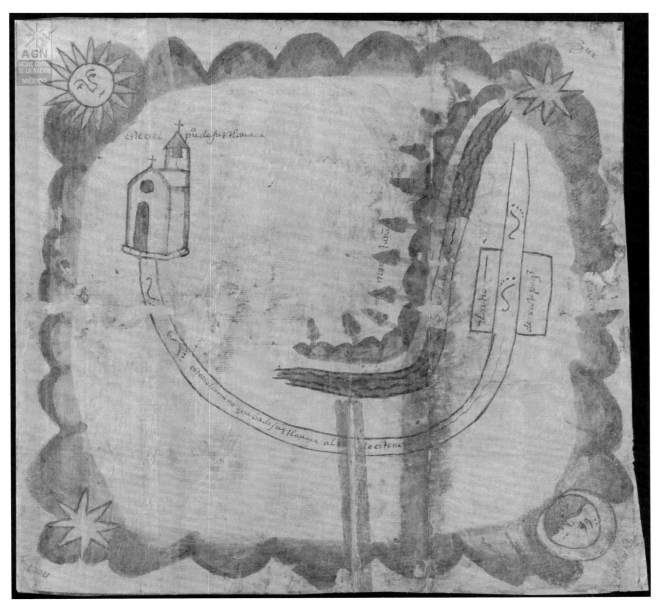

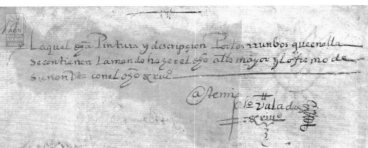

4.1. *Map of Juxtlahuaca (1609), no. 1271, Tierras, vol. 1871, exp. 11, f. 11. Archivo General de la Nación, Fondo Hermanos Mayo, concentrados, sobre 363.*

4.2. *Pedro Valadés's authentication, map of Juxtlahuaca (1609), no. 1271, Tierras, vol. 1871, exp. 11, f. 11. Archivo General de la Nación, Fondo Hermanos Mayo, concentrados, sobre 363.*

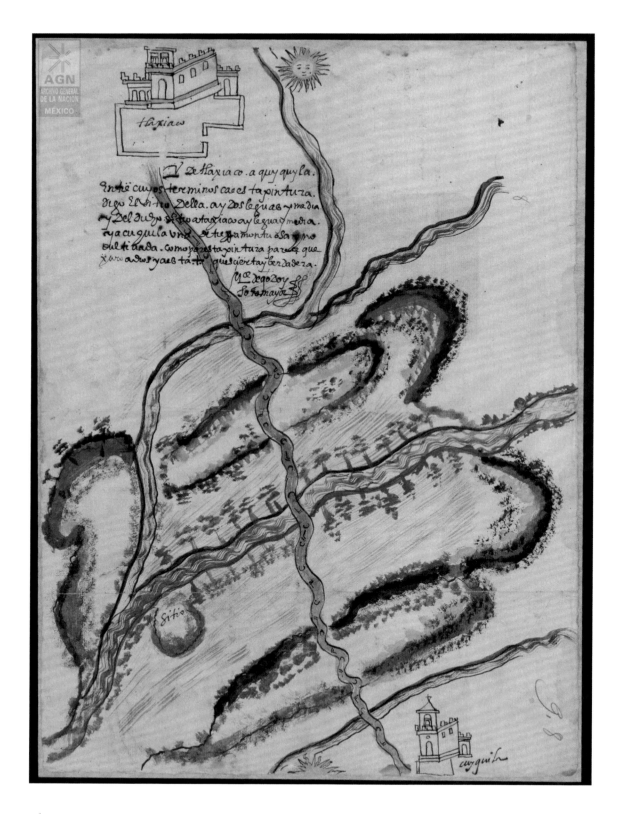

For Spanish officials, land grant maps needed to fulfill criteria centered on the identification of petitioned sites. The painter of the map of Tlaxiaco and Cuquila (Figure 4.3) displayed a sophisticated sense of style when applying a palate of earth tones, shading, and three-dimensionality in a 1588 composition submitted to authorities for a livestock ranch and two *caballerías*.[24] When the corregidor, Melchor de Godoy Sotomayor, inspected the map, he identified the important Mixtec center of Tlaxiaco at the top of the page represented by a church. The feet and hoof marks moving away from Tlaxiaco toward Cuquila in the bottom frame led to the petitioned site labeled "*sitio.*" The painter focused on representing the relationship between the two towns, the land in between, and the road that connected them. Below Tlaxiaco, Godoy translated the elements of the map into writing, noting the distance between the two towns and the parcel. The corregidor commented on the nature of the land ("uncultivated and mountainous as is registered in this map") and proceeded to sign it (Figure 4.4)—the ultimate act of authentication. In concert with imperial policies, Godoy's attention on places, distance, and land use defined his intervention as an act of authentication grounded in the language of the state. Although each painter generated distinct and often visibly striking maps, annotations flagged important geographical markers used to determine the location of petitioned or contested sites.

Joseph de Chávez, a scribe in the Huajuapan region in northwestern Oaxaca, did the same with the map made in 1616 (Figure 4.5) for a livestock ranch in favor of a cacique named Juan Bautista.[25] Along with the jurisdiction's corregidor, and most likely with a cadre of indigenous leaders and townspeople, the group traveled northwest from Suchitepetongo to survey the site known as Ahuehuetitlán. Chávez's carefully placed signposts along different parts of the map prioritized certain geographic features, including the mountain ranges (*sierras*), the densely forested landscape (*arcabucos*), and the vacant

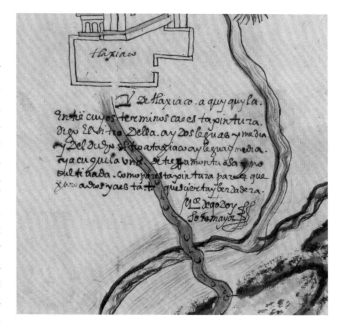

4.4. *Melchor de Godoy Sotomayor's certifying gloss, map of Tlaxiaco and Cuquila (1588),* no. 1692.9, Tierras, vol. 2692, exp. 17, f. 8. Archivo General de la Nación, Fondo Hermanos Mayo, concentrados, sobre 363.

lots (*baldíos*) of Huajuapan, though he made no effort to gloss the multiple rivers that seemed to flow through the region. At the intersection of two roads in the bottom center of the map, next to the church that marked the town of Suchitepetongo, the scribe noted that the petitioned site was one league away. As the viewer moves from the bottom of the page to the top (from west to east) along the road to Huajuapan, a manicule in the left center points to an area surrounded by trees, mountains, and a river with a caption that reads: "Here is the petitioned site known as Ahuehuetitlán."[26] Above it, the scribe used a small blank space on the page to attest to the true and faithful execution of the map and that both he and the corregidor had "walked and personally seen" the site.

Spanish officials submitted their own maps on occasion, although these were much less elaborate than some of the maps presented by Indian painters. The corregidor Diego de Santa Cruz Olguín's 1611 map (Figure 4.6) described the site where Luis Quijada intended to establish a roadside inn near the town of Cuscatlán in

the northern part of Oaxaca that currently neighbors the state of Puebla.[27] Santa Cruz used few pictorial details and as many words to convey his message, a characteristic of Spanish notarial maps Serge Gruzinski described as "extremely restrained, spare, and unadorned."[28] Santa Cruz's quickly sketched map includes a small church representing the town, plus two straight parallel lines that stretch from one corner of the page to another in a diagonal fashion, representing the road from Puebla to Oaxaca. Although the top corner of the page where the road ends is torn, a cartographic symbol no doubt marked the petitioned site. Even in this restrained sketch, the corregidor made sure to annotate the map in order to give it clarity.

With more complex pictorial records and maps, some authorities made separate records to guide the user. In 1558, the cacique Diego Cortés used a pictorial manuscript to renegotiate a *tasación* (appraisal) for him and his brothers, Bartolomé and Hernando. The tasación served to determine which privileges Spanish authorities bestowed on select members of the Indian nobility. Over the course of two days, the Valley's alcalde mayor reviewed the petition and interviewed a host of *principales* from Cuilapa about the Cortés brothers and about a *pintura* Diego presented as evidence of his status. From this experience, one can glean the extent to which some

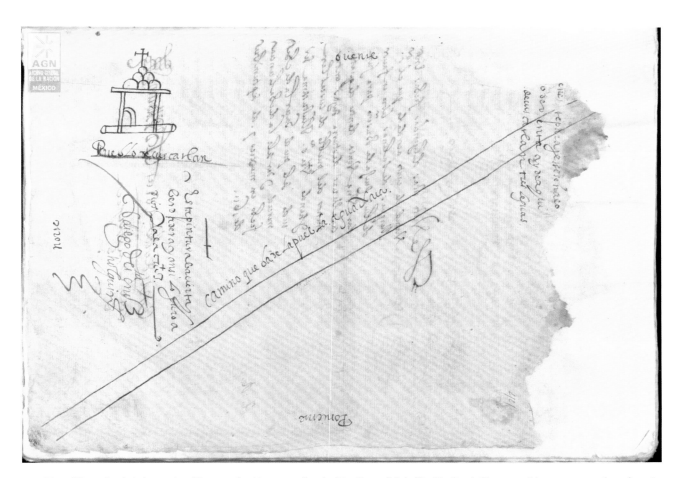

4.6. *Map of Cuscatlan (1611), no. 1607, Tierras, vol. 2682, exp. 4, f. 9. Archivo General de la Nación, Fondo Hermanos Mayo, concentrados, sobre 363.*

officials in Oaxaca examined pictorial documents within the legal environment of the region.

The public reading of the painting brought together native leaders—including, perhaps, a painter or two—and Christian clerics who together with the alcalde mayor examined its contents over the course of two days. On September 4, the alcalde mayor remarked that, having "seen the painting herein contained, and examined it with the principales of this town and with its [Spanish] clergy, it was determined that the *macehuales* [Indian commoners] depicted in this pintura were a gift of birth from his father Don Luis."[29] The alcalde mayor's declarations from the second day reflect the consensus the parties reached concerning its interpretation. "There are 1,148 married Indian commoners," he said, "tributaries of the Marques del Valle; from the [illustrated figures] in the pictorial, it seems Don Diego is a *tequitlato*."[30] As a tequitlato, Cortés could collect tribute on behalf of the Crown as well as the harvest of a plot of land from the macehuales under his authority.[31] Diego pushed his petition further by claiming that his older brother, Hernando, "suffered extreme need," for which he requested a stipend from the surplus in Cuilapa's community chest, a fund used for a range of activities associated with town affairs.[32] The alcalde mayor remarked that, because Cortés had a second tasación with another set of Indian tributaries, he had "plenty to eat and [means] with which to support himself, his home and family, and Don Hernando."[33] Although it is not clear whether the alcalde mayor granted the stipend, he did, in effect, authorize Diego Cortés's petition, recognizing his cacique status and his role as a tequitlato. The pictorial used by Cortés possessed qualities associated with genealogical manuscripts and tribute records. Despite the fact the painting is lost, the accompanying manuscript provides an avenue from which to assess the way in which some officials viewed and inspected pictorial records and the methods they applied to make them legible.

In another instance, the task of authentication seemed so daunting, and the map so complex, that the reviewing official thought it best to prepare a key. When the alcalde mayor, Juan de Torres de Lagunas, commissioned a map for the Relaciones Geográficas survey, he followed a royal mandate dated May 25, 1577, that explained to officials in New Spain and Peru the overall purpose of the project and the type of information sought. It stated that in order to "attend to their good government, it has seemed a proper thing to decree that a general description be made of the whole condition of our Indies, islands, and their provinces, the most accurate and certain possible."[34] Instructions called for the use of native informants ("persons knowledgeable of the things of the land") who could discuss a region's history, politics, and rituals. In addition, the questionnaire asked for the mapping of individual towns, coasts, and islands. "Make a map of the layout of the town, its streets, plazas and other features, noting the monasteries, as well as can be sketched easily on paper," it instructed respondents on item ten.[35] Question forty-two asked about "the ports and landings along the coast" and requested "a map showing their shape and layout," and number forty-seven asked about islands close to shore, instructing respondents to "make a map, if possible, of their form and shape, showing their length, width, and lay of the land."[36] Torres de Lagunas recruited the painter of Tehuantepec featured in chapter 2 to compose such a map. The map (Figure 2.10) submitted by the painter to the alcalde mayor included substantial geographical features recorded separately.[37] Without the intervention of provincial bureaucrats and scribes to untangle copious evidence generated during lengthy cases, Audiencia judges and officials would have found it much more difficult to process petitions.

The most compelling aspect of the commission and authentication of the Tehuantepec map has only partially to do with its inspection. Torres de Lagunas was not alone in turning to native painters in the late sixteenth century to produce maps. In an uncoordinated effort, authorities across New Spain tapped into a pool of native artists—astute bilingual caciques often dressed in European clothing—accustomed to dealing with scribes and officials. What motivated officials to delegate the task of mapping to natives? The reasons reflect a series of choices derived from a reading of the instructions, an estimation of the work involved, knowledge of the region, and an official's network of relationships with royal officers, priests, and native intermediaries.

Scribes and officials of Mediterranean notarial cultures had developed traditions of linguistic mapping during the later Middle Ages, but maps of towns and regions had not played a significant part in these practices.[38] Not surprisingly, provincial bureaucrats in New Spain seldom attempted to map a region, and when they did they put on display their notorious skills as doodlers more than their geographical observations, as Diego de Santa Cruz Olguín's 1611 map (Figure 4.6) described above illustrates.[39] More than disdain for visual images or lack of interest, most scribes, alcaldes mayores, and corregidores did not have the background or instruction to render spatial relationships visually. And while there is no doubt that Spaniards prized writing and the power of the written word, officials also recognized, sometimes reluctantly, the value of local expertise. The act of commissioning a map reflects an exchange based on the recognition of someone's ability to make a pictorial representation that considered the region's geographical and political space.

HURDLES

In their effort to authenticate maps, provincial bureaucrats faced numerous hurdles, including lack of fluency in native languages, unfamiliarity with geographical spaces, and the assimilation of an endless stream of competing narratives that claimed authority over land. Limited knowledge of indigenous languages forced the intervention of interpreters at the local and regional levels who facilitated communication between authorities, settlers, and natives.[40] Translators provided valuable services as mediators between towns and authorities. Officials understood that, as much as the use of translators represented an essential tool of expansion and colonization, the process also carried with it considerable disadvantages. Since officials drew interpreters from the Spanish and Indian worlds to help mediate affairs, the fear of misrepresentation, abuses of power, and lying tempered early modern encounters and left provincial bureaucrats, natives, and settlers distrustful of each other.

When Torres de Lagunas, the alcalde mayor described above, commissioned an earlier map (Figure 2.11) from the painter of Tehuantepec in 1580 for a livestock ranch,

he required translation for Zapotec and Nahuatl speakers testifying about the petitioned site.[41] Torres de Lagunas also enlisted the services of Antonio Jiménez, an *yndio interprete* (Indian interpreter) fluent in Nahuatl and Zapotec, and Diego Gutiérrez, who translated Zapotec into Spanish. They both swore under oath to faithfully interpret the testimony of the witnesses.[42] Invoking God in a legal proceeding placed, in theory, a higher burden on the witness to testify truthfully, especially since accusations of lies and deceit traditionally spilled into the testimony of plaintiffs and associated characters. Complaints about scribes that centered on abuses of power and inexperience reveal the limitations and weaknesses associated with authentication.[43] While Indians turned out in large numbers to the courts, a majority of them did not speak Spanish with royal interlocutors.[44] Fluency in native tongues and their effective translation represented a valued commodity but could generate tension and misrepresentation as well as abuse.

Officials also fielded accusations of abuse from social actors across ethnic divisions who called out translators on suspicious and unsavory methods. In 1675, the *cabecera* of Teozapotlán and its four subject towns pleaded with the court to remove Juan Ramírez from his post as interpreter (*deponer de dicho oficio*), a salaried post that, as the case suggests, allowed him to coerce the natives of the region.[45] Ramírez, they said, had continually extorted and "greatly harassed" them. A judge found their argument compelling enough to rule in their favor, but with "considerable craftiness" (*mucha maña*) the translator had managed to retain his post for several months after the verdict arrived in Oaxaca. The natives feared retribution and took the initiative to propose a new candidate to replace Ramírez, a man named Sebastián de Ricaldes, who they said possessed the qualities they desired in a translator. Having used his services on a prior occasion, Teozapotlán testified that Ricaldes was "docile and humble . . . and does not extort or take away anything" from us.[46] The court did, in fact, select Ricaldes as a translator for Teozapotlán, though it is not clear whether or not Ramírez lost his appointment.

The possibility for misrepresentation tempered the very fabric upon which authentication and an official's quest for sameness resided. As Robert Haskett has contended regarding the Cuernavaca region, services provided by interpreters produced misrepresentations only on occasion, a statement that aligns nicely with formal complaints from the Oaxaca region.[47] And yet the constant slippage of poorly understood languages, and the mediation of translators and scribes who recorded portions of what witnesses and clients spoke, brings to mind what Rappaport and Cummins describe as "double overlay," a reference to the complexity of documents written in Spanish that recorded translated Quechua testimony of native Pasto speakers.[48] The failure to fully capture the intention of those who testified across several languages could have debilitating consequences on disadvantaged groups. In the Mixe regions that bordered Zapotec domains, widespread use of Nahuatl among Zapotecs posed a serious disadvantage to Mixe speakers who did not enjoy the same fluency. Although natives had spoken Nahuatl for trade before the arrival of Europeans, in Oaxaca's northern sierra the Spaniards' Nahua allies extended the language's use into the administrative realm.[49] Because of their fluency in Nahuatl, Zapotecs gained a tremendous advantage over Mixe speakers when competition over land intensified during the seventeenth century, gradually appropriating vast portions of Mixe territory.[50]

When authorities visited the towns under their jurisdiction, they also relied on the geographic knowledge of local caciques, interpreters, litigants, and witnesses to define spatial boundaries. These individuals guided officials during surveys, provided testimony, translated, and, most important, helped to legitimize agrarian administration in their regions. What to some people appeared as vacant and unused land, to others had meaning and history. In their annotations, officials routinely described on maps the type of soil represented—"uncultivated," "mountainous," "rugged," "forested"—to signal not only the type of terrain but also the possibility of exploiting it. Recognition of indigenous rights to land thrived in many areas of the Hispanic world, yet this practice generated changes that centered on the Spanish emphasis on ranching and cultivation, that is to say on making land productive.[51] This idea clashed with indigenous visions

of ownership focused on territorial holdings passed down through generations of leading nobles. Interested parties often found themselves under fire after petitions for identified sites received opposition.

Don Pedro Martín de Velasco introduced a map in 1591 (Figure 3.3) to support his petition for a livestock ranch near the town of Santa Cruz Ixtepec.[52] The site was located about a league and a half away from Santa Cruz on a small mountain known as Queguquilapa claimed by Velasco as part of his patrimonial lands. The site appears on the map surrounded by a chain of hills on the upper-left portion, an empty banner drawn across the landscape with black ink, signaling to viewers where on the page one could find the petitioned site. Painted in red, a road connects the site to the town of Santa Cruz, its church encircled by houses of different sizes, on the right side of map. Two other settlements on the bottom portion of the page reflect local interests in the region. Directly below the site, the *hacienda* of Diego Calbo flanks the town of Santa Ana on the right, and a road connects both to Santa Cruz. In early January 1592, Velasco and Calbo, as well as representatives from Santa Cruz and Santa Ana, guided the region's corregidor, a scribe, and a translator to survey the chosen site. The records they produced to document the merced reveal the way diverse social actors prioritized space and the manner in which they used and assimilated the close bond between the visual and the textual.

The scribe's narrative after they arrived at Queguquilapa moved swiftly from recognizing individuals present for the survey to asking about any potential harm that granting a merced would cause to local residents. The text included few details about the local geography. His report recorded no discussion about the three *mojoneras* (boundary markers) identified on the map next to a mound of rocks that helped to situate the petitioned site. Neither did it mention any of the relative distances from the primary settlements to the site. Those details he reserved for the map's annotation, an action that would force future users to consult the two records in tandem in order to gain a fuller appreciation of the relationship between geographical markers. Each of the four major places on the map—two native towns, one hacienda, and the petitioned site—include a banner to identify them by name. The petitioned estancia's banner remained conspicuously empty, perhaps as a strategy by the painter to force the reviewing official to focus his attention on this portion of the map. Whatever the case, the official did not annotate the blank space, preferring to instead identify the site directly above it as *sitio que se pide* (petitioned site).

We get a sense of the importance of the geographic area in the upper-left portion of the map because of the reviewing official's exacting comments. The land Don Pedro petitioned for the livestock ranch pushed against a boundary that separated the towns of Santa Cruz and Santa Ana. On the map, the road appeared to delineate part of this border, the reviewer noting on its left side *términos de Santa Ana* (limits of Santa Ana) and *tierras de Santa Cruz* (lands of Santa Cruz) on the right. Not until examining the transcript of witness testimony, however, do we get a sense of the underlying strains that lay below the surface of the map. Although native witnesses who were asked about the site did not object to awarding the land to Don Pedro, the testimony of a *vecino* (Spanish resident) from Antequera suggests that, behind the scenes, tensions ran high. Sixty-five-year-old Lupe de Anaya testified that he had visited the same site four or five years earlier with the local monastery's vicar, another friar, and the scribe assigned to Don Pedro's case. He noted that the petitioned site had "gravelly soil that had never been broken or cultivated" and that, after survey-ing it in its entirety, they found no evidence of "maguey, house, or shack."[53] When they visited the site the previ-ous day during the official survey, he noticed that a straw shack, presumably Don Pedro's, had been burned down. Anaya said no one knew for sure who was responsible but that he had heard that "the Indians of Santa Ana had done it maliciously and to stir confrontation."[54] In this case, the alphabetic and pictorial records were, as Rappaport and Cummins have suggested, "mediated by orality," a custom shared by both cultures.[55] Oral testi-mony served to disseminate local knowledge, as did the off-the-record conversations that informed all activities associated with surveying land.

In other instances, judges and scribes examined and compared native maps during their boundary surveys in order to locate important geographic features. Such was the case with a group of Spanish and indigenous offi-cials who met on May 10, 1687, at the plaza of San Ana Zegache, a Zapotec town in the southern range of the Valley of Oaxaca. Led by Antonio de Abellán y Carrasco, the alcalde mayor of the Cuatro Villas del Marquesado, an alignment of four principal towns in the Valley, the group headed west at daybreak aided by a sturdy painted map (Figure 4.7).[56] Although a majority of the maps from this period often bear little resemblance to earlier maps from the sixteenth century and early seventeenth century, efforts within indigenous communities to illus-trate the landscape showcase the evolution of pictorial traditions rooted in early contact. The map served as a navigation tool that helped the party identify geographi-cal elements, ranches, and natural and manmade bound-ary markers during a survey and demarcation (*deslinde y reconocimiento*) of nearby lands. The property belonged to the Marquesa del Valle, an absentee landlord consolidat-ing her assets in the region. *Oficiales de república* (native political officers) from Zimatlán and San Pablo helped guide the group through a portion of the estate they con-tested. The alcalde mayor of Chichicapa and Zimatlán, towns under the authority of the Crown (not the absent Marquise), and a deputy (*teniente*) for the city of Ante-quera, the Spanish seat of power in the region and also controlled by the Crown, accompanied the expedition. Though some natives spoke Spanish, an interpreter trav-eled with the group to translate when necessary.

After traveling nearly a league and a half, they reached the hacienda of Captain Cristobal Ramírez, who produced a *título y merced* (title and royal deed) confirm-ing the limits of his property. The group remained on the hacienda long enough to compare the deed to the property's boundary markers, after which point the scribe noted: "Guided by him [the alcalde mayor] and the [native] informants, and the map's demonstrations, we veered left leaving said hacienda until it was out of sight."[57] They headed south along what the Indians from San Pablo considered their patrimonial lands. During this particular leg of the journey, San Pablo introduced manuscripts, including various *autos de posesión* (formal

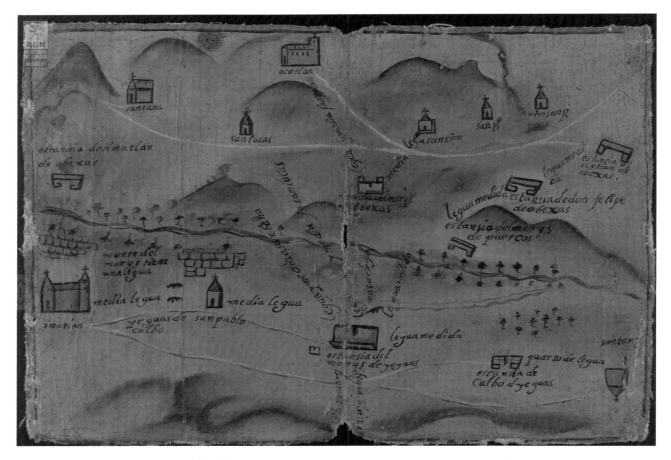

4.7. *Map of Simatlán and Ocotlán, 1686 [1639], no. 3009, Hospital de Jesús, leg. 85, exp. 4. Archivo General de la Nación, Fondo Hermanos Mayo, concentrados, sobre 363.*

edits of possession) they claimed verified their control of the land. Abellán ordered the survey to continue in spite of their objections but asked the natives from San Pablo to show him the boundaries described in the map. "Having mandated that the land titles be incorporated into these proceedings, the alcalde mayor [also] ordered that [the natives] guide him to the limits they know to be theirs including the sites depicted on the map," the scribe observed.[58] Officials looked to the map to identify and determine boundaries, the scribe referencing it another four times during the survey with such statements as "according to the map's demonstration" and "they fall within the map's delimitations."[59] Scribes and officials engaged with maps, annotating and codifying them to

make them legible for the immediate use of authorities, but also in preparation for their transition into one of various local or regional archives where documents rested for future reference.

MOVEMENT

After individuals and *cabildos* transacted petitions with scribes and officials or when a legal dispute ended, copies and original dockets (including maps) ended up in archives across Oaxaca and Mexico City, sometimes making it as far away as Seville. After completing the surveys for the Relaciones Geográficas in the early 1580s, officials returned their responses to Mexico City en route to Spain. On November 21, 1583, administrators at the

Council of the Indies in Seville turned over to Juan López de Velasco, the recently appointed royal chronicler and cosmographer who designed the survey, three *legajos* (large bundles) of relaciones and maps to inform the King's project.[60] Speculation about López de Velasco's reaction, described in some cases as one of disappointment, masks a collective curiosity over the reception of the mapped portion of the survey. For one thing, a large quantity of the responses did not include any maps. The majority of the maps he did receive reflected indigenous authorship, at best a mixture of native and European pictorial traditions, at worst an unreadable—to European eyes—visual portrayal of the New World landscape. Whatever the case, the cosmographer scrutinized the maps and relaciones, cataloging them in a file labeled "Descripción y Población."[61] Note the two different inscriptions (Figures 4.8a and 4.8b) on the map of Amoltepec: One indicates the area represented, and the second specifies the name of the town where it originated; a catalog number followed. In 1596, a new cosmographer, Andrés García Céspedes, reorganized the "Descripción y Población" file, his work noticeable via his signature and multiple annotations of regions, ethnic states, bishoprics, and towns on the margins of many of the responses (Figure 4.9). Later chroniclers, including Antonio de Herrera y Tordesillas and the jurist Antonio de León

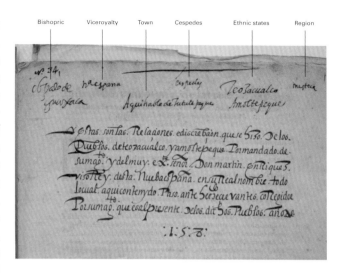

4.9. *Céspedes annotations, Relación of Teozacoalco and Amoltepeque, 1580. Relaciones Geográficas of Mexico and Guatemala, 1577–1585, Nettie Lee Benson Latin American Collection, University of Texas Libraries, University of Texas at Austin.*

4.8. *Cataloging inscriptions: (a) Amoltepeque, Relaciones Geográficas map of Amoltepeque (1580); (b) Amoltepeque, Relaciones Geográficas map of Amoltepeque (1580). Relaciones Geográficas of Mexico and Guatemala, 1577–1585, Nettie Lee Benson Latin American Collection, University of Texas Libraries, University of Texas at Austin.*

Pinelo, accessed material from the Relaciones Geográficas in the "Descripción y Población" file for their own works on the Indies.[62]

Historians have typically described this considerable imperial project as an unsuccessful venture despite the evident use and circulation of the materials produced for the project. Howard Cline, for instance, observed that "little or no administrative use was apparently ever made of them. With some few exceptions they seemingly lay untouched in files until . . . the late eighteenth century." Along similar lines, Barbara Mundy has noted that "when López de Velasco compiled a terse catalogue of the texts and maps of the Relaciones that had arrived to Spain by 1583, he must have been afflicted with an overriding sense of the project's failure."[63] Admittedly, López de Velasco's desire to produce the most up-to-date atlas and chronicle of the Indies did not come to fruition. But as María Portuondo suggests, the changing standards of cosmography during the sixteenth century allowed López de Velasco to think about the responses as an archive of individual, firsthand accounts that could support the needs of the Council of the Indies when the need arose.[64] The responses certainly exceeded any past efforts to measure New World resources.

More typically, maps traveled from various regions of New Spain to the Audiencia in Mexico City, where a cast of actors engaged with them in an extension of the authentication process initiated at the local level. The movement of titles, maps, and other important records tied to the authentication process carried risks for litigants as well as authorities. When Zimatlán addressed the court in the fall of 1686 about the impending survey of the Marquise's land that would affect their town boundaries, native officials directed royal authorities to a legal docket supposedly stored in Mexico City:

> Our ascendants and we have held some lands since time immemorial that fall within our town's eastern boundaries; [they] are named in our [Zapotec] language Guiyalana y Secbichi [and are located] by some small mountains. The titles and maps to these [lands] are in the Real Audiencia of this New Spain [to support] the dispute we had with the natives from Santa María Magdalena. The survey your grace intends would seriously damage and impair us, and with all due respect and reverence, we request your lordship not prevent our grievance. We contradict this survey once, twice, and three times, and as many as is necessary according to our rights and we petition that the titles be drawn [from the Audiencia] for our defense.[65]

Seventeen members of the town council signed their names to the request. After reviewing Zimatlán's petition, a user (most likely a scribe or lawyer who worked on the case) wrote a cautionary *ojo* (literally, "eye") on the margins of the page to warn the reviewer (Figure 4.10). A note below it warned: "Watch out, these titles have not appeared, only a merced without a name, survey, or possession."[66]

The incident exposes the difficulties of archiving in the early modern period. The town's claim that the map and titles resided in Mexico City may have been false, an allegation implied by the reader who wrote on the margin, but it was not far-fetched. Maps presented by

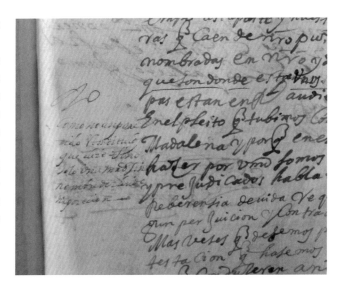

4.10. Ojo *detail (1686), Hospital de Jesús, leg. 85, exp. 4, f. 104. Archivo General de la Nación, Fondo Hermanos Mayo, concentrados, sobre 363.*

individuals, towns, and legal representatives to local authorities typically went to Mexico City for review by magistrates, notaries, and legal aides. The circulation of maps opened the possibilities of loss, theft, misplacement, and damage when individuals surrendered their manuscripts over to notaries, royal officials, or lawyers as evidence. From an Audiencia perspective, the accumulation of paper represented a serious challenge for authorities fielding cases from all over the viceroyalty. Often, they unloaded "old paper" by selling it to various local stores. By the end of the colonial period, Antonio de León y Gama, a highly regarded bureaucrat-intellectual who spent his career as a midlevel administrator at the Audiencia, lamented that its archive had "perished almost in its entirety," further noting it had been a truly "irreparable and painful" loss.[67] In other words, the threats of displacement were real.

Conflict over land filled the archive in the first place. In many regions of Oaxaca, contestation reached new heights beginning in the second half of the seventeenth century when the native population started to recover after devastating epidemics during the sixteenth and early seventeenth centuries. New regulations that sought to administer land tenure, growing tensions between head and subject towns, and among residents of various ethnic backgrounds all contributed to the increase in litigation. In response, native mapmaking underwent a transformation based on an imagined pictorial aesthetic of the pre-Colombian and early colonial past. Efforts to archaize, or artificially age, cartographic representations, either through material technology or through visual forms and colors as discussed in chapter 2, represent one of the major features of maps produced for litigation from the 1680s until the end of the eighteenth century. The new generation of painters presented to authorities a unique patchwork of maps that, in keeping with tradition, drew from native intellectual circles, family and patrimonial archives, and oral history. Although a majority of the maps from this period often bear little resemblance to earlier maps from the sixteenth century and early seventeenth century, efforts within indigenous communities to map the landscape showcase the evolution of pictorial traditions rooted in early contact. But just how did judges, lawyers, and translators in Mexico City contend with the flood of paper that trickled in from surrounding areas? How did these individuals engage with maps and other forms of pictorial evidence used to negotiate land and privileges?

Towns and legal aides themselves played a pivotal role in the authentication process by subjecting maps to rigorous critique. Litigants and lawyers often traveled to the capital to testify or attend hearings to present or contest maps in support of their petitions.[68] Any hint of foul play could set off accusations from opposing parties that quickly pointed out inconsistencies and, sometimes, offered profound reflections on the nature of maps in the early modern period. Diego Fernández de Córdoba's acute observation, discussed in the introduction of this book, that maps were subject to the will of those who made and commissioned them, suggests the level of scrutiny they received. As we learned in chapter 1, Fernández de Córdoba questioned the timing of the map's submission by the natives of Xoxocotlán against his client, rebuking their "deceitful" tactics. In Mexico City, officials relied on the work of provincial bureaucrats and notaries, on the one hand, and on the legal representatives of settlers and natives who prepared arguments on behalf of their clients in the language of the state on the other. The case of San Dionisio del Mar against their longtime rival, San Francisco del Mar, over control of a profitable salt lake highlights the way in which natives and legal aides forced discussions about maps that got tangled up with other forms of evidence presented by litigants to substantiate their claims. The episode marks a moment during which differences of oral testimonies, past rulings, and visual records collided at the local and regional courts where plaintiffs litigated their cases.

Francisco Xavier de Herrera, San Dionisio's legal aide, addressed Audiencia authorities in September 1745 in an attempt to resolve the matter of his client's dispossession of the lake. He brought officials up to speed with the history of the contested lake, noting that, a century earlier in 1645, the court ruled in favor of San Dionisio over control of the salt lake they called "Quispalapa." In the intervening years, residents from San Francisco Ixaltepec del Mar, San Dionisio's old rival, reclaimed the lake and its profitable salt business, prompting a new round of litigation starting in the late 1720s. When confronted, San Francisco claimed that several generations of caciques had controlled the lake they knew as "Amatitlán," and they produced a series of witnesses who testified on their behalf. All of them confirmed it belonged to San Francisco. When asked how San Francisco could ignore the previous court ruling that awarded possession of Quispalapa to San Dionisio, they responded that, in fact, San Dionisio's lake was another one located several leagues away from their lake, Amatitlán.

Herrera reminded authorities of the verdict issued in 1645 in favor of San Dionisio for possession of Quispalapa, noting its location between two *parajes* (sites) known as Agua Blanca and Colotepec. Since San Francisco disputed the location of a lake, the parajes served to situate the lake between recognized geographic boundaries during a land survey. Herrera called into question testimony on behalf of San Francisco, noting the witnesses greatly miscalculated the distance of the lake, all of them claiming it lay seven leagues from San Dionisio when in fact it was only three. The legal aide believed such a serious miscalculation indicated the witnesses had been coached as part of San Francisco's malicious ploy to deprive his clients of the salt lake.

More important, Herrera called into question the use of San Francisco's map (Figure 4.11), a key piece of evidence that, according to him, clearly signaled San Francisco had lied because it made no mention of Quispalapa—or even of what San Francisco called Amatitlán.[69] "Your Excellency will find that the map made by the Indians of San Francisco del Mar does not conform to the *autos*, and not only is it not in tune with them, but entirely out of tune and opposite," he wrote.[70] How could a map that did not plot the referenced parcel effectively serve San Francisco's petition? Herrera observed that San Francisco, with "malice" but also "lack of experience," simply "accumulated a string of places that are neither under litigation, nor will delineating them produce any

[bearing on the case]." "The best of all," he mocked, "was that the places under litigation are not illustrated or plotted."[71] Herrera pressed his case further by contrasting the map of San Francisco with the one presented by his clients (Figure 4.12).[72] In his brief, he pointed out to the Audiencia judges how the visual elements of San Dionisio's map coincided with natural markers discussed in an earlier act of possession that affirmed the town's control of the salt lake. "It started," he reminded them, "at a narrow pass that is between two small mountains, where there is a rock of four faces (Figure 4.13), the same one that is depicted in the map of p. 55, notebook 4, made by my clients."[73] Herrera wished to prove to authorities that the possession of the lake—a strong piece of evidence built around a site visit that required the physical presence of officials and witnesses—gained strength by

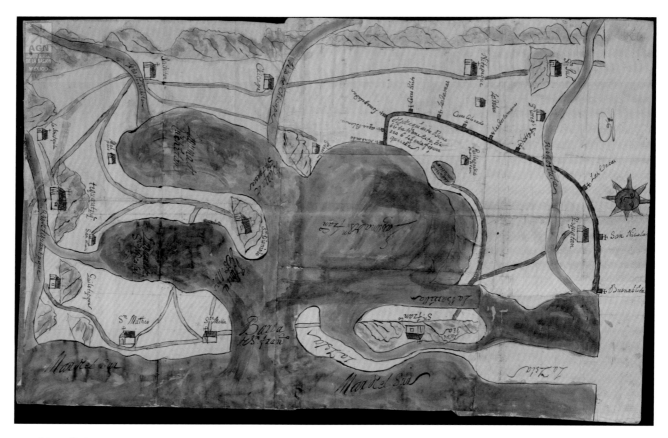

4.11. *Map of Tehuantepec, Juchitlán, Chicapa, Niltepec, Isguatán, San Francisco and San Dionisio (1746), no. 0785, Tierras, vol. 584, exp. 1, cuad. 4, f. 26. Archivo General de la Nación, Fondo Hermanos Mayo, concentrados, sobre 363.*

4.12. *Map of San Dionisio del Mar (1740), no. 0784, Tierras, vol. 584, exp. 1, cuad. 2, f. 55. Archivo General de la Nación, Fondo Hermanos Mayo, concentrados, sobre 363.*

4.13. *"The four-faced rock," map of San Dionisio del Mar (1740), no. 0784, Tierras, vol. 584, exp. 1, cuad. 2, f. 55. Archivo General de la Nación, Fondo Hermanos Mayo, concentrados, sobre 363.*

the presence of the properly adjusted map, a benefit his counterparts could not depend on.

Before authorities made a judgment in the matter, Herrera requested that an officer of the court authenticate San Francisco's map. The legal aide sought to discredit San Francisco's claim by pointing to the absence of the disputed site and its geographic markers. Herrera wanted the scribe to confirm that the map presented by San Francisco did not include an important geographical reference point known as Colotepec and that nowhere on the map could one identify a clearly illustrated salt lake. Further, he requested confirmation on the absence of the rock of four faces, a key boundary marker, as well as the omission of three lagoons that witnesses testified bordered San Dionisio.[74] Pointed commentary from opposing sides obligated the parties to clarify their positions, gather additional witnesses, enter pleas, retain legal counsel, contract scribal services, and in general extend litigation. Making sure someone else officially recognized the imperfect nature of San Francisco's map—most of all its many silences on the matter of the salt lake—illustrates one of the tactics used by reviewers to discredit it as cartographic evidence.

The task to authenticate the map fell to Juan Joseph de Zarazua, a royal scribe attached to the oldest and most prestigious notarial office in the capital city.[75] Zarazua reviewed the proceedings from the dispute, then homed in on San Francisco's map. He began by identifying a string of places that started with "Las Vacas" (The Cows) on the right-hand margin of the map near the sun; he then moved counterclockwise, passing through Agua Blanca, a paraje found on both maps. Eighteen towns represented by churches, including important economic centers such as Juchitán and Tehuantepec, dotted San Francisco's map, and crosses identified mountains and other geographic markers. The map's lacustrine environment engulfed half of the visible surface of the map, with the Pacific Ocean, known then as the South Sea, framing the bottom half of the page. Sandbars, rivers, lagoons, and islands shaped the region's coastline and, as this dispute attested, contributed to the local economies of individual towns. Yet none of the place-names depicted on the map mentioned the salt lake, the four-faced rock, or

the three contiguous lakes described by San Francisco's witnesses. San Francisco's attorney later told authorities that "it doesn't really matter if these natives in their map did not represent the site"; what mattered was that the map clearly showed the town's boundaries.[76] Zarazua confirmed Herrera's assessment that the map made no mention of the sites relevant to the case.

Placing pressure on authorities to consider evidence more closely, towns and their legal aides forced discussions about the use of maps and the maps' content when it suited their cause. The Mixtec town of San Juan Chapultepec in Oaxaca's central valley accused its rival, San Martín Mexicapan, of introducing false titles that bore the signature of a notorious counterfeiter named Juan Roque. In 1701, they described Roque as a meddlesome Indian who had produced similar titles in the region, and they pointed out that the testament (dated 1602) and the primordial title (dated 1525) submitted by San Martín bore his style.[77] Intending to mislead authorities, these types of records represented a challenge for the regional scribes, judges, legal aides, and litigants who used, but also contested, the introduction of maps and other indigenous records as evidence.[78] Despite raising doubts about the legitimacy of the titles presented by the Nahua community of San Martín Mexicapan, the Mixtecs from San Juan had also presented their own title in 1696. Purportedly made in 1523 (two years before that of their rivals), and written in Mixtec, the title included a painted map (Figure 4.14) that tied San Juan's boundaries to historical memory.[79] A written gloss on the map verified the boundaries and the day of their inspection, conveniently tying San Martín to the supposed boundary survey: "Today, Monday, the eighth day of the month of February, the title and painted map belonging to the ñuu of San Juan Yuchayta were made, concerning all the borders agreed upon and recognized by the Mexican people of the tayu of San Martin."[80]

Although the use of native maps was nothing new in litigations over land, the timing and content of these

(OPPOSITE PAGE) 4.14. *Map of San Juan Chapultepec (1523?)*, *no. 0660, Tierras, vol. 236, exp. 6, f. 2. Archivo General de la Nación, Fondo Hermanos Mayo, concentrados, sobre 363.*

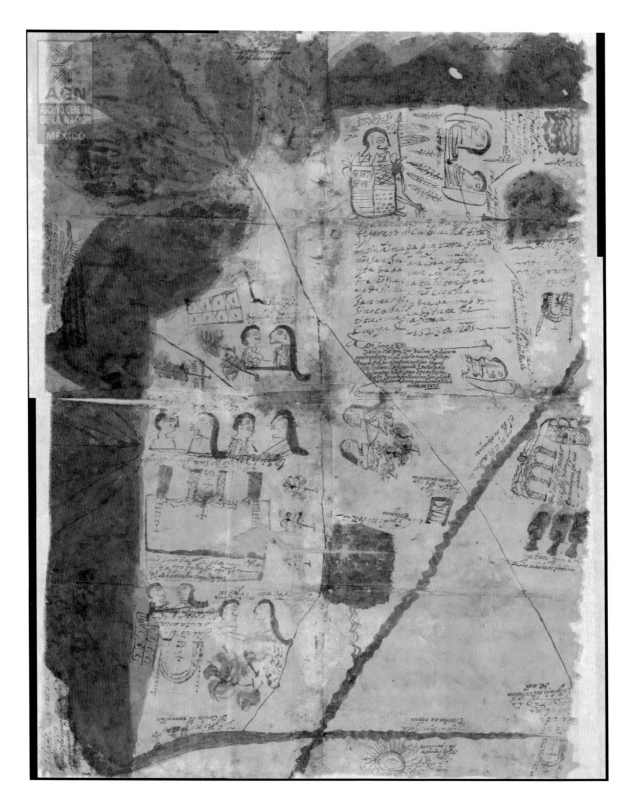

records raised some eyebrows for those charged with authenticating them at the local level. At the alcalde mayor's behest, two translators—one of them a cacique from nearby Atzompa, the other most likely a Spanish vecino from Antequera—inspected the title and the map. As they reviewed the map, they wrote a series of glosses that translated Mixtec into Spanish text. Portions of the mountains that framed the upper and left-hand portion of the map include their annotations signaling mountains and boundary markers, as did their identification of the ordered pairs used to signify ruling couples. The practice of dynastic representation imitated pictorial writing from the early contact period (Figure 2.5), but the style clearly did not apply lines and color in the same way. The two translators also noted that the map included "defective" written passages that could not be easily understood.[81] Perhaps they sensed the dating was off. Supposedly created in 1523, the map did not share the style and characteristics of earlier models. How much of this variance authorities could actually recognize is hard to say, but clearly they had misgivings. Lisa Sousa and Kevin Terraciano observe that the date attributed to the title and map predated Mixtec alphabetic writing by about half a century, casting serious doubt on their authenticity.[82] Although native maps informed early Spanish colonization in varied ways, no discernable pattern emerged until the 1570s and 1580s, when imperial policies directed at New World administration went into effect.

The map's brownish hues and faded ink may well have been the result of Juan Roque's experimentation with smoke or ovens, tools that counterfeiters used to give materials an aged appearance.[83] Well into the eighteenth century, workshops in central Mexico churned out titles for native towns that employed similar methods to archaize (artificially age) their products in order to give them an air of authenticity.[84] The mysterious death of one Pedro de Villafranca in Toluca in 1761 prompted an investigation that blew off the lid on one such enterprise in central Mexico. According to his widow, Villafranca had the uncanny ability to reproduce notarial formulas, sixteenth-century writing, signatures of high-ranking officials, and painted maps; he had done so for a host of indigenous towns in and around Mexico's Central Valley during the course of his profitable career. Earlier in the century, another Indian cacique from central Mexico, Don Diego García de Mendoza Moctezuma, headed an illicit manuscript workshop that likewise catered to disenfranchised indigenous towns. Unlike Villafranca, who favored replicating the formula of *mercedes de tierras* (a system to distribute land), Don Diego's method applied native elements, most notably maguey paper, to invoke the past. Joseph de Luna, a lawyer who had translated several of the cacique's titles from Nahuatl to Spanish, told authorities that Don Diego provided his service to Indian towns that needed it—for a hefty fee, of course.[85] Don Diego's agents scouted for clients at the Audiencia, where they referred vulnerable litigants who lacked the necessary titles to legitimize their land to the counterfeiter.

Maps, then, were hardly inconsequential documents in the quest for land. For the midlevel bureaucrats in the trenches charged with inspecting maps, authenticating them and other pictorial sources of indigenous origin represented part of a long-standing process of adaptation to New World realities that stretched back to the sixteenth century. For others, the Audiencia represented a library of sorts that allowed the intellectually curious to dabble in the history of the region. Antonio de León y Gama, the noted eighteenth-century bureaucrat-intellectual mentioned above, considered his years of experience as an Audiencia official to be his strongest qualification to interpret two Aztec stones uncovered during an excavation at Mexico City's Plaza Mayor in 1790. A driven scholar of limited means, León y Gama struggled to get his work published because of the elevated cost of reproducing the images he prepared to accompany his study.[86] When he finally succeeded in publishing his work, León y Gama told readers, somewhat immodestly, that it would be difficult for another person to interpret the findings correctly because they would lack his bureaucratic experience. "Thirty-six years handling ancient papers and cases of Indians and Spaniards," he explained to his readers, had given him special insight into the interpretation of these historical sources.[87] He argued that, through the study of place-names and geography, scholars could launch a deeper discussion of pre-Colombian antiquities. He relied heavily on original sources for his work, in particular the "pinturas" and "other precious documents from that time" that dated to the "founding of the first Real Audiencia." In addition, he enjoyed access to important indigenous documentary groups, including those assembled by the Italian Lorenzo Boturini in the 1730s and 1740s, other records preserved at the Royal and Pontifical University, and those stored by individual collectors.

Yet mere access to sources did not suffice for León y Gama. Knowledge required fluency in languages, understanding of historical context, and time to review complex pictorial and alphabetic sources. "Only he who knows how to combine and interpret at will . . . can gain fruit from them," León y Gama cautioned. He presented himself as a new type of intellectual alchemist, one with authority rooted not merely in bookish culture but in the practical experience of the judicial bureaucrat. During his decades at the Audiencia, he learned about native tenacity in matters related to land, about defense strategies and encroachment, and about maps and titles used to inform litigation. In his comments, León y Gama anchored his personal expertise in the knowledge he acquired as an agent of the state, working on a regular basis with titles, maps, and other pictorial records. The bureaucrat's emphasis on this aspect of his intellectual development served as a shield against European intellectuals who for generations had disparaged indigenous sources without truly analyzing them. This "all-consuming concern for assessing the power of outsiders to comprehend local realities," as Jorge Cañizares-Esguerra has described it, framed León y Gama and other creole intellectuals' relationship with maps.[88]

CONCLUSION

As a result of their contact with mapmakers and other intermediaries, officials established parameters of use that attempted to guide cartographic production. At the same time, commissioning the task of mapmaking to indigenous painters forced authorities to surrender a measure of power by leaving these mapmakers to sort out the details of their cartographic productions. Using the notarial template as a model, attempts at authentication supported the legitimization of maps, a process fused to legal and notarial writing, on the one hand, and social memory and tradition on the other. Certification hinged upon spatial routines, including ritual boundary-walking, surveying, witness testimony, mapping, and place-naming, which served to define and control the natural environment. When the priorities of late-sixteenth-century mapping—that is to say those centered on petitions for land and the execution of imperial policy—shifted to issues related to defense of patrimonial lands by the late seventeenth century, so too did common sense and the standards used to petition and measure maps.

AFTERLIFE

Authorities in Mexico City descended upon the modest home of Lorenzo Boturini in the late winter of 1743. Lorenzo, a native of Milan with a patrician pedigree, a facility for languages, and a fervent devotion for the Virgin of Guadalupe, had attracted the attention of the newly appointed viceroy of New Spain, the Count of Fuenclara. Shortly after arriving in New Spain, the viceroy received word that Lorenzo had taken it upon himself to raise funds for a crowning ceremony dedicated to Our Lady of Guadalupe. Adding insult to injury, Boturini sidestepped viceregal authorities in the capital city, turning directly to the Vatican instead to gain approval for the celebration. While a thorough investigation into Boturini's dealings did not produce any evidence of wrongdoing, officials learned the Italian had traveled to New Spain in 1736 without proper passage, an infraction that gave them a motive to take him into custody. As they prepared to sequester Boturini's possessions for collateral to cover legal fees, meals, and other expenses associated with imprisonment, they stumbled upon a most impressive sight.

Since his arrival in Mexico City seven years earlier,

the Italian Boturini had assembled a collection of several hundred Mesoamerican and early colonial records, including Aztec calendar wheels, annals, painted tributary records, cartographic histories, land grant maps, and genealogical drawings painted over large linen surfaces. In addition, he had collected printed chronicles, language manuals, historical works, and testimonials of the apparition, which reflected Boturini's devotion to the Holy Patroness. But how did someone like Boturini—a foreigner with no established connections in the New World and no steady stream of income—gain access to such closely guarded sources? This epilogue considers the role that archival practice and notarial culture played in the formation of the Boturini collection. Royal officials, scribes, translators, lawyers, clerics, *caciques*, and corporate entities engaged in a variety of archiving pursuits to safeguard valuable records and knowledge, in the process gaining unrestricted access to important pictorial sources. As the case of Boturini demonstrates, these networks jealously guarded the flow of maps and other records of Mesoamerican origin that the Italian desired.

While the story of Boturini's misadventures is well

known among specialists, the formation of the collection and the discursive strategies used to account for pictorial and alphabetic records of the early colonial period are not.[1] Boturini's collecting efforts succeeded by leaning on the social networks associated with the map trade. As documents from every part of the realm flooded the Audiencia and other viceregal institutions in Mexico City, translators, scribes, and officials continued to wrestle with the authentication of multiple forms of evidence used by indigenous groups to negotiate diverse aspects of colonial life. The interpretation of these types of records depended on what Ann Laura Stoler describes as the "emotional economy," that is to say the mixture of personal experience, shared culture, and use of reason that allowed colonial bureaucracies to classify data in search of order, knowledge, and power.[2] Correspondence and a series of inventories prepared between February 1743 and July 1745 reveal the way a cast of characters clustered around the capital city's notarial circuits, rendering complex pictorial manuscripts into written form.[3] The catalog prepared by Boturini and a separate one compiled by a Zapotec cacique named Patricio Antonio López shed light on the complex assimilation of non-alphabetic sources within existing archival frameworks that guided the use of documents in New Spain. Maps in the collection ceased documenting spatial boundaries and instead formed part of a mosaic whose pieces, scattered across a network of local and regional archives, revealed the secrets of the past.

BUILDING AN ARCHIVE

Archives in New Spain functioned on privilege. In the eighteenth-century Hispanic world, *archivar*, the verb form of "archive," meant to "place in public custody and to secure legal records and public documents."[4] *Archiveros*, the gatekeepers who literally and figuratively held the keys to the safe, protected but also restricted the use of documents. A set of qualifications based on learning, family and social networks, employment, and capital served as a prerequisite for scrutinizing potential users interested in accessing important manuscripts. More important, archival privilege operated based on knowledge. On the one hand, individuals acquired

privilege by understanding what Stoler describes as "the administrative forms that shaped the circuits of reportage, accountability, and decision making that in turn produced densities of documents."[5] On the other, archival privilege relied on knowledge acquired through everyday interaction with lawyers, litigants, translators, legal agents, Indian lords, and merchants who, through their dealings with authorities, introduced local forms of knowing. These "grids of intelligibility" served to classify and store information drawn from the confusion that defined colonial bureaucracies.[6] Colonial officials used these frameworks to interpret and articulate in writing the contents of the complex pictorial records that they often reviewed in court.

The seizure of the Italian's collection generated a series of inventories prepared by historians, translators, and bureaucrats that bear witness to multiple strands of archiving used in the colonial world. Monastic libraries, secular and clerical archives, native *cabildo* archives, collections of records held by important Indian families, and individual collections all stored valued documents and books from which the Italian drew.[7] Boturini's status as a foreigner, along with the climate of Guadalupan devotion that swept the region in the eighteenth century, allowed him to establish relationships with Indian translators, nuns, Audiencia judges, clerics, and collectors who helped him track down important sources.[8] But as Francisco Hernández and others had discovered in earlier centuries, Indians would not give up their secrets easily.

Boturini's interest in ethnography and history, his religious fervor, and his ease with languages drove his investigation on Mesoamerican culture and the apparition of the Virgin of Guadalupe. He believed that the use of original records represented the most effective way to assess the history of the Americas, but he struggled early in his quest to gain access to any pictorial records. Writing from Spain years after his residence in the New World, he observed:

I will not tire of referring to the immense labor, and expenses, that these priceless jewels from Indian antiquity cost me. I will, however, give notice that because the natives from that vast region had them, and have others, I had to cover vast ground, guessing and asking. And despite my unwavering determination, and that I never let go of the mission [I had] undertaken, notwithstanding, two years passed without being able to acquire even a single map, or to see the face of some manuscript, many times trekking from one place to another for five or six straight months, before returning to the city.[9]

In his travels across the Mexican countryside, Boturini experienced the insular nature of indigenous archives firsthand. "It is so difficult to deal with the Indians, [for] they are distrustful of Spaniards in the extreme," he recounted. Boturini learned that, in fact, many towns buried their titles and important records to prevent them from falling into Spanish hands. Two centuries of colonial rule had generated a thick layer of distrust when it concerned the use and control of pictorial records.

For generations, caciques and indigenous town councils in New Spain jealously guarded important documents, especially those concerning history, territorial boundaries, and privileges. The Indian elite learned soon after the arrival of Europeans that documents mattered in the Hispanic world. Native archiving reflected an appreciation of law and notarial practices used to petition authorities for privileges and goods, as well as to defend corporate interests. When native officers from Tehuantepec along Oaxaca's Pacific Coast complained to the viceroy in 1660 about the abusive behavior of the alcalde mayor, their grievance made light of the fact that they, too, stored important papers that structured their rights and obligations. "No other alcalde mayor has attempted [to extract so much tribute from us] until now," they claimed, "because of the many royal provisions we have in *our archives* which are obeyed by the other justices for our protection."[10] As we saw in chapter 1, within the towns themselves, maps and other pictorial sources enhanced the status of those who stored and cared for them; they were coveted items of a shared history that often predated the arrival of Spaniards. For ambitious landholders, farmers, townships, and confraternities, indigenous pictorial records conjured mixed feelings,

since these visual representations of space purportedly validated land they desired. Population growth, changing legislation, and increased competition for agricultural and ranching plots fed the production and use of pictorial records of indigenous origin up until the eighteenth century.

By writing letters, Boturini could communicate with a broad array of actors, among them lay and ecclesiastic officials, regional judges, caciques, military captains, residents of various social ranks, and miners from across the region. Boturini wrote about his efforts to crown the image of Our Lady of Guadalupe, enclosed a sketch of the crown he proposed to make, and requested donations to help fund the coronation ceremony. In his letters, Lorenzo revealed in a postscript his intention to write a history of the apparition based on original sources. For the project, he requested that they help him "obtain from the natives all the painted maps with figures and characters, the ancient songs, the historic [books], and every manuscript in any language that deals with the pagan era, as well as the systems of their calendars and planets."[11] Boturini instructed the priests to send the letters and any records they could compile to his home in Mexico City under whatever conditions they saw fit, and he assured them he would comply promptly with their terms.

When Boturini penned a letter addressed to town council officials from indigenous hamlets across the region, he turned to one of their own for help. Patricio Antonio López, a Zapotec cacique and royal interpreter, assisted the Italian in drafting a petition in Nahuatl. López shared with Boturini a strong interest in the region's history and played a pivotal role in the Italian's ventures.[12] According to Boturini, the Zapotec lord sent a missive in advance of Boturini's letter notifying native authorities of the project and the request for documentary sources, a measure that sought to mitigate the distrust the Italian had witnessed during his travels. "Do not see my petition, lords, as [an effort] to take away your lands, or to usurp your [holdings]," Boturini assured them, "but only to investigate the history of said apparitions with the ancient and faithful accounts of those Indians that lived contemporaneous to the miracle."[13]

As a way to legitimize his petition while also highlighting the originality of his proposal, he made a point to mention his use of primary sources to reconstruct the history of the miraculous event. Implicitly, Boturini castigated earlier Spanish historians who, in his view, had failed to adequately write about the region's past and about the apparition.[14] Boturini instructed native authorities to send any pertinent manuscripts directly to López, noting: "I hope Your Lords will take great care to exhibit all maps and manuscripts to Don Patricio, for once viewed and examined, they shall be returned to their owners," an assurance that sought to assuage native fears.[15] Boturini's difficulty in accessing the records he so desired speaks directly to archival privilege: safeguarding pictorial manuscripts did not always conform to the idea of the public good. In another respect, not all publics were created equal, especially in a region such as New Spain, where distrust and apathy tempered the protection of and access to indigenous records.

CATALOGING

Inventories formed an intimate part of notarial language in the Hispanic world. Postmortem estate evaluations, wills, indices of prohibited books, and commercial logs helped to catalog and describe goods from across the empire. In Boturini's case, imprisonment prompted a register of sequestered property. After his arrest in February 1743, Antonio de Roxas y Abreu, the district judge assigned to the case, prepared an initial report of the goods and documents in Boturini's possession. Accompanied by two witnesses, a depositary, and a scribe, the judge divided the documentary collection into four groups that he placed into an *arca* (chest). The first included "volumes of paintings, characters, and hieroglyphs" associated with pre-Colombian history up to the conquest. Groups two and three included "maps and manuscripts of the conquest made by the subjugated Indians" and "some papers in the shape of a wheel that the gentleman [Boturini] said were mathematical systems used by the ancient Indians." In the last group, the judge identified "various rare manuscripts and printed books pertaining to the history of the apparitions" of Our Lady of Guadalupe.

Roxas y Abreu did not intend for his list to describe the documents exhaustively. His report—a cursory evaluation of the records—transferred jurisdiction of the collection to court officials, who sequestered it inside Boturini's house on Stamp Street in the city's northwest quadrant. The collection's depth and sophistication, however, made it a challenge to document. Roxas y Abreu seemed intimidated by the task, making it clear Boturini would "explain more diffusely" the meaning of "the messages, histories, maps, and manuscripts" in a more detailed inventory prepared under the Italian's guidance.[16] Prior to this initial inventory, Boturini had advised the judge as to the contents of the archive. "According to said gentleman," noted Roxas y Abreu, the paintings and hieroglyphs in the collection described the peoples of the Americas "from the confusion of tongues in Babylonia, [to] the origin of the Indians, their migration to these parts, their length of stay, their empires, [and] their princes who ruled including individual narratives of the reign of each one."[17] When describing the calendar wheels, the judge said "the gentleman" had declared they "were mathematical systems of the ancient Indians and first founders of this Empire."[18] This initial survey of records registers what Stoler describes as "the febrile moments of persons off balance" and spaces of "epistemic anxiety" that emerged from misunderstandings that nonetheless had to be rendered into the idiom of empire.[19]

Inventories represent an important source of information that help situate objects in time and space. For the early modern period, travel across oceans meant the circulation of exotic and everyday goods traded and carried over vast distances by a diverse cast of characters that included merchants, sailors, clerics, bureaucrats, bankers, aristocrats, intellectuals, apothecaries, and soldiers.[20] Recent studies have likewise revealed the way in which people regularly found new uses for old artifacts, shedding light on a vibrant culture of repurposing and recycling.[21] As Peter Miller notes, "Objects speak to us through the memories that belong to them, [and] the more we know of the lives they have lived, the more loudly they speak."[22] Catalogs and lists captured in writing the movement of objects, but they were by no means value-free records. As Jessica Keating and Lia Markey observe, inventories "were also authored documents compiled under particular temporal, legal, political, and social constraints that affected their organization and the ways in which the objects they list were described."[23] The catalogs prepared to account for the Boturini collection were no exception.

Boturini attempted to use the allure of a descriptive catalog to gain some sympathy from his captors. From prison, the Italian pleaded with authorities to allow him to catalog his prized manuscripts, for he feared for the safety of his archive. To the King he promised "a most sumptuous inventory," an effort that sought to reveal for the monarch the extent of available records to write about the history of the region's past. On April 2, 1743, Boturini wrote a letter asking the viceroy to review his case and to allow him to make an inventory of the archive. "Once you see it," he urged, "you will understand its great importance."[24] Boturini's insistence on an annotated list that would capture the extent of his impressive holdings signals the importance of arranging objects textually, a fixation of collectors during the early modern era.[25] For the Italian, an inventory had the power to bring objects to life, a sensory experience for armchair travelers who could not directly view the artifacts. Lists, as James Delbourgo and Staffan Müller-Wille observe, have the power to organize and weave objects together, "abstracting, enumerating, and linking them" to form a thematic unit.[26] In lieu of the originals, Boturini's inventory would allow people to imagine the magnificent sources he collected and to think about his efforts to bring them together in a coherent, albeit subjective, textual display.

The second phase of the inventory took place on March 29, 1743, nearly two months after the first assessment. To prepare the collection for the move from Stamp Street to the treasury office, Roxas y Abreu and a scribe transferred the records into a large cedar armoire with two locks. The choice to reassign the collection to a different storage unit signals the need to host it in a more suitable repository, one with protective mechanisms designed to keep unauthorized users away from the contents held within. During the transfer, the judge prepared a more detailed

inventory, generating fifty-two individual entries instead of the four broad categories he used in his earlier catalog. The two men must have felt overwhelmed as they sifted through manuscript treatises, notebooks, printed material, bundles of loose folios, and correspondence. Sixteen of the entries accounted for 104 maps of various shapes and sizes made on native bark paper, cloth, animal hides, linen, and rag paper. The largest piece in the collection, "a map on maguey paper, twenty-two feet long and six and a half feet wide," appeared in the first entry, followed by "another of rotten linen, fifteen feet long."[27] The judge privileged the larger pieces, allotting many of them an individual entry. Smaller maps he lumped into groups: "forty-eight maps on paper, mistreated and very old," "twenty-four old maps of various sizes," "another nine maps on paper, small," and so on.

The choice of categories, especially the emphasis on describing an object's material condition, casts light on the importance authorities gave to historical records of the early contact period. Materials forced officials to recognize that differences existed in the production of historical, cultural, and administrative records and to establish parameters of use. "How objects were made and what they were made from," observes Ulinka Rublack, "may have a bearing on how they were perceived and gained significance."[28] By the eighteenth century, any court official worth his salt knew, for instance, that *amate* paper reflected native craftsmanship, a tradition tied to centuries old pictorial practices. Roxas y Abreu made an effort to recognize the fibrous material along with others, including sheepskin, vellum, and cloth, all of which helped to establish origin and age in place of titles, years of production, or descriptions of subject matter generally absent from each catalog entry. He took note, for instance, of "an unbound book in the Mexican language on old thick paper," and in another entry he recorded "a large notebook with characters and writings largely in Mexican." The term "Mexican" indicated that the original author wrote in Nahuatl, thereby placing the record more firmly within the indigenous world, whereas the materiality of the first ("old thick paper") and the visuality of the second ("characters and writing") helped to situate the documents in the distant past.

Authorities ordered Boturini in July 1743 to work on a catalog of the archive, but he refused to cooperate even after months of pleading. Boturini believed the complexity of the records he collected and his detailed knowledge of them would allow him some leverage to secure his freedom. For months in prison, the Italian expressed concern that his precious archive would tempt judges "or worse, the officers of the treasury," to plunder its depths.[29] Boturini suspected the viceroy had set him up in order to acquire the manuscripts himself, intimating to the King in June 1743 that the top colonial official had offered him a generous sum for the collection. But according to the letter, Boturini declined the offer, snubbing New Spain's most powerful man by suggesting no one, even the viceroy, could purchase his collection "with money or gems." The Italian believed his complex holdings would indeed force authorities to seek his help: "Without an interpreter," he said, "the archive remains mute forever."[30]

As it turned out, Boturini had no leverage, and the judge had little patience for petulance. Boturini's refusal to prepare the inventory earned him a temporary transfer to one of the city's dreaded *bartolinas*, or "dungeon cells," where within three torturous days he succumbed to the added discomfort of his surroundings and proceeded to assist authorities in identifying the goods in his collection. The Italian's involvement in the cataloging of his own collection captures an important moment that bridged the world of notaries and scribes who typically handled such matters with that of intellectuals and antiquarians such as Boturini. General practice delegated the task of reviewing and inventorying the belongings of wrongdoers or the deceased to officials with little or no knowledge of the recorded objects.[31] Keating and Markey observe that, while inventories "attempt to translate material things into linguistic statements," such statements are generally vague phrases focused on "size, form, provenance, and adornment or iconography."[32] One need only consider Roxas y Abreu's anemic inventory from March 29 to get a sense of the extent to which officials could, or even wished, to engage specialized collections. But Boturini's situation was highly unusual: never before had someone assembled such a dizzying array of indigenous books and manuscripts. Boturini's quip about the viceroy's offer to purchase the collection suggests authorities understood its importance but had failed to properly account for its content. Conscripting the Italian made this moment a unique instance where an inventory of goods benefited directly from the knowledge of the person who brought the objects together in the first place.

The Italian reunited with his precious archive over the course of two weeks in September 1743. The experience generated eight individual inventories that recorded more than five hundred books and manuscripts, a handful of gems presumably destined to adorn the crown for the Virgin, personal correspondence between the Italian and his network of contacts, and even one giant's tooth in the shelves.[33] Descriptions by those who came into contact with the collection attempted to capture its complexity with a few well-chosen words. Juan de Balbuena, the principal scribe assigned to assist Boturini in cataloging the records, described it as an "historic Indian archive and museum" in one instance, and as an "Indian museum of the general history of the realm" one month later.[34] His choice of terms reveals the way those close to the records understood the scope of what the Italian had assembled. References to the native origin of many of the manuscripts and to their pictorial and physical dimensions defied the traditional boundaries of an archive defined by standardized paper organized into bundled *legajos*. Sebastián de Covarrubias, the father of the first monolingual Spanish dictionary (published in 1611), defined *archivo* (archive) as "the drawer or cabinet where original manuscripts, privileges, and reports are stored." For Covarrubias, the term found its maximum expression in the "order" and "safety" bestowed upon documents by the Spanish monarchs in the royal archive of Simancas, qualities understood to extend to the custody of records by "lords, cities, churches, convents, and communities," at least in spirit if not in practice.[35]

By the first half of the eighteenth century, the meaning of an archive matured into a term more suggestive of civic responsibility that explained archives as "the public place where documents and legal records are stored."[36] The Real Academia Española retained the example of

Simancas, "the public one in the realm," as the gold standard, adding that records "bore more truth and authority based on the circumstances of the place."[37] The definition shifted from a focus on cabinets and small storage units to imposing physical buildings representative of power and authority. And yet, in the practical sense, both notions lived peacefully alongside each other. After all, the archive described by Balbuena, Roxas y Abreu, and others associated with Lorenzo's arrest fit into a large cedar cabinet, one presumes, by folding and stacking records that did not conform to standard sizes. Perhaps these subtle changes in meaning, combined with the unique nature of the documentary records he assembled, convinced the Italian to introduce a catalog of the collection in print years later as a *museo indiano*, or "indigenous museum."[38]

The collection brought together such a sophisticated assortment of artifacts from the region's past that it also constituted a space of reflection beyond the more utilitarian and administrative nature of an archive. By adopting the term "museum" to describe what in the past he had called an archive, Boturini aligned himself with the great European collectors who gained prestige by making their objects available for public display in their homes.[39] Balbuena's description of the collection as a museum attempted to capture this important dimension associated with the promotion of learning and knowledge.[40] Archives lock objects, hide them, protect them; museums shelter them too, but they also display them, thus inviting contact and contemplation. In the eighteenth and early nineteenth centuries, "part of the attraction of museums and of the cabinets of curiosity that preceded them," observes Constance Classen, "in fact, seemed to be their ability to offer visitors an intimate physical encounter with rare and curious objects."[41] Following established European patterns of collecting that witnessed elites bring together objects as tools of diplomacy as much as "sites of cultural and technological production," Boturini made his museum available to Mexico City's intelligentsia in an attempt to further his status and credibility as a specialist in the history of the realm.[42] "In all the time of my long sojourn in the Indies," the Italian boasted, "I opened my house, and the

Museum, to the public. It gave me the greatest pleasure that the most illustrious scientific minds frequented it."[43] The exceptional nature of the literary and scientific treasures he assembled would, he believed, serve as the basis for a definitive multivolume history of native peoples.

Unprecedented in scale, Boturini's collection did not, however, represent the first or the only attempt at building an assortment of early historical records to write about the viceroyalty's past. Collections tied to old families—including, most notably, the Alva Ixtlilxochitls—preserved archives stocked with legal and historical manuscripts of various sorts, kept in large part to help protect familial assets. Seventeenth-century efforts by creole elites turned toward the early contact period to strengthen their positions in colonial society by explaining the way local sons of Spanish ancestry inherited the mantle of power from early conquistadors, missionaries, and in some cases prominent native lords.[44] Fernando de Alva Ixtlilxochitl (1578–1650), a *castizo* intellectual with familial ties to the cultured Texcocan rulers of the Triple Alliance as well as to Spanish actors who established the new order after the fall of the Mexica Empire, not only safeguarded his family's treasures but also incorporated them into the historical accounts he wrote.[45] "The ability to access a hidden truth through the creative recombination of objects," argues Anna More, "was especially powerful in areas in which indigenous traditions themselves had become dislodged from endogamous transmission, either through active or passive imperial policy."[46] After years of research, Boturini claimed such authority in his own time.

In his prison correspondence, Boturini typically made reference to "his archive," sharing with the monarch his fears and anger over the fate of the records. "Not everyone was given the opportunity to go to Corinth to meet the painted images of the Indians . . . and their hieroglyphs," he wrote on June 17 while incarcerated. His reference to the famous city of the ancient world stressed Lorenzo's fear about the allure his archive would have over its new custodians as much as his mistrust of their assessment when inventorying the records.[47] His bitterness over the separation he had endured from his collection spilled into his letters. On August 3, he wrote to the King that authorities had imprisoned not only him but also his "very valuable archive," one "built on great expense and ceaseless vigils." On September 29, he complained that authorities had "sequestered my archive, and had it stripped away from me under the dubious pretext of [holding it] in custody."[48] Lorenzo's anger stemmed not only from fear and frustration but also from genuine disappointment over access to the collection of records he had painstakingly assembled since his arrival in New Spain.

INTERPRETATION

As much as the eight-part inventory documented a wide swath of pre-Colombian and early colonial manuscripts, it also demonstrated the difficulties of interpreting such a sophisticated set of sources. On the first day, Lorenzo guided authorities through his personal files, documenting a dizzying array of letters to and from officials from across New Spain and the Vatican as well as to an assortment of local priests, caciques, prelates, and notables of the realm with whom he discussed matters surrounding the coronation of the Virgin. He also retained receipts for miscellaneous manuscripts people sent him, his power of attorney over the Countess of Santibañez's holdings in New Spain, and records about his family, including a book and a genealogy that documented the history of his forbearers. The set offers unique insight into Lorenzo's overall research and collecting strategy—a mixture of archival investigation, ethnographic fieldwork, strategic communication, and fundraising that allowed him to gradually build his archive and advance the cause of the ceremony dedicated to Our Lady of Guadalupe. His efforts bordered on the fanatical, a quest for what Jean Baudrillard coined a "paradigm of perfection," a phrase that describes the sense of completion achieved through "seeking out, categorizing, gathering, and disposing" of objects to form thematic units.[49]

Each item received a number used to fix its place within the string of manuscripts and books that populated the eight inventories. The numbers worked in tandem with the textual description to give meaning to a record by establishing material, size, and length and, in some instances, also author, language, provenance,

and genre. The Matrícula de tributos (Figure e.1), a registry of gold, feathers, cacao, beans, military regalia, and other tribute items paid to the Triple Alliance, still bears traces of its connection to the collection. On the last page of the manuscript, a large "35" followed by "2°" designated its position in the second inventory that took place on September 17, 1734. Boturini described the item as "a tribute registry paid to the Empire, on maguey paper, its pages [measured] about a marquilla, fully illustrated, in sixteenth pages, without a beginning or end."[50] Besides the illusion of order, numbering gave a new life and identity to each record, and it established relationships between the documents that had formerly not existed. Above the large numeric inscription that registered a divinatory manuscript on amate paper (Figure e.2), a short inscription rechristened it "idolatrous calendar in sixteenth pages."[51] Known in Nahuatl as a tonalamatl, or "book of days," a reference to the 260-day ritual calendar, this almanac resided in the catalog adjacent to a "tanned leather, one vara in length and half in width, painted with what appear like a wheel of calculations of the indigenous century of fifty-two years, and surrounding it different figures of dreadful idols," and a booklet of a "Mexica calendar" Boturini had copied by hand.[52] The numbers and the annotation helped to classify the collection, establishing in the process a new truth about each object.[53]

Assembling the archive relied heavily on reproduction, a process that reveals details about classification, circulation, storage, and accessibility. Boturini had copied manuscripts, for instance, that formed part of the Alva Ixtlilxochitl collection, including a "volume that contains the history of the Toltec nation, and the history of the Chichimec lords up until the arrival of the Spaniards, and other accounts of conquest, its author Don Fernando de Alva Ixtlilxochitl; all pieces were copied from their originals, written in Spanish, in 116 pages."[54] The collection resided in the Jesuit College of San Pedro and San Pablo in Mexico City, where Boturini also copied a rare unpublished manuscript by the sixteenth-century jurist Alonso de Zorita titled Breve relación de los señores de la Nueva España [Brief Account of the Lords of New Spain], written around 1570. The Italian's annotation at

the end of the document reveals rich details about his methodology:

> I, Lorenzo Boturini, Lord of Hono, made this copy in the month of November 1738 from its original, found in the library of the Colegio of San Pedro y San Pablo of the Society of Jesus of Mexico, est. 48 n. 10. Its original contains 124 written pages and a note at the front that says, "In the year 1683, it reached my hands – Lic. Pensado."[55]

As Iván Escamilla observes, the historian's trade rests on personal and professional relationships that allow access to primary sources.[56] Boturini's methodology paid careful attention to the way archival privilege functioned in New Spain, and his annotations in the catalog bear witness to the way he took advantage of the resources in the

capital of the viceroyalty. Besides San Pedro y San Pablo, Boturini also gained access to Mexico City's Cathedral archive and to that of the Jesuit Oratory of San Felipe Neri, more commonly known as La Profesa.[57] Entry 31 from September 28 indicated Boturini "copied and ordered copies" of seven folio-size notebooks related to the apparition of the Virgin.[58] Reproduction—an essential element of the viceroyalty's vibrant manuscript culture—often required the assistance of skilled scribes who could faithfully copy important texts and documents.

The inventory captured the ravages that time had inflicted on the documentary record, as well as the difficulties associated with its interpretation. Maps, in particular, suffered. A pictorial history "of about two varas on maguey paper" experienced some damage but showed evidence of repair (*algo maltratado y remendado*), and a square map also on native paper was "mistreated and torn at the center."[59] The Plano Parcial de la Ciudad de México (Figure e.3), a large sixteenth-century map of Mexico City made on amate paper, appeared "very

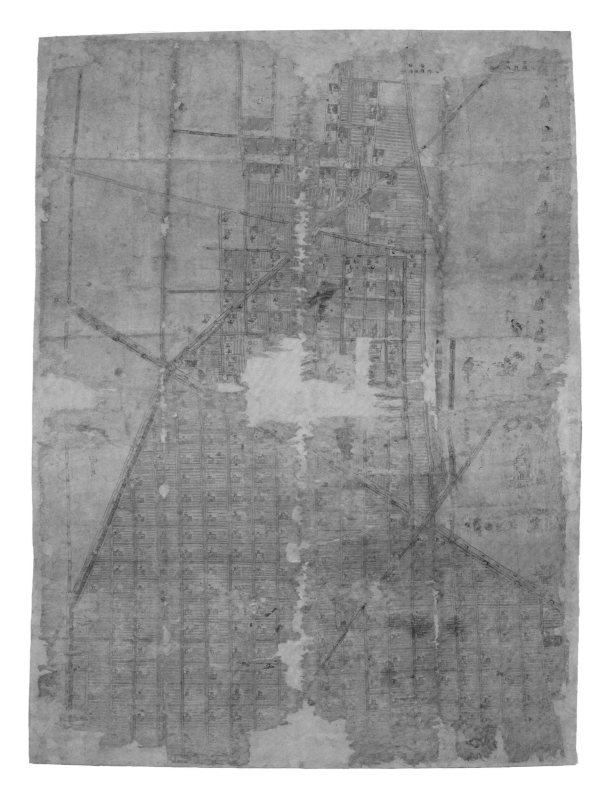

mistreated" (*muy maltratado*).[60] Along the map's frayed edges on the right, one can still discern a successive line of Nahua nobles that stretched back to the early fifteenth century, while irreparable damage along its central axis has erased nearly 10 percent of the more than four hundred plots of land parceled among the city's indigenous residents. A map of Lake Texcoco also on native paper recorded on September 25, revealed someone had pasted a piece of European paper (*papel de Castilla*) on the back of the map to repair damages it had endured.[61] Water, paper's mortal enemy, threatened the archive at every turn. "A map fragment on maguey paper of the old Mexica Empire" had rotted, and at least another two had suffered extensive water damage.[62] Paper fragments of pictorial records and alphabetic sources, including "a bundle of pieces of maps, very mistreated," and "two pieces of maps, [on] European paper, highly damaged, sown with thread, about some parcels of lands," limited interpretation.[63]

Boturini experienced difficulty deciphering the meaning of some records in his archive. The scribe working on the inventory observed the Italian had not yet determined the significance (*no ha inteligenciado*) of "a map on European paper, with crude figures of about a vara in length and half a tercia in width, damaged."[64] The Italian had also failed to determine the meaning of another item, "a map on tanned leather, about one tercia in width and about two and a half varas long," that he received from an unnamed source in Oaxaca.[65] The presence of this record indicates that Boturini's aggressive letter-writing campaign had paid off in the end. Yet the historical investigation undertaken by the Italian brings to the fore the challenges faced by the team tasked with documenting the collection. Except for Boturini, the individuals assigned to sequester and later inventory the records did not seem to understand how to make sense of the rich documentary trove. While the Italian attempted to leverage his knowledge of the records, authorities denied him his freedom and instead coerced him to prepare a catalog of the collection, a condition

that must have influenced his work when crafting the inventory. During the survey of records, the written descriptions demonstrated that Boturini did not always enjoy a clear grasp of the documents he professed to know so much about.

Boturini worked with the collection for the last time on September 28, 1743, when the group documented records associated with the apparition of the Virgin. The Italian had assembled an impressive range of print and manuscript sources, including hagiographies, novenas, religious histories, testimonials, sermons, and hymnals. When they concluded the inventory, the scribe noted all the "papers, maps, and books" were securely deposited in the cabinet and that the cabinet itself resided in the Royal Treasury's Main Chamber.[66] Within days, authorities concluded their investigation into Boturini's activities, noting the Italian acted out of zeal, not self-interest. Nevertheless, he had traveled undocumented to New Spain, and his punishment for this offense resulted in an unceremonious expulsion from the realm. The records, the viceroy determined, would stay in Mexico. Unfortunately, the dark cloud that had followed Boturini for the previous few months did not dissipate after his release. The official in charge placed Boturini in the custody of Sebastián de Torres, the royal freight conductor, who escorted him to Veracruz and turned him over to the city's prefect. In the port city, the Italian waited for passage in San Juan de Ulúa along with the general prison population until he finally boarded *La Concordia*, a vessel bound for Spain that carried a large shipment of silver. After years of dedicated research, Boturini's departure from New Spain must have felt like a horrifying nightmare designed to endlessly torment him. Near the Spanish coast, English pirates captured his ship, took him prisoner, and stripped him of his last remaining possessions. Freed at Gibraltar in March 1744, Boturini made his way to the House of Trade in Cádiz in rags, physically weak, and entirely demoralized.[67]

THE ZAPOTEC POET

After Boturini recounted his misfortunes at court in Madrid, officials in Spain wrote to the viceroy in America, requesting proper care of the collection while they determined the fate of the records.[68] In Mexico City, the letter from the court triggered another inventory to assess the collection. Not satisfied with Boturini's catalog, authorities recruited the Zapotec cacique Patricio Antonio López to complete the task. A poet and chronicler who enjoyed steady work as a court interpreter in the capital, López also gained recognition in his own time as a specialist in Mesoamerican history.[69] Domingo Varcarcel, the Audiencia judge that presided over Boturini's case, appointed López, noting he was "an ideally suited person, practical and very intelligent, because of his *profesión* [occupation as a translator] in the Mexican language and with the maps and characters that the natives used in these kingdoms in the past."[70] The cacique's fluency in Zapotec and Nahuatl, coupled with his knowledge of notarial forms and legal protocol, made him an ideal candidate for the job. Likewise, López had direct knowledge of the Boturini collection, having helped draft letters of introduction between the Italian and a number of indigenous towns across the viceroyalty. When officials in Spain suggested to the viceroy creating a specialized academy devoted to the history of New Spain, the viceroy agreed, nominating López as its first chronicler.[71]

López's reading of the collection considerably expanded the previous inventory. In his entries, the cacique often added detailed bibliographic information about a source or offered a fuller description of its contents. López described the ninth item in the second inventory in the following way: "The one in this number is also a manuscript, Nahuatl, with only a few notes in Spanish. It is an original from the Archive of Tlaxcala, where the cabildos they had had been established by order of the government of that city. It starts in the year 547 and ends in 627; in 177 pages."[72] Boturini had noted simply in his catalog "another mistreated vellum tome, manuscript, with some accounts in Spanish and Nahuatl that happened in Tlaxcala." When compared, López's moderately longer entry offered a richer description of the record, including a range of dates, page count, information on the document's origin, and even a measured corrective. Despite Boturini's assertion, López noted, the author wrote primarily in Nahuatl, minimal Spanish

notes notwithstanding. In another entry, López historicized a manuscript by observing it dealt with the history of the Teochichimecas and that it explained the Nahua calendar. The author of the source, the cacique observed, "copied it apparently from the ancient paintings made by the first Indians who learned to write"; Boturini, López noted, made a copy of it from the one held in the collection of the Jesuit Library of San Pedro and San Pablo.[73]

In some instances, the Zapotec lord's analysis of a source provided important historical context and shed light on issues that troubled the viceroyalty in the eighteenth century. In the thirty-first entry of the second inventory, Boturini had observed "a book, quarto, covered (between two boards) in black tanned leather; it deals with the history of the Aztec nation [illustrated] with signs and figures, on Spanish paper, twenty fojas."[74] For López, the entry represented an opportunity to provide a detailed account of the Nahua manuscript, and it formed part of a handful of records the cacique prioritized in the catalog. A chronological account of Mesoamerican rulers, Catholic clergy, and Spanish viceroys, the record functioned as a political genealogy of the region up to the year 1609. In addition to political information, the manuscript documented "two epidemics that the Indians suffered in this realm," one from 1545 when, according to the account, 800,000 people perished, and the *cocolixtli* epidemic of 1577 that killed more than two million natives.[75] López indicated that, at the time of the cocolixtli outbreak, Juan de Torquemada observed a "horrendous comet, and [that] there appeared on the sun three circles that looked like three inflamed and bloody suns."[76] The painter-scribe who prepared the native manuscript illustrated cocolixtli by depicting a seated male figure expelling blood through the nose. López had special reason to comment on the terrifying scene, since he lived through the deadly *matlazahuatl* epidemic that raged through the region in 1736 and 1737, an event presaged, according to the Zapotec lord, by the presence of a clearly visible comet in the western sky.[77] The cacique's fluency in indigenous languages, coupled with his knowledge of notarial forms and legal protocol, allowed him a close reading of the native record that often eluded Boturini.

López formed part of a distinguished line of indigenous caciques who as royal interpreters gained privileged access to the institutions of government that administered justice across the viceroyalty. The Zapotec lord followed in the footsteps of Alva Ixtlilxochitl, a "cacique descended from the kings of Texcoco [and] an interpreter for this supreme government" whose works he annotated for the catalog.[78] As part of this tradition, López cast himself as an advocate for the underprivileged native patrons he served. In his *Mercurio yndiano*, an historic poem on indigenous history published in 1740, the Zapotec lord observed that a "natural inclination to defend my own" compelled him to write about the native past. The cacique proudly wrote that, despite its best attempts, the powerful Nahua state had failed to subdue the Zapotec kingdom, and that Zapotec leaders had aligned voluntarily with Spanish forces in the sixteenth century "without ever being conquered."[79] The title of López's work referenced Mercury, the Roman god associated with eloquence and communication, who he described as "an interpreter and ambassador." In a century and a half of Spanish rule, López observed, "only native caciques of recognized nobility and virtue" had ever served as interpreters.[80] Despite his patriotic narrative, López's work articulated a forceful vision of the past that accounted for indigenous voices.

In 1737, authorities in the Tribunal of the Holy Crusade, an arm of the church designed to oversee financial contributions to combat enemies of the faith, appointed López as a translator. The cacique filled a post previously occupied by Manuel Mancio, a recently deceased interpreter of indigenous origin who, over a thirty-year period, had translated oral, pictorial, and alphabetic forms of evidence presented by indigenous litigants in the courts.[81] Between 1704 and 1708, Mancio authenticated three maps and other pictorial records made on native paper submitted as evidence in a dispute between the *parcialidad* of Santiago Tlatelolco, an urban subdivision of Mexico City, and neighboring towns over rights to marshland. In 1710, Mancio examined a folding screen made of eight painted leaves with a few alphabetic annotations in Nahuatl presented by Santa María Magdalena Mixihuca in the Valley of Mexico.[82] The

representatives from Mixihuca submitted the ancient record to resolve a dispute with San Gregorio Atlapulco, who themselves introduced a set of annals written in Nahuatl that included pictorial elements.[83] Mancio's experience brings into focus the continued use of indigenous records in the courts and the role interpreters played in the negotiation of land.

Patricio Antonio López's trained eye paid close attention to the age and provenance of the maps he annotated for the catalog. "In this one you find a map on *marca mayor* paper," he wrote in one entry, "[a] description of the town of San Juan Teotihuacan. Modern painting."[84] Boturini had, in fact, commissioned the map from a local painter to include in his future study of the realm.[85] In the following item, López noted the recent creation of another map: "This other one is on a cotton sheet; [it is a] modern painting with different towns with its divisions and boundary markers."[86] He distinguished the new maps from the old ones by pointing to deterioration and their material characteristics. In item twenty-one of the second inventory, López identified two map fragments on native bark paper that had gone through an early process of authentication. "These are two small pieces of maps with figures," he observed, "explained in some parts with letters of the Spanish alphabet, it is on paper they [the natives] used." López determined from his paleographic analysis that the pictorial document recorded events starting in 1480, "according to the numbers one can see next to one of its figures, superimposed after the arrival of the Spaniards."[87] The keepers of the maps in question had, like countless other indigenous towns across the viceroyalty, presented their pictorial records to authorities to negotiate some aspect of Spanish rule, and in the process officials had left written traces that López followed.

As a royal interpreter, the cacique had acquired specialized knowledge of notarial practices and understood the priorities that drove indigenous litigants. He applied these skills to describe a pictorial manuscript on European rag paper that Boturini had failed to decipher. López wrote that the painted figures "denoted the names of the common pasture lands and plots that the caciques divided among their Indian tenants because it was customary for all of these people to name each location and place, as it is today."[88] The Zapotec translator further asserted that place-names functioned to define *mojoneras* (boundary markers) and *límites* (borders), alluding to the complex spatial practices that regulated land tenure. In his annotation of item number 44 of the fourth inventory, a boundary map on amate from the Valley of Puebla known today as the Map of Cuauhtinchan no. 4 (Figure e.4), López took note of the process of authentication that had taken place years earlier.[89] "In this other one made on vast [quantities of] paper from the Indies," the cacique observed, "are described the towns of the province of Tepeaca, Cuauhtinchan, Tetela, and others; it is very old, it has some letters superimposed that decipher the boundary markers."[90] Officials in the sixteenth century had annotated the native records to allow future users to clearly identify the elements they prioritized. López recognized these practices with ease.

But the cacique's annotations carried with them more than simply bureaucratic savvy. Historical knowledge allowed the native lord to peddle his vision of the past in the catalog to a sophisticated audience that included the viceroy, high-ranking members of the Audiencia, the Council of the Indies, and possibly the King of Spain himself. In *Mercurio yndiano*, he had challenged those who viewed natives as "irrational, rude, barbarous, timid, cowardly, and servile," using the history of the Zapotec people to position indigenous groups on their own terms within a historiography that traditionally belittled Indian society.[91] The inventory allowed López to frame a narrative about the conquest period that presented the Zapotec as a fierce, proud, an independent nation that willingly aligned with Spanish forces after the fall of Tenochtitlan. In his reading of a genealogy on tanned leather, he represented Zapotecs as "allies of the Mixtecs, they were independent empires feared greatly by the Mexica Empire," establishing autonomy for what he viewed as the two most powerful nations in Oaxaca.[92] López zeroed in on a ruling pair in the genealogy's central frame that, according to him, depicted the last Zapotec leader, Ray of Wind, sitting face to face with Hernán Cortés. "The saddled horse that can be spotted behind him," the cacique observed, "and the harquebus laid on the ground with its butt turned to face the prince, denoted that those lands and people were not conquered, nor that victory was achieved through the thunder of these arms or cavalry."[93] The close reading of the source allowed López to historicize another important pictorial record Boturini had not managed to read.

No other historian of the New World since Ixtlilxochitl had displayed such a clear understanding of the relationship between memory, ritual, and writing that structured native views about the past as Patricio Antonio López. And yet the cacique's understanding of historical memory also shared an intimate connection with the rich literature about early encounters in the New World, a body of work he drew upon to strengthen his analysis of the maps and pictorial sources, as well as to legitimize their content in the eyes of his powerful audience. Throughout the inventory of records, López drew generously from the influential studies of Spanish historians such as Antonio de Herrera y Tordesillas (1549–c. 1625), a prolific scholar who served as chronicler in the Habsburg court, and Juan de Torquemada (c. 1562–1624), the revered Franciscan historian whose interpretation of the theft of an ancient cross on the coasts of Huatulco he challenged.[94] In his lengthy annotation of an old Mixtec *lienzo* that documented the family line of the legendary eleventh-century warrior Eight Deer, he credited the work of another writer from Oaxaca, the creole historian Francisco de Burgoa (c. 1600–1681) after historicizing the pictorial elements of the large cloth surface.[95] Burgoa's important historical-geographic study of the region appealed to the cacique's strong sense of identity, one clearly tied to his native land and his Zapotec roots. By invoking these and other European works to unpack the contents of the collection, López demonstrated the way the rich array of native pictorial and alphabetic manuscripts could enter into dialogue with each other to provide a more nuanced understanding of history.

(OPPOSITE PAGE) E.4. *Map of Cuauhtinchan no. 4 (c. 1563), no. 35-31, Biblioteca Nacional de Antropología e Historia.*

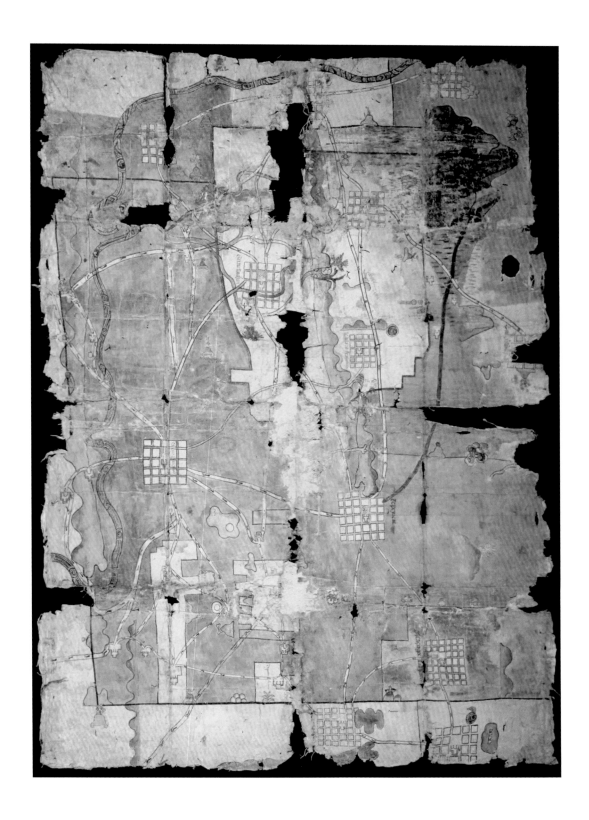

Over the course of the next fifty years, word of the collection spread among specialists in Mexico City and Madrid. As part of their centralization policies, Bourbon officials in Spain during the 1780s and 1790s made numerous attempts to acquire the records in the Boturini collection, but these efforts largely failed in the face of creole opposition in New Spain reluctant to see the region depleted of its treasures.[96] In Mexico City, prelates, military officers, antiquarians, bureaucrats, and intellectuals consulted, borrowed, copied, admired, and pillaged the contents of the archive. A report of the collection prepared in 1791 indicates that the military officer and avid collector Diego de Panes had borrowed "three lienzos, fourteen loose folios, three notebooks, and a map on cloth" and that the Conde de Gálvez, New Spain's viceroy from 1785 to 1786, borrowed "an unspecified number of maps and papers."[97] By 1823, when Ignacio de Cubas, an archivist and future director of Mexico's National Museum and later of its first National Archive, conducted a survey of the records, more than half of the items had disappeared.[98] Indeed, as Antoinette Burton shrewdly observes, "the history of the archive is a history of loss," of stolen and misplaced records, silenced voices, and abandoned projects.[99] The inventories prepared after authorities sequestered the records in the first place point to the way loss had shattered knowledge of pictorial writing, as well as how individuals and towns stored, used, and sold painted manuscripts, books, and legal records of various types. Despite numerous efforts to order and decode its holdings, the collection demanded fluency in indigenous languages, specialized historical knowledge, and a strong measure of cultural awareness—a combination of elements found in limited supply.

In another respect, the formation of the Boturini collection functions as a metaphor to contextualize the major themes analyzed in this book. The distrust the Italian witnessed upon which natives built relationships with Spaniards speaks volumes about the tense and adversarial encounters surrounding maps and land negotiations. Boturini learned that, across indigenous towns in the viceroyalty, various forms of archiving—including burying records underground—constituted an important way for social actors to safeguard their documentary treasures in order to hone power and negotiate privilege. The Italian learned about these practices, in part, because of his association with individuals such as Patricio Antonio López, an officer of the state with deep ties to native society, as well as to the network of copyists, translators, intellectuals, judges, scribes, and clerics that gave shape to the region's vibrant manuscript culture. The cacique's years of experience working as an interpreter for various institutions demonstrates the way bureaucratic practice and notarial culture shaped knowledge about maps and pictorial records, as well as the way social memory and custom, in turn, fashioned different, often competing, visions of the past.

NOTES

INTRODUCTION

1. See www.unesco.org/new/en/communication-and-information /flagship-project-activities/memory-of-the-world/register/full-list -of-registered-heritage/registered-heritage-page-8/sixteenth-to -eighteenth-century-pictographs-from-the-maps-drawings-and -illustrations-of-the-national-archives-of-mexico/#c200811.

2. "Sixteenth to Eighteenth-Century Pictographs from the Record Group 'Maps, Drawings, and Illustrations' of the National General Archives of Mexico," Reference no. 2010–41, Archivo General de la Nación, Mexico City.

3. As a result of these efforts, the AGN published its *Catálogo de ilustraciones*, a fourteen-volume register of the archive's graphic material. For Mapilu, its online counterpart, see www.agn.gob.mx /mapilu. For indigenous pictorial records, also see Joaquín Galarza, *Códices y pinturas tradicionales indígenas en el Archivo General de la Nación. Estudio y catálogo*.

4. Susan Pearce, *On Collecting: An Investigation of Collecting in the European Tradition*, 25–26.

5. For instance, see María de los Ángeles Romero Frizzi, "El título de San Mateo Capulpan, Oaxaca: Actualidad y autenticidad de un título primordial"; Arnold Bauer's captivating *Search for the Codex Cardona: On the Trail of a Sixteenth-Century Mexican Treasure*; and Michel Oudijk and Sebastián van Doesberg, *Los lienzos pictográficos de Santa Cruz Papalutla, Oaxaca*.

6. Harley's influence extended over geographic and temporal boundaries. See, for example, Christian Jacob, "Toward a Cultural History of Cartography"; Matthew Edney, *Mapping an Empire: The Geographical Construction of British India, 1765–1843*; D. Graham Burnett, *Masters of All They Surveyed: Exploration, Geography, and a British El Dorado*; Ricardo Padrón, *The Spacious Word: Cartography, Literature, and Empire in Early Modern Spain*; Mary Sponberg Pedley, *The Commerce of Cartography: Making and Marketing Maps in Eighteenth-Century France and England*; and Alex Hidalgo and John F. López, eds., "The Ethnohistorical Map in New Spain."

7. See the essays edited by David Buisseret in *Monarchs, Ministers, and Maps: The Emergence of Cartography as a Tool of Government in Early Modern Europe*; Neil Safier, *Measuring the New World: Enlightenment Science and South America*; Burnett, *Masters of All They Surveyed*; Edney, *Mapping an Empire*; J. B. Harley, "Silences and Secrecy: The Hidden Agenda of Cartography in Early Modern Europe," in *The New Nature of Maps*; and María Portuondo, *Secret Science: Spanish Cosmography and the New World*.

8. Serge Gruzinski, "Colonial Indian Maps in Sixteenth-Century Mexico: An Essay in Mixed Cartography"; Dana Leibsohn, "Primers for Memory: Cartographic Histories and Nahua Identity," in *Writing without Words*, and "Colony and Cartography: Shifting Signs on Indigenous Maps of New Spain," in *Reframing the Renaissance: Visual Culture in Europe and Latin America, 1450–1650*, ed. Claire Farago; Barbara Mundy, *The Mapping of New Spain: Indigenous Cartography and the Maps of the* Relaciones Geográficas, and "Mesoamerican Cartography," in *The History of Cartography*. In addition, see Alessandra

Russo, *El realismo circular: Tierras, espacios y paisajes de la cartografía novohispana, siglos XVI y XVII*; and Mercedes Montes de Oca Vega, Dominique Raby, Salvador Reyes Equiguas, and Adam Sellen, *Cartografía de tradición hispanoindígena: Mapas de Mercedes de tierras, siglos XVI y XVII*, vol. 1–2.

9. See George Kubler, "On the Colonial Extinction of the Motifs of Pre-Colombian Art," in *Essays in Pre-Colombian Art and Archaeology*, ed. Samuel Lothrop; and Donald Robertson, "The Pinturas (Maps) of the Relaciones Geográficas, with a Catalogue," in *Handbook of Middle American Indians* v. 12, ed. Robert Wauchope and Howard F. Cline (hereafter cited as *HMAI*). Compare Mundy, *The Mapping of New Spain*, xix; and Russo, *El realismo circular*, 19.

10. Mundy, *The Mapping of New Spain*, 216.

11. Leibsohn, "Colony and Cartography," 266.

12. Mundy, *The Mapping of New Spain*, 210.

13. Gruzinski, "Indian Maps," 51.

14. See *Límites, mapas y títulos primordiales de los pueblos del estado de Oaxaca: Índice del Ramo de Tierras*, ed. Enrique Méndez Martínez and Enrique Méndez Torres; Enrique Méndez Martínez, *Índice de documentos relativos a los pueblos del estado de Oaxaca*; *Documentos para la etnohistoria del estado de Oaxaca: Índice del Ramo de Mercedes del Archivo General de la Nación*, ed. Ronald Spores and Miguel Saldaña; and *Colección de documentos del Archivo General de la Nación para la etnohistoria de la Mixteca de Oaxaca en el siglo XVI*, ed. Ronald Spores.

15. See Mary Elizabeth Smith, *Picture Writing from Ancient Southern Mexico: Mixtec Place Signs and Maps*; John Monaghan, "The Text in the Body, the Body in the Text: The Embodied Sign in Mixtec Writing," in *Writing without Words*; Kevin Terraciano, *The Mixtecs of Colonial Oaxaca: Ñudzahui History, Sixteenth through Eighteenth Centuries*, 15–65; Lisa Sousa and Kevin Terraciano, "The 'Original Conquest' of Oaxaca: Nahua and Mixtec Accounts of the Spanish Conquest"; and María de los Ángeles Romero Frizzi, ed., *Escritura zapoteca: 2,500 años de historia*. For Indian manuscripts in general, see Donald Robertson, *Mexican Manuscript Painting of the Early Colonial Period: The Metropolitan Schools*; Elizabeth Hill Boone, *Stories in Red and Black: Pictorial Histories of the Aztecs and Mixtecs*; Arellano Hoffman et al., eds., *Libros y escritura de tradición indígena*; Serge Gruzinski, *La colonización de lo imaginario: Sociedades indígenas y occidentalización en el México español. Siglos XVI-XVIII*, esp. 15–148; Walter Mignolo, *The Darker Side of the Renaissance: Literacy, Territoriality, and Colonization*, 87–96; and James Lockhart, *The Nahuas after the Conquest: A Social and Cultural History of the Indians of Central Mexico, Sixteenth through Eighteenth Centuries*, 326–418.

16. Recent work includes Daniela Bleichmar, "History in Pictures: Translating the *Codex Mendoza*"; Diana Magaloni Kerpel, *The Colors of the New World: Artists, Materials, and the Creation of the Florentine Codex*; Justina Olko, *Insignia of Rank in the Nahua World: From the Fifteenth to the Seventeenth Century*; Dana Leibsohn, *Script and Glyph: Pre-Hispanic History, Colonial Bookmaking, and the Historia Tolteca-Chichimeca*; Catherine DiCesare, *Sweeping the Way: Divine Transformation in the Aztec Festival of Ochpaniztli*; and Elizabeth Hill Boone, *Cycles of Time and Meaning in the Mexican Books of Fate*.

17. See Arni Brownstone, ed., *The Lienzo of Tlapiltepec: A Painted History from the Northern Mixteca*; Byron Hamman, "Object, Image, Cleverness: The Lienzo de Tlaxcala"; Oudijk and van Doesberg, *Los lienzos pictográficos de Santa Cruz Papalutla, Oaxaca*; Travis Barton Kranz, "Visual Persuasion: Sixteenth-Century Tlaxcalan Pictorials in Response to the Conquest of Mexico," in *The Conquest All Over Again: Nahuas and Zapotecs Thinking, Writing, and Painting Spanish Colonialism*, ed. Susan Schroeder; Florine Asselbergs, *Conquered Conquistadors: The Lienzo de Quauhquechollan: A Nahua Vision of the Conquest of Guatemala*; Michel Oudijk and Maarten Jansen, "Changing History in the Lienzos de Guevea and Santo Domingo Petapa"; and Ross Parmenter, "The Lienzo of Tulancingo, Oaxaca: An Introductory Study of a Ninth Painted Sheet from the Coixtlahuaca Valley."

18. Terraciano, *The Mixtecs*, 347–348.

19. For resettlements in the Valley of Oaxaca, see Peter Gerhard, *A Guide to the Historical Geography of New Spain*, 51–52, 90–91, and 159; and William Taylor, *Landlord and Peasant in Colonial Oaxaca*, 21, 26–27, and 37. For the neighboring Mixteca region, see Terraciano, *The Mixtecs*, 119–121. On *congregaciones* in the Valley of Mexico, see Charles Gibson, *The Aztecs under Spanish Rule: A History of the Indians of the Valley of Mexico, 1519–1810*, 28, 54, and 282–286; and Lockhart, *The Nahuas*, 44–46 and 415–416. Also, Ethelia Ruiz Medrano, *Mexico's Indigenous Communities: Their Lands and Histories, 1500–2010*, 91–96.

20. Gibson, *The Aztecs*, 264.

21. Gibson, *The Aztecs*, 265.

22. See Yanna Yannakakis, *The Art of Being In-Between: Native Intermediaries, Indian Identity, and Local Rule in Colonial Oaxaca*, 150; Terraciano, *The Mixtecs*, 230–231; and Taylor, *Landlord and Peasant*, 35.

23. Taylor, *Landlord and Peasant*, 44.

24. Terraciano, *The Mixtecs*, 339.

25. John K. Chance, *Race and Class in Colonial Oaxaca*.

26. Sylvia Sellers-García, *Distance and Documents at the Spanish Empire's Periphery*.

27. On unlicensed legal agents, see Woodrow Borah, *Justice by Insurance: The General Indian Court of Colonial Mexico and the Legal Aides of the Half-Real*, 297–302.

28. Demetrio Ramos, "La crisis indiana y la Junta Magna de 1568."

29. *Transcripción de las Ordenanzas de descubrimiento, nueva población y pacificación de las Indias dadas por Felipe II, el 13 de julio de 1573, en el Bosque de Segovia, según el original que se conserva en el Archivo General de Indias de Sevilla*.

30. See John F. López, "Indigenous Commentary on Sixteenth-Century Mexico."

31. Portuondo, *Secret Science*.

32. Mundy, *The Mapping of New Spain*, 17–27.

33. Ramos, "La crisis Indiana," 1–2.

34. Taylor, *Landlord and Peasant*, 21, 26–27, 37; Peter Gerhard,

A Guide to the Historical Geography of New Spain, 51–52, 90–91, 159; Terraciano, *The Mixtecs*, 119–121; Gibson, *The Aztecs*, 28, 54, 282–286; and Lockhart, *The Nahuas*, 44–46, 415–416.

35. Mundy, *The Mapping of New Spain*, 183.

36. Gerhard, *A Guide*, 51, 93.

37. As the case of Xoxocotlán analyzed in chapter 1 clearly demonstrates.

38. Ruiz Medrano, *Mexico's Indigenous Communities*, 96–103.

39. Brian Owensby, *Empire of Law and Indian Justice in Colonial Mexico*, 97.

40. Archivo General del Estado de Oaxaca (AGEO), Alcaldías Mayores, leg. 62, exp. 12; Enrique Florescano, *Historia de las historias de la nación mexicana*, 241; Taylor, *Landlord and Peasant*, 6–7, 68. Each vara equaled roughly 33 inches.

41. Raymond Craib, *Cartographic Mexico: A History of State Fixations and Fugitive Landscapes*, 64–65.

42. Elías Trabulse, "Científicos e ingenieros en la Nueva España: Don Diego García Conde en la historia de la cartografía mexicana," in *Una visión científica y artística de la Ciudad de México: El plano de la capital virreinal (1793–1807) de Diego García Conde*.

CHAPTER 1

1. AGN, Tierras, vol. 129, exp. 4.

2. A *medida*, or "measure," equaled about one-half acre. An *estancia de ganado menor* measured around three square miles; the larger *estancia de ganado mayor*, or "cattle ranches," measured close to seven square miles.

3. They belonged to the town's cabildo, the municipal council that administered local matters. The size of each cabildo varied according to the size of each municipality. In 1691, Xoxocotlán's cabildo included two *alcaldes*, five *regidores* (councilmen), two *alguacil mayores* (chief bailiffs), and a scribe. The town received a license in 1640 to elect its own officials, a growing trend among Indian republics that sought independence from head towns known as *cabeceras* as the native population recovered from epidemics. See Taylor, *Landlord and Peasant*, 30; Yannakakis, *The Art of Being In-Between*, 100–102.

4. Map of Santa Cruz Xoxocotlán (1686), AGN, no. 625, Tierras, vol. 129, exp. 4, f. 249.

5. Michael Baxandall, *Painting and Experience in Fifteenth-Century Italy: A Primer in the Social History of Pictorial Style*, 1.

6. Clifford Geertz, *The Interpretation of Cultures: Selected Essays*, 10.

7. Chance, *Race and Class*.

8. Taylor, *Landlord and Peasant*, and François Chevalier's *Land and Society in Colonial Mexico: The Great Hacienda*, trans. Alvis Eustis. Also, see James Lockhart, "Encomienda and Hacienda: The Evolution of the Great Estate in the Spanish Indies," in *Of Things of the Indies: Essays Old and New in Early Latin American History*; and Eric Van Young, *Hacienda and Market in Eighteenth-Century Mexico: The Rural Economy of the Guadalajara Region, 1675–1820*, and his "Mexican Rural History Since Chevalier: The Historiography of the Colonial

Hacienda." More recent scholarship has drawn on Oaxaca's unique landholding patterns to examine the role of native intermediaries in the negotiation of power and natural resources in the region's Northern Sierra; see Yannakakis, *The Art of Being In-Between*, 131–157.

9. Taylor, *Landlord and Peasant*, 198.

10. Taylor, *Landlord and Peasant*, 82–89, 209–210. Also see Méndez Martínez and Méndez Torres, eds., *Límites, mapas y títulos primordiales*.

11. Robert Haskett, "Paper Shields: The Ideology of Coats of Arms in Colonial Mexican Primordial Titles," 111.

12. Taylor, *Landlord and Peasant*, 13–17.

13. Taylor, *Landlord and Peasant*, 111–140.

14. See Terraciano, *The Mixtecs*, 102–132; John M. D. Pohl, "Mexican Codices, Maps, and Lienzos as Social Contracts," in *Writing without Words*; and Yannakakis, *The Art of Being In-Between*, 20. The *ñuu*, or "ethnic state," formed the basic unit of organization for Mixtec societies in Oaxaca equivalent to the *altepetl* in central Mexico. See Lockhart, *The Nahuas*, 14–47.

15. Marcello Carmagnani, *El regreso de los dioses: El proceso de reconstitución de la identidad étnica en Oaxaca. Siglos XVII y XVIII*, 13.

16. Carmagnani, *El regreso de los dioses*, 104.

17. Terraciano, *The Mixtecs*, 15–65; Monaghan, "The Text in the Body"; Smith, *Picture Writing from Ancient Southern Mexico*; and Boone, *Stories in Red and Black*.

18. María de los Ángeles Romero Frizzi, "Los caminos de Oaxaca," in *Rutas de la Nueva España*, ed. Chantal Cramaussel, 127.

19. Chantal Cramaussel, "Introducción," in *Rutas de la Nueva España*.

20. Romero Frizzi, "Los caminos de Oaxaca," 122.

21. Romero Frizzi, "Los caminos de Oaxaca," 134.

22. AGN, Tierras, vol. 129, exp. 4, f. 67.

23. Margot Beyersdorff, "Covering the Earth: Mapping the Walkabout in Andean *Pueblos de Indios*," 130.

24. Yanna Yannakakis, "Witnesses, Spatial Practices, and a Land Dispute in Colonial Oaxaca," 164.

25. The original transcription reads: "Hasta llegar al Camino Real que se viene de la Ciudad de Antequera a la Villa de Cuilapa de donde así mismo pareció otro mojón de piedras que dijeron los dichos naturales ser antiguo y allí pusieron una cruz y pidieron al dicho alcalde mayor se les diese por testimonio de cómo habían puesto los dichos mojones." AGN, Tierras, vol. 129, exp. 4, f. 6.

26. AGN, Tierras, vol. 129, exp. 4, f. 20.

27. A copy of the original document included in the case states that a *merced* was issued to "Don Juan de Guzmán, indio principal de la Villa de Cuilapa, de un sitio de estancia para ganado menor de ella en la parte y lugar que en lengua zapoteca dicen Tepeacatontze y en mixteca dicen Cuyen; una loma yerma que va a dar [a] unas tierras altas peladas que por la una baja una quebradilla y por las dichas lomas a sus lados están unas quebradillas la cual por mi mandato y comisión fue a ver y vido Luis Suárez de Peralta, alcalde mayor de la Ciudad de Antequera." AGN, Tierras, vol. 129, exp. 4, f. 68–69.

For the sale of the estancia to Francisco Muñoz de Tejada, Guzmán's heirs described the location of the property in more detail: "Decimos que nosotros [the Guzmán caciques] tenemos y poseemos un sitio de estancia despoblado en una loma yerma a la falda de un cerro alto en el pago que llaman Tepeacatonstui en términos de la Villa de Cuilapa que linda por la parte del oriente con tierras del pueblo de Xoxocotlán de esta jurisdicción y por la parte del norte con unos cerros altos que son tierras realengas y por la del poniente con tierras del cacicazgo de Mecatepeque y Huihui que son dos barrios de la dicha Villa de Cuilapa y por la del sur con tierras patrimoniales del cacicazgo de Doña María de Mendoza cacique que fue de la dicha villa." AGN, Tierras, vol. 129, exp. 4, f. 19–20.

28. AGN, Tierras, vol. 129, exp. 4, f. 67.

29. The section that regulated land tenure in the *Recopilación de las leyes de los reinos de Indias* includes numerous edicts issued during the course of the sixteenth and seventeenth centuries instructing cabildos to divide lands but to leave Indian lands untouched. The fact that authorities reissued them on a regular basis reflects the difficulties in upholding these prescriptions. *Recopilación de leyes*, 118–122.

30. Joanne Rappaport and Tom Cummins, *Beyond the Lettered City: Indigenous Literacies in the Andes*, 169.

31. Rappaport and Cummins, *Beyond the Lettered City*, 167.

32. Helen Nader, *Liberty in Absolutist Spain: The Habsburg Sale of Towns, 1516–1700*; and Richard Kagan, *Lawsuits and Litigants in Castile, 1500–1700*.

33. Susan Crane, "Writing the Individual Back into Collective Memory," 1373–1377; and Pierre Nora, "Between Memory and History: Les Lieux de Mémoir," 9.

34. Yannakakis, "Witnesses, Spatial Practices," 173.

35. Brian Owensby, *Empire of Law*, 20.

36. Owensby, *Empire of Law*, 49–89.

37. AGN, Tierras, vol. 129, exp. 4, f. 1.

38. AGN, Tierras, vol. 129, exp. 4, f. 291.

39. AGN, Tierras, vol. 129, exp. 4, f. 293.

40. AGN, Tierras, vol. 129, exp. 4, f. 2.

41. AGN, Tierras, vol. 129, exp. 4, f. 81.

42. Ruíz's *traspaso*, a transfer of rights and responsibilities from one individual to another, on November 16, 1676, included the transfer cost (1,300 pesos) and the mortgage (*censo*) on the property and stipulated: "Antonio Rendón otorga que traspasa el dicho sitio y tierras de labor y casas en el edificadas con todas sus tierras, mercedes, pastos, aguas, y abrevaderos." The parties agreed to survey the property in the near future, noting "se obliga de entregarle un mandamiento [a Bartolomé Ruíz] para ajustar la medida del dicho sitio y estancia que se le despachó en virtud de los títulos," but no such document accompanied the docket. Ruíz did obtain the original merced awarded to Don Juan de Guzmán described in note 27 as well as subsequent transfer agreements, boundary surveys, and other related documents associated with the property. AGN, Tierras, vol. 129, exp. 4, f. 77–78.

43. The original reads "ha visto que sin embargo de dichos mojones ha sembrado cogiéndolos dentro el dicho Antonio Rendón y después el dicho Capitán Bartolomé Ruíz sin que sepa que los dichos Indios lo hayan hecho nunca ni contradicho sino es en esta ocasión." AGN, Tierras, vol. 129, exp. 4, f. 100.

44. AGEO, Alcaldías Mayores, leg. 48, exp. 10.

45. AGN, Tierras, vol. 129, exp. 4, f. 401.

46. "Don Félix de Mendoza, principal del dicho pueblo de Xoxocotlán, enemigo de mi parte y quien por dicha ocasión le movió dicho pleito persuadiendo a los demás naturales de dicho pueblo a ello con la mucha mano que tenía como principal y poderoso." AGN, Tierras, vol. 129, exp. 4, f. 129.

47. Owensby, *Empire of Law*, 62.

48. Yannakakis, *The Art of Being In-Between*, 165.

49. In the Valley of Oaxaca, eighteen cases—political disputes from 1582 to 1762; and land disputes, twelve cases from 1576 to 1814. See Taylor, *Landlord and Peasant*, 239.

50. AGN, Tierras, vol. 129, exp. 4, f. 415.

51. AGN, Tierras, vol. 129, exp. 4, f. 172.

52. In the AGN, examples of copies made in the Valley of Oaxaca include Map of Simatlán and Ocotlán (1636), AGN, no. 3009, Hospital de Jesús, leg. 85, exp. 4; Map of Ocotlán and Simatlán (1686), AGN, no. 3039, Hospital de Jesús, leg. 146, exp. 13, f. 33; Map of Hocot[l]án and Cimatlán (1734), AGN, no. 3018, Hospital de Jesús, leg. 102, exp. 33, f. 24; Map of Xoxocotlán (1686), AGN, no. 625, Tierras, vol. 129, exp. 4, f. 249; and Map of Santa María Guelaxé, San Gerónimo Tlacochaguaya and Santa Cruz Papalutla (1690 [1778]), AGN, no. 0956, Tierras, vol. 1206, exp. 1, cuad. 8, f. 21. At the Mapoteca Orozco y Berra, see Xoxocotlán, 1718, MOB no. 1176-OYB-7272-A; 1660 original lost; 1771 copy lost, but image available in Smith, *Picture Writing from Ancient Southern Mexico*, 338. For the Mixteca, see the Map of Guaytlatlauca, Tosatengo, Coaxochtla, Mimichtla, Tisacovaya, and Socontitlán (1609), AGN, no. 2500, Tierras, vol. 3619, exp. 4, f. 7; and its copy, the Map of Quatlatlauca and Socotitlán, made in 1709, AGN, no. 0663, Tierras, vol. 254, exp. 2, f. 24bis.

53. Barbara Mundy and Dana Leibsohn, "Of Copies, Casts, and Codices: Mexico on Display in 1892," 340.

54. Smith, *Picture Writing from Ancient Southern Mexico*, 37.

55. See, for instance, Marta Herrera, Santiago Muñoz, and Santiago Paredes, "Geographies of the Name: Naming Practices among the Muisca and Páez in the Audiencias of Santafé and Quito, Sixteenth and Seventeenth Centuries."

56. Mundy, *The Mapping of New Spain*, 175.

57. Though not mentioned on the map, the prominent size of each church and their positioning on the map suggest the original painting described the Villa of Oaxaca and Cuilapa, to which Xoxocotlán was subject.

58. Leibsohn, "Colony and Cartography," 273.

59. Frances Karttunen, in "After the Conquest: The Survival of Indigenous Patterns of Life and Belief," 242, argues that sacred

directions (east, north, west, south, and center) represented one of the most enduring aspects of pre-Hispanic culture during the colonial period. I find Louise Burkhart's assertion (*The Slippery Earth: Nahua-Christian Moral Dialogue in Sixteenth-Century Mexico*, 59–60) that the layout of native homes, "a microcosmic establishment of order, laid out to the four directions with the fire at the center of the house," reflected indigenous ideas of spatial ordering found on some maps.

60. J. B. Harley, "Deconstructing the Map," in *The New Nature of Maps*, 157.

61. Harley, "Deconstructing the Map," 163.

62. Exceptions to this rule include the Lienzo of Analco, the Lienzo of Tlaxcala, and the Lienzo of Quauhquechollan, all of which deal with the Spanish conquest. See Yanna Yannakakis, "Allies or Servants? The Journey of Indian Conquistadors in the Lienzo de Analco"; Travis Kranz, "Visual Persuasion: Sixteenth-Century Tlaxcalan Pictorials in Response to the Conquest of Mexico," in *The Conquest All Over Again: Nahuas and Zapotecs Thinking, Writing, and Painting Spanish Colonialism*, ed. Susan Schroeder; and Florine Asselbergs, *Conquered Conquistadors: The Lienzo de Quauhquechollan, A Nahua Vision of the Conquest of Guatemala*.

63. See Cummins, "From Lies to Truth: Colonial Ekphrasis and the Act of Crosscultural Translation," in *Reframing the Renaissance: Visual Culture in Europe and Latin America, 1450–1650*.

64. Yannakakis, "Witnesses, Spatial Practices," 176.

65. The original inscription reads: "Por orden del Capitan Don Antonio de Abellan . . . cupie [copié] este Mapa según su original que se me dio sin estrepar [estropear?] ni disminuir cosa alguna según se acostumbra en mi arte de la pintura." Map of Xoxocotlán (1686), AGN, no. 625.

66. Mundy, *The Mapping of New Spain*, 62.

67. AGN, Tierras, vol. 129, exp. 4, f. 176.

68. Cummins, "From Lies to Truth," 158.

69. Elizabeth Hill Boone, "Pictorial Documents and Visual Thinking in Postconquest Mexico," in *Native Traditions in the Postconquest World*, ed. Elizabeth Boone and Thomas Cummins, 149.

70. Yannakakis, "Witnesses, Spatial Practices," 166.

71. On this point, see Sousa and Terraciano, "The 'Original Conquest' of Oaxaca," 351.

72. Map of Xoxocotlán (1718), Mapoteca Orozco y Berra, MOB no. 1176-OYB-7272-A. Map of Xoxocotlán (1771), lost; image available in Smith, *Picture Writing from Ancient Southern Mexico*, 338.

73. Smith, *Picture Writing from Ancient Southern Mexico*, 202–210; Maarten Jansen, "Monte Albán y Zaachila en los códices mixtecos," in *The Shadow of Monte Alban: Politics and historiography in postclassic Oaxaca, Mexico*, ed. Maarten Jansen, Peter Kröfges, and Michel Oudijk; and Maarten Jansen, Dante García Ríos, Ángel Rivera Guzmán, "La identificación de Monte Albán en los códices Mixtecos: Nueva Evidencia." Enrique Méndez Martínez and Enrique Méndez Torres recently published the 1686 map with a transcription of the written glosses and a short passage of the court case between

Xoxocotlán and Bartolomé Ruíz. See *Historia de Zaachila, Cuilapan, y Xoxocotlan: Tres pueblos unidos por sus orígines*, 432–440.

74. Mary Elizabeth Smith has argued the written glosses do not necessarily reflect the glyph sign used in each case: *Picture Writing from Ancient Southern Mexico*, 204–210.

75. AGN, Tierras, vol. 129, exp. 4, f. 184.

76. Florescano, *Historia de las historias*, 241.

77. Yannakakis, "Witnesses, Spatial Practices," 166.

78. "Porque como nuevo trasunto supone la pintura del original antiguo que no se haya presentado, que cuando pudiera aprovechar a dichos naturales, de necesidad precisa se reúsa exhibir." AGN, Tierras, vol. 129, exp. 4, f. 184.

79. AGN, Tierras, vol. 129, exp. 4, f. 197.

80. The scribe recorded virtually the same response for thirty-eight-year-old Joseph de Santiago: "Por constarle de que tienen mapa pintura y títulos que los ha visto y oído leer"; as he did for Lucas de los Santos: "que sabe este testigo que los susodichos tienen mapa y títulos por haberlos visto y oídolos leer y que en ellos se incluye este pedazo de tierra." See AGN, Tierras, vol. 129, exp. 4, f. 210–211.

81. Sousa and Terraciano, "The 'Original Conquest' of Oaxaca," 351; and Yannakakis, "Witnesses, Spatial Practices," 164.

82. Miguel Aguilar-Robledo, "Contested Terrain: The Rise and Decline of Surveying in New Spain, 1500–1800."

83. "Se fue caminando de oriente a poniente como media legua de distancia de dicho pueblo a llegar a un paraje [de] tierras de sembrado de maíz que está en rastrojo en *donde dijeron así dichos naturales como el dicho* Cap. Bartolomé Ruíz ser donde estaban los árboles de ciruelas que se contenían en dicho Real *despacho de que se hallaban todavía las raíces patentes de dichos árboles*," AGN, Tierras, vol. 129, exp. 4, f. 213. Unless otherwise noted, use of italics reflects annotations from the original record.

84. The decree directed officials in New Spain "to designate and give agricultural land to all Indian towns from all the provinces of New Spain, not simply the 500 varas of land surrounding the town. The distance should be measured from the [town's] last house, not from the churches . . . and not only will it be the aforementioned 500 varas, but one hundred more to equal six hundred ['se dé y señale generalmente a los Pueblos de Indios de todas las provincias de Nueva España sus sementeras no solo las 500 varas de tierra del rededor de la Población y que estas sean medidas no desde las iglesias, sino de la última casa . . . y que no solo sean las referidas 500 varas sino 100 más a cumplimiento de 600']." Authorities intended the royal decree to curb Spanish encroachment of Indian lands: "Se van entrando los dueños de estancia y tienen la de los indios quitándoselas y apoderándose de ellas unas veces violentamente, y otras con fraude, por cuya razón los miserables indios dejan sus casas y pueblos (que es lo que apetecen)," AGEO, Alcaldías Mayores, leg. 62, exp. 12, 1687.

85. "*Por lo que ha visto y reconocido dicho señor alcalde mayor halla que no tan solamente tiene dicho pueblo las 600 varas de ordenanza*

y nueva Real cédula sino que le sobran 918 varas y media hasta dichos mojones.” AGN, vol. 129, exp. 4, f. 215.

86. Tamar Herzog, “Colonial Law and ‘Native Customs’: Indigenous Land Rights in Colonial Spanish America,” 315.

CHAPTER 2

1. Map of Ystepeq and Zixitlan (1598), AGN, no. 2084, Tierras, vol. 2764, exp. 22, f. 302.

2. George Vaillant, “A Correlation of Archeological and Historical Sequences in the Valley of Mexico”; H. B. Nicholson, “The Mixteca-Puebla Concept in Mesoamerican Archeology: A Re-examination,” in *Men and Cultures: Selected Papers from the Fifth International Congress of Anthropological and Ethnological Sciences*, ed. Anthony F. C. Wallace; and “The Mixteca-Puebla Concept Re-visited,” in *The Art and Iconography of Late Post-Classic Central Mexico*, ed. Elizabeth H. Boone.

3. Córdova, *Vocabulario en lengua zapoteca*, 183v, 252v–253.

4. Alvarado, *Vocabulario en lengua mixteca*, 102v, 142v.

5. Lockhart, *The Nahuas*; Terraciano, *The Mixtecs*; and Matthew Restall, “A History of the New Philology and the New Philology in History.”

6. Reyes, *Arte en lengua mixteca*, 11.

7. Alonso de Molina, *Vocabulario en lengua castellana y mexicana*, 120.

8. Luis Reyes García, ed., *¿Cómo te confundes? ¿Acaso no somos conquistados? Anales de Juan Bautista*.

9. Robertson suggests Ixtlilxochitl may have drawn his insight about this connection from the *Codex Xolotl*, an early-sixteenth-century pictorial history; *Mexican Manuscript Painting*, 13.

10. Robertson, *Mexican Manuscript Painting*, 13. For a recent analysis of native manuscript production in the Texcoco region, see Eduardo de J. Douglas, *In the Palace of Nezahualcoyotl: Painting Manuscripts, Writing the Pre-Hispanic Past in Early Colonial Period Tetzcoco, Mexico*.

11. See, for instance, Jeanette Favrot Peterson, *Paradise Murals of Malinalco: Utopia and Empire in Sixteenth-Century Mexico*.

12. Map of Aztatla (1576), AGN, no. 1578, Tierras, vol. 2679, exp. 15, f. 15; and Map of Nochistlán (1602), AGN, no. 1082, Tierras, vol. 1520, exp. 2, f. 57.

13. Useful works to understand the role of painters include Robertson, *Mexican Manuscript Painting*, 25–58; Dana Leibsohn, “Colony and Cartography”; Mundy, *The Mapping of New Spain*, 61–89; and Carmen Arellano Hoffmann, “El escriba mesoamericano y sus utensilios de trabajo,” 220–234. For a more recent study that uses indigenous maps from the Archivo General de la Nación, see Ana Pulido Rull, “Land Grant Painted Maps: Native Artists and the Power of Visual Persuasion in Colonial New Spain.”

14. Lockhart, *The Nahuas*, 94.

15. See Lockhart, “Encomienda and Hacienda.”

16. See AGN Indios, vol. 36, exp. 444; Indios, vol. 36, exp. 299; and Indios, vol. 41, exp. 63.

17. Judith Francis Zeitlin, “Ranchers and Indians on the Southern Isthmus of Tehuantepec: Economic Change and Indigenous Survival in Colonial Mexico,” 52–53.

18. Map of Santo Domingo Tepenene (1617), AGN, no. 2225, Tierras, vol. 2812, exp. 11, f. 312.

19. Map of Santo Domingo Tepenene (1617), AGN, no. 2225.

20. My views here take a cue from Oscar Martínez, *Border People: Life and Society in the U.S.-Mexico Borderlands*, 20.

21. Alida Metcalf, *Go-Betweens and the Colonization of Brazil, 1500–1600*, 9–10.

22. Robertson, *Mexican Manuscript Painting*, 40.

23. Map of Teozacoalco and Relación of Teozacoalco and Amoltepeque (1580), Benson Latin American Collection (BLAC), Folder XXV-3.

24. Mundy, *The Mapping of New Spain*, 159.

25. Relación of Teozacoalco, BLAC, Folder XXV-3.

26. Serge Gruzinski, *Man-Gods in the Mexican Highlands: Indian Power and Colonial Society, 1550–1580*, trans. Eileen Corrigan, 34–36.

27. Map of Mystequilla and Tegoantepec (1573), AGN, no. 2378, Tierras, vol. 3343, exp. 4, f. 43v and 44; Map of Tzanaltepec, Tonaltepec, and Oztutlan (1580), AGN, no. 1903, Tierras, vol. 2729, exp. 4, f. 107v y 108; Relación Geográfica Map of Tehuantepec (1580), BLAC; Map of Tlapanatepec (1583), AGN, no. 1964, Tierras, vol. 2737, exp. 25, f. 8; Map of Tlapanaltepeque (1585), AGN, no. 2391, Tierras, vol. 3343, exp. 20, f. 8; Map of Tlapa[na]tepeque (1586), AGN, no. 1965, Tierras, vol. 2737, exp. 25, f. 29; and Map of Ystepeq and Zixitlan (1598), AGN, no. 2084, Tierras, vol. 2764, exp. 22, f. 302.

28. See Zeitlin, “Ranchers and Indians”; and Lolita Gutiérrez Brockington, *The Leverage of Labor: Managing the Cortés Haciendas in Tehuantepec, 1588–1688*.

29. Zeitlin, “Ranchers and Indians,” 51.

30. Zeitlin, “Ranchers and Indians,” 49–50.

31. Map of Mystequilla and Tegoantepec (1573), AGN, no. 2378.

32. Elinor Melville, *A Plague of Sheep: Environmental Consequences of the Conquest of Mexico*.

33. Relación Geográfica Map of Tehuantepec (1580), BLAC.

34. Brockington, *The Leverage of Labor*, 13–17; Gerhard, *A Guide to the Historical Geography of New Spain*, 266.

35. Zeitlin, “Ranchers and Indians,” 47.

36. Map of Tzanaltepec, Tonaltepec, and Oztutlan (1580), AGN, no. 1903.

37. Map of Tlapanaltepeque (1585), AGN, no. 2391; and Map of Tlapa[na]tepeque (1586), AGN, no. 1965.

38. Mundy, *The Mapping of New Spain*, 201.

39. Georges Baudot, *Utopia and History in Mexico: The First Chroniclers of Mexican Civilization (1520–1569)*, trans. Bernard R. Ortiz de Montellano and Thelma Ortiz de Montellano.

40. Inga Clendinnen, *Ambivalent Conquests: Maya and Spaniard in Yucatan, 1517–1570*; and Fernando Cervantes, *The Devil in the New World: The Impact of Diabolism in New Spain*.

41. Sarah Cline, "The Spiritual Conquest Reexamined: Baptism and Christian Marriage in Early Sixteenth-Century Mexico," 478.

42. Terraciano, *The Mixtecs*, 277.

43. The neighboring school of San José de los Naturales focused on such crafts and technical skills as carpentry, shoemaking, sculpting, and painting. Robertson, *Mexican Manuscript Painting*, 42–45; Gibson, *The Aztecs*, 382.

44. Terraciano, *The Mixtecs*, 15.

45. Mundy, *The Mapping of New Spain*, 77.

46. Burgoa, *Geográfica descripción*, 13.

47. See entries for the years 1564 and 1565 that list religious work registered to indigenous painters: Luis Reyes García, ed., *Anales de Juan Bautista*.

48. Serge Gruzinski, *Images at War: Mexico from Columbus to Blade Runner (1492–2019)*, trans. Heather MacLean, 34–48.

49. See Samuel Edgerton, *Theatres of Conversion: Religious Architecture and Indian Artisans in Colonial Mexico*; and Jaime Lara, *City, Temple, Stage: Eschatological Architecture and Liturgical Theatrics in New Spain*.

50. For a detailed study of Dominican architecture, see Robert Mullen, *Dominican Architecture in Sixteenth-Century Oaxaca*. For the Dominican presence in Oaxaca, see Daniel Ulloa, *Los predicadores divididos (Los dominicos en Nueva España, siglo XVI)*.

51. *Manuscritos del Concilio Tercero Provincial Mexicano (1585)*, vol. 1–2, ed. Alberto Carrillo Cázares.

52. Russo, *The Untranslatable Image: A Mestizo History of the Arts in New Spain, 1500–1600*, 7.

53. Map of San Miguel Cuestlavaca (1582), AGN, no. 1609, Tierras, vol. 2682, exp. 9, f. 8.

54. Gruzinski, *Images at War*; Edgerton, *Theatres of Conversion*; and Kelly Donahue-Wallace, "Picturing Prints in Early Modern New Spain."

55. Ellen Taylor Baird, "The Artists of Sahagún's *Primeros Memoriales*: A Question of Identity," in *Work of Bernardino de Sahagún: Pioneer Ethnographer of Sixteenth-Century Aztec Mexico*, ed. Jorge Klor de Alva, H. B. Nicholson, and Eloise Quiñones Keber, 212.

56. James C. Scott, *Domination and the Arts of Resistance: Hidden Transcripts*, 138.

57. Nancy Farriss, *Maya Society under Colonial Rule: The Collective Enterprise of Survival*, 99.

58. Map of Guaxilotitlan (1586), AGN, no. 1726, Tierras, vol. 2702, exp. 2, f. 10.

59. Map of Santo Domingo Tepenene and Couayxtlabaca (1590), AGN, no. 1904, Tierras, vol. 2729, exp. 5, f. 117.

60. Smith, *Picture Writing*, 184.

61. Map of Tepenene (1600), AGN, no. 1812, Tierras, vol. 2719, exp. 23, f. 9.

62. Eleanor Wake, "The Dawning of Places: Celestially Defined Land Maps, *Títulos Primordiales*, and Indigenous Statements of Territorial Possession in Early Colonial Mexico," in *Indigenous Intellectuals: Knowledge, Power, and Colonial Culture in Mexico and the Andes*, ed. Gabriela Ramos and Yanna Yannakakis, 203.

63. Wake, "The Dawning of Places," 214.

64. Reinvention through reproduction in many ways characterizes the history and historiography of visual culture, especially indigenous pictorial documents, in New Spain. See Clara Bargellini, "Originality and Invention in the Painting of New Spain," in *Painting a New World: Mexican Art and Life, 1521–1821*; Mundy and Leibsohn, "Of Copies, Casts, and Codices"; Baird, "The Artists," 222–226; and Robertson, *Mexican Manuscript Painting*, 107, 112, 130, 132, 150, 185–186.

65. AGN, Indiferente Virreinal, Civil, exp. 23, n. p.

66. AGN, Indiferente Virreinal, Civil, exp. 23, f. 4.

67. Yannakakis, "Witnesses, Spatial Practices," 164.

68. Map of San Andrés Tlacozahuala (1704), AGN, no. 0658, Tierras, vol. 220, 1a. pte., exp. 1, f. 277. For capellanías, see Gisela von Wobeser, "La función social y económica de las capellanías de misas en la Nueva España del siglo XVIII"; and Candelaria Castro Pérez, Mercedes Calvo Cruz, and Sonia Granado Suárez, "Las capellanías en los siglos XVII-XVIII a través del estudio de escritura de fundación."

69. Map of San Andrés Sinaxtla (1704), AGN, no. 0670, Tierras, vol. 308, exp. 4, f. 29.

70. Map of San Pablo Mitla (1730), AGN, no. 0719, Tierras, vol. 489, 1a. parte, exp. 1, f. 271.

71. Richard Kagan, *Urban Images of the Hispanic World, 1493–1793*, 45–70.

72. Aguilar-Robledo, "Contested Terrain," 30.

73. See edict issued by Viceroy Gaspar de la Cerda Sandoval Silva y Mendoza, Conde de Galve, in the late seventeenth century, *Orden para la correspondencia de pesos, varas, medidas*; and Cecilio Robelo, *Diccionario de pesas y medidas mexicanas, antiguas y modernas y de su conversión. Para uso de los comerciantes y las familias*. See also Manuel Carrera Stampa, *El sistema de pesas y medidas colonial*; and Marcos Matías Alonso, *Medidas indígenas de longitud, en documentos de la Ciudad de México del siglo XVI*.

74. Nuria Valverde and Antonio Lafuente, "Space Production and Spanish Imperial Geopolitics," in *Science in the Spanish and Portuguese Empires, 1500–1800*, ed. Daniela Bleichmar, Paula de Vos, and Christine Huffine, 199.

75. Map of Santa María Guelaxé, San Gerónimo Tlacochaguaya, and Santa Cruz Papalutla (1690 [1778]), AGN, no. 0956, Tierras, vol. 1206, exp. 1, cuad. 8, f. 21.

CHAPTER 3

1. Transcription in María Teresa Sepúlveda y Herrera, *Procesos por idolatría al cacique, gobernadores y sacerdotes de Yanhuitlán, 1544–1546*, 170; original in AGN, Inquisición, vol. 37, exp. 7, f. 167.

2. For examples of this practice in other parts of Mesoamerica, see Few, *For All of Humanity: Mesoamerican and Colonial Medicine in Enlightenment Guatemala*, ch. 1.

3. Terraciano, *The Mixtecs*, 17.

4. Bernardino de Sahagún, *Historia general de las cosas de Nueva España*, vol. 3, ed. Ángel María Garibay, 115 (hereafter cited as *HGNE*).

5. Gabriela Ramos and Yanna Yannakakis, "Introduction," in *Indigenous Intellectuals*, 2.

6. See Simon Varey, *The Mexican Treasury: The Writings of Dr. Francisco Hernández*; Simon Varey, Rafael Chabrán, and Dora B. Weiner, *Searching for the Secrets of Nature: The Life and Works of Dr. Francisco Hernández*; Martín de la Cruz, *The Badianus Manuscript (Codex Barberini, Latin 241) Vatican Library: An Aztec Herbal of 1552*, ed. Emily Walcott Emmart; José María López Piñero and José Pardo Tomás, *La influencia de Francisco Hernández (1515–1587) en la constitución de la botánica y la materia médica modernas*; and Diana Magaloni, "Painters of the New World: The Process of Making the *Florentine Codex*," and *The Colors of the New World*.

7. Patrizia Granziera, "Huaxtepec: The Sacred Garden of an Aztec Emperor," and "Concept of the Garden in Pre-Hispanic Mexico." Also see William Dunmire, *Gardens of New Spain: How Mediterranean Plants and Foods Changed America*.

8. See Ryan Kashanipour, "A World of Cures: Magic and Medicine in Colonial Yucatán."

9. See Gerhard Wolf, Joseph Connors, and Louis Waldman, eds., *Colors Between Two Worlds: The Florentine Codex of Bernardino de Sahagún*; Ursula Klein and E. C. Spary, eds., *Materials and Expertise in Early Modern Europe: Between Market and Laboratory*; Daniela Bleichmar, Paula de Vos, and Christine Huffine, eds., *Science in the Spanish and Portuguese Empires, 1500–1800*; Paula de Vos, "Natural History and the Pursuit of Empire in Eighteenth-Century Spain," and "The Science of Spices: Empiricism and Economic Botany in the Early Spanish Empire"; Antonio Barrera-Osorio, *Experiencing Nature: The Spanish American Empire and the Early Scientific Revolution*; Gabriela Siracusano, *El poder de los colores: De lo material a lo simbólico en las prácticas culturales andinas, Siglos XVI–XVIII*; Pamela H. Smith and Paula Findlen, eds., *Merchants and Marvels: Commerce, Science, and Art in Early Modern Europe*; and Pamela O. Long, *Openness, Secrecy, Authorship: Technical Arts and the Culture of Knowledge from Antiquity to the Renaissance*.

10. Gruzinski, "Colonial Indian Maps," 51–52.

11. "Painting of one color," Alvarado, *Vocabulario en lengua mixteca*, 168.

12. He noted in his *Vocabulario de la lengua mexicana* that monochromatic paintings were known as *çancecni ycac tlacuilolli* and *çancecnic tlachia tlacuilolli* which he translated from the Spanish as "painting of a single color," 96.

13. "El *tetlilli* o piedra negra es una tierra que se extrae principalmente en la región llamada de las Mixtecas, de esta Nueva España, y que usan a veces los pintores para dar dicho color," Hernández, *Historia natural de Nueva España*, vol. 2, in *Obras completas*, vol. 3, 409 (hereafter cited as *HNNE 2*).

14. See Jorge Cañizares-Esguerra's treatment of Hernández in *How to Write the History of the New World: Histories, Epistemologies, and Identities in the Eighteenth-Century Atlantic World*, 63–64, 357, f. 10.

15. "An Epistle to Arias Montano," in Varey, *The Mexican Treasury*, 262.

16. "An Epistle to Arias Montano," in Varey, *The Mexican Treasury*, 263.

17. About sixty of these paintings survive in the *Codex Pomar*. José María López Piñero, *El Códice Pomar (ca. 1590): El interés de Felipe II por la historia natural y la expedición Hernández a América*; and Varey, *The Mexican Treasury*, 4.

18. "An Epistle to Arias Montano," in Varey, *The Mexican Treasury*, 262–263.

19. *HNNE 2*, 408–409.

20. "Hacen estos naturales tinta del humo de las teas, y es tinta bien fina; llámanla *tlilliocotl*; tiene para hacerla unos vasos que llaman *tlicomalli*, que son a manera de alquitaras; vale por muchas tintas para escribir." *HGNE*, 343.

21. Map of Mistepec, Chicaguastla, and Coquila (1595), AGN, no. 0867, Tierras, vol. 876, exp. 1, f. 122.

22. Gerhard, *A Guide*, 288.

23. Granziera, "Huaxtepec."

24. "Su naturaleza es muy astringente y algo cálida. Se prepara con él una tinta muy buena," *HNNE 2*, 65–66.

25. Bernard Ortiz de Montellano, "Empirical Aztec Medicine."

26. Noemí Quezada, "The Inquisition's Repression of *Curanderos*," in *Cultural Encounters: The Impact of the Inquisition in Spain and the New World*, ed. Mary Elizabeth Perry and Anne J. Cruz.

27. *HGNE*, 353, 356–357. Also see Martha Few, "Indian Autopsy and Epidemic Disease in Early Colonial Mexico," in *Invasion and Transformation: Interdisciplinary Perspectives on the Conquest of Mexico*, ed. Rebecca Brienen and Margaret Jackson; and Diana Magaloni Kerpel, "Painters of the New World," 49–52.

28. Map of Coquila (1599), AGN, no. 2463, Tierras, vol. 3556, exp. 6, f. 175. Coquila (Santa María Cuquila) was a small head town known as a *cabecera* in the Tlaxiaco region of the Mixteca Alta with a rich pictorial tradition. Other native maps from the Cuquila region include the Map of Tlaxiaco and Cuquila, 1588, AGN, no. 1692.9, Tierras, vol. 2692, exp. 17, f. 8; Map of Tlaxiaco, Cuquila, and Mistepec, 1595, AGN, no. 1614, Tierras, vol. 2682, exp. 17, f. 18; and Map of Mistepec, Chicaguastla, and Coquila, 1595, AGN, no. 0867, Tierras, vol. 876, exp. 1, f. 122.

29. The Codices Bodley, Nutall, Selden, Colombino, Yanhuitlán, the Lienzo de Zacatepec, and the Map of Teozacoalco (1588) all share this pattern in association with imperial buildings, temples, and place-names. Detailed studies on each of these manuscripts can be found in *The Codex Nuttall: A Picture Manuscript from Ancient Mexico*, ed. Zelia Nuttall; *Interpretación del Códice Bodley 2858*, ed. Alfonso Caso; *Interpretación del Códice Selden*, ed. Alfonso Caso; Alfonso Caso, "El mapa de Teozacoalco," in *Obras: El México antiguo*, vol. 8; *Códice Colombino: Interpretación del Códice Colombino por Alfonso Caso*. *Las glosas del Códice Colombino por Mary Elizabeth Smith*; and *Códice*

Yanhuitlán, ed. Wigberto Jiménez Moreno and Salvador Mateos Higuera. For the Lienzo de Zacatepec, see Smith, *Picture Writing from Ancient Mexico*, 89–121, 264, 266–290.

30. James Kiracofe, "Architectural Fusion and Indigenous Ideology in Early Colonial Teposcolula: La Casa de la Cacica: A Building at the Edge of Oblivion"; and Terraciano, *The Mixtecs*, 160.

31. Ursula Klein and E. C. Spary, "Introduction: Why Materials?," in *Materials and Expertise*, 1.

32. *HGNE*, 342–343.

33. *HGNE*, 343.

34. Maximino Martínez, *Catálogo de nombres vulgares y científicos de plantas mexicanas*, 354.

35. "Hasta de tintas negras, así para teñir, como para escribir, ha dado Dios minerales en acuestas partes. . . . En acuesta sierra de Zacapulas, junto al pueblo de Cuzal, está un mineral de tierra negra, que solo con que se desborote en agua, se hace una tinta muy negra para escribir. Aunque es menester echarle goma, porque sola se borra como es tierra." Francisco Ximénez, *Historia natural del Reino de Guatemala compuesta por el reverendo padre predicador general fray Francisco Ximénez, de la orden de predicadores escrita en el pueblo de Sacapulas en el año de 1722*, 343. My thanks to Kevin Gosner for pointing me to this source.

36. Map of Santa Ana and Santa Cruz (1591), AGN, no. 0581, Tierras, vol. 56, exp. 5, f. 16.

37. Sylvia Sellers-García traces documents' lives, arguing that the composite nature of records helped mitigate the distance that separated Spain from its overseas territories; see *Documents and Distance at the Spanish Empire's Periphery*. In the case of the map of Coquila (AGN no. 2463), besides the painter's tracings of the landscape, at least two different hands are discernable from observation of the annotated text.

38. Elisabeth Butzer, "The Roadside Inn or 'Venta': Origins and Early Development in New Spain," 12, note 1.

39. Paula de Vos, "Apothecaries, Artists, and Artisans: Early Industrial Material Culture in the Biological Old Regime."

40. See Antonio Mut Calafell's exhaustive catalog of Iberian formulas collected from print and manuscript sources: "Fórmulas españolas de la tinta caligráfica negra de los siglos XIII a XIX y otras relacionadas con la tinta (reavivar escritos, contra las manchas y goma glasa)," in *El papel y las tintas en la transmisión de la información*.

41. Andrés Flórez, *Doctrina christiana del ermitaño y el niño*, in Mut, "Fórmulas españolas," 160. Another edition of this work was printed in Valladolid in 1552; see José Antonio González Salgado, "Contribución al estudio de la ortografía en el siglo XVI: La reforma del padre Flórez."

42. Diego Bueno, *Arte nuevo de enseñar a leer, escribir, y contar príncipes y señores*, 26, in Mut, "Fórmulas españolas," 165.

43. The original text reads: "De la [tierra] negra sé decir, que me enviaron un poco para que de ella hiciese tinta, la cual echada en agua, o vino se hace de ella muy buena tinta, con que se escribe muy bien, y es algo azul que la hace de mejor gracia." Nicolás Monardes,

Primera y segunda y tercera parte de la historia medicinal de las cosas que se traen de nuestras Indias occidentales que sirven en medicina, 115v, Library of Congress, Rare Books and Special Collections (hereafter LCRB).

44. José María López Piñero, "Las 'Nuevas Medicinas' Americanas en la Obra (1565–1574) de Nicolás Monardes."

45. Juan de Icíar, "Recepta de tinta para papel," in *Arte sutilísima, por la cual se enseña a escribir perfectamente*.

46. "Luego se pondrá una caldera grande, a buena lumbre, y se echará en ella la vasija donde están las agallas y cocerá una hora." Ignacio Pérez, *Arte de escribir*, in Mut, "Fórmulas españolas," 161.

47. Icíar, "Recepta de tinta para papel."

48. "Yo he hecho experiencia con muchas recetas que andan escritas y con ninguna he hallado tan buen efe[c]to como con ésta." José de Casanova, *Primera parte del arte de escribir todas formas de letras*, 10.

49. "Sirve la tinta con que escribimos, a las llagas llenas de corrupción, y a las quemaduras del fuego: sobre las cuales debe aplicarse espesa con agua, y dejarse hasta que las dichas llagas se encoren." Andrés Laguna, *Pedacio Dioscorides Anazarbeo, acerca de la materia medicinal, y de los venenos mortíferos*, 568.

50. Johns, "Ink," 108.

51. Joseph Moxon, *Mechanic Exercises, or, the Doctrine of Handy-Works*, 77–79, LCRB.

52. Moxon, *Mechanic Exercises*, 75.

53. Johns, "Ink," 108.

54. Inventory of Juan de Junta, originally in Archivo Histórico Provincial de Burgos, no. 5542 (1557), f. 100–134v, transcribed in William Pettas, "A Sixteenth-Century Spanish Bookstore: The Inventory of Juan de Junta."

55. Pettas, "A Sixteenth-Century Spanish Bookstore," 8.

56. Robert Pask, "Advertisement," Early English Books Online, Record No. E4:2[18b], original in British Library.

57. Marta Straznicky, "Introduction: What Is a Stationer?," in *Shakespeare's Stationers: Studies in Cultural Bibliography*, ed. Marta Straznicky; and Harold Love, *The Culture and Commerce of Texts: Scribal Publication in Seventeenth-Century England*.

58. Klein and Spary, "Introduction," 5.

59. See José Torre Revello, "Algunos libros de caligrafía usados en México en el siglo XVII."

60. Map of Teutitlán (1583), AGN, no. 0560, Tierras, vol. 35, exp. 7, f. 11.

61. Map of Santo Domingo Tepenene (1617), AGN, no. 2225, Tierras, vol. 2812, exp. 11, f. 312.

62. Size led one nineteenth-century cataloger to file the map simply as *enorme*, or "huge," a description still used today in its current home in the Nettie Lee Benson Latin American Collection, University of Texas at Austin.

63. Caso, "El mapa de Teozacoalco," 149.

64. Fernando Martínez Cortés, *Pegamentos, gomas y resinas en el México prehispánico*, 15.

65. Martínez Cortés notes that, even though Hernández refers to roots (*raíces*), the parts of the plants used to make the binder are the pseudobulbs; *Pegamentos*, 18.

66. "La raíz es fría, húmeda y glutinosa; se prepara con ella un gluten excelente y muy tenaz que usan los indios, y principalmente los pintores, para adherir más firmemente los colores de suerte que no se borren fácilmente las figuras." Francisco Hernández, *Historia natural de Nueva España*, vol. 1, in *Obras Completas*, vol. 2, 118 (hereafter cited as *HNNE* 1).

67. Gerhard, *A Guide*, 275–277.

68. In response to the questionnaire, Spanish officials in New Spain often assigned this task to native painters. Cervantes, in fact, commissioned a second map from another painter that portrayed the nearby town of Amoltepeque, a subject considered in detail in chapter 4; and Mundy, *The Mapping of New Spain*, 61–62.

69. Ulinka Rublack, "Matter in the Material Renaissance," 84.

70. Rublack, "Matter," 44.

71. "Y así mismo algunas historias pintadas, en papel de cortezas de árboles, y pieles curtidas." Burgoa, *Geográfica descripción*, 134.

72. Alvarado, *Vocabulario en lengua mixteca*.

73. Alvarado, *Vocabulario en lengua mixteca*, 161.

74. Sahagún, *Historia general de las cosas de la Nueva España*, vol. 2, ed. Juan Carlos Temprano (hereafter cited as *HGNE*, 90), 967.

75. "Se cortan sólo las ramas gruesas de los árboles, dejando los renuevos; se maceran con agua y se dejan remojar durante la noche en los arroyos o ríos. Al día siguiente se les arranca la corteza, y, después de limpiarla de la cutícula exterior, se extiende a golpes con una piedra plana pero surcada de algunas estrías, y que se sujeta con una vara de mimbre sin pulir doblada en círculo a manera de mango. Cede aquella madera flexible; se corta luego en trozos que, golpeados de nuevo con otra piedra más plana, se unen fácilmente entre sí y se alisan; se dividen por último en hojas de dos palmos de largo y un palmo y medio aproximadamente de ancho, que imitan nuestro papel más grueso y corriente, pero son más compactas y más blancas, aunque muy inferiores a nuestro papel más terso." Hernández, *HNNE* 1, 183–184. One *palmo*, a unit associated with the distance from the thumb to the little finger, measured roughly 20.95cm.

76. *HGNE*, 143.

77. The AGN describes this pictorial record as a codex and uses the original spelling of the town. Códice de Tecomastlabaca, 1578, AGN, no. 1692.8, Tierras, vol. 2692, exp. 16, f. 24.

78. Sebastián van Doesburg, "Documentos pictográficos de la Mixteca Baja."

79. Arellano Hoffmann, "El escriba mesoamericano," 239.

80. *HNNE* 1, 348.

81. Barbara Mundy, "Pictography, Writing, and Mapping in the Valley of Mexico and the Beinecke Map," in *Painting a Map of Sixteenth-Century Mexico City: Land, Writing, and Native Rule*, ed. Mary Miller and Barbara Mundy, 40.

82. Hernández noted: "[El papel] es propio para envolturas y muy adecuado y útil entre estos indios occidentales para celebrar las fiestas de los dioses, confeccionar las vestiduras sagradas, y para adornos funerarios." *HNNE* 1, 83.

83. Códice de Teguantepeque, c. sixteenth century, AGN, no. 3122, Hospital de Jesús, leg. 450, exp. 1, f. 3; and *Codex Mendoza*, ed. Frances Berdan and Patricia Anawalt. For paper in a ritual context, see Philip Arnold, "Paper Ties to Land: Indigenous and Colonial Material Orientations to the Valley of Mexico"; and Franke Neumann, "Paper: A Sacred Material in Aztec Ritual."

84. On indigenous toponyms associated with paper or papermaking activities, see Arellano Hoffmann, "El escriba mesoamericano," 238–239.

85. "Contra Nicolás de la Cruz y socios de San Francisco Cajonos por idolatría," Archivo del Juzgado de Villa Alta, Oaxaca, Mexico. Cited in Hans Lenz, "Paper and Superstitions."

86. Long, *Openness, Secrecy, Authorship*, 5.

87. Bodil Christensen, "Bark Paper and Witchcraft in Indian Mexico"; and Lenz, "Paper and Superstitions."

88. Karl Mayer, "Cover: Amate Manuscripts of the Otomí of San Pablito, Puebla."

89. Mayer, "Cover," 130.

90. Arnold, "Paper Ties," 28.

91. For detailed studies of these codices, see *Interpretación del Códice Bodley 2858*; *Interpretación del Códice Selden 3135 (A.2)*; and *Codex Fejérváry-Mayer: M 12014 City of Liverpool Museums*, ed. C. A. Burland, *Codices selecti*, vol. 26.

92. Terraciano, *The Mixtecs*, 16.

93. Alvarado, *Vocabulario en lengua mixteca*, 59, 166.

94. Joyce Marcus, *Mesoamerican Writing Systems: Propaganda, Myth, and History in Four Ancient Civilizations*, 60.

95. Córdova, *Vocabulario en lengua çapoteca*, 101–102.

96. *HGNE*, 90, 966.

97. "El año de setenta, o por allí cerca, me certificaron dos religiosos dignos de fe que vieron en Oaxaca, que dista de esta ciudad sesenta leguas hacia el oriente, que vieron unas pinturas muy antiguas, pintadas en pellejos de venados, en las cuales se contenían muchas cosas que aludían a la predicación del Evangelio." *HGNE*, 90, 1061.

98. Anna More, *Baroque Sovereignty: Carlos de Sigüenza y Góngora and the Creole Archive of Colonial Mexico*, 69–90.

99. *Los códices de México*, 54.

100. See *Códices cuicatecos Porfirio Díaz y Fernández Leal: edición facsimilar, contexto histórico e interpretación*, ed. Sebastián van Doesburg; *Códice Baranda*, ed. René Acuña; *Códice Dehesa, largo: 5 metros 20 centímetros; ancho: 17 centímetros; pintado por ambos lados; existente en el Museo Nacional de México*; and Ana G. Díaz Álvarez, "El *Códice Dehesa*: Reflexiones en torno a un documento mixteco colonial a partir de su análisis codicológico."

101. María Cristina Sánchez Bueno de Bonfil, *El papel del papel en la Nueva España*, 18.

102. Sylvia Rogers Albro and Thomas Albro define the *reçute* ("small") size of paper according to a Bolognese papermaker's stone

from which Spain acquired paper; it measured 31.8 × 43.6 centimeters. See their "The Examination and Conservation Treatment of the Library of Congress Harkness 1531 Huejotzingo Codex," 99 and 106. Emma Rivas Mata notes that the basic sheet of paper known as *in plano* measured 32 × 44 centimeters. See "Impresores y mercaderes de libros en la ciudad de México, siglo XVII," in *Del autor al lector: Libros y libreros en la historia*, ed. Carmen Castañeda, 95, n. 63.

103. José Piedra, "The Value of Paper," 102.

104. Juan de Zumárraga to Charles V, May 6, 1538, in *Cartas de Indias*, 786, University of Arizona Special Collections.

105. The decree of 1638 required the use of paper bearing the royal seal for official use and prohibited its production to anyone without a license. Lenz, *Historia del papel*, 89.

106. "Para que por 20 años use la exclusiva de cierto modo para la fabricación de papel en esta Nueva España," June 8, 1575; duplicate in AGN, Reales Cédulas Duplicadas, vol. 1, exp. 18; transcription in Sánchez Bueno de Bonfil, *El papel del papel*, 51–53.

107. The passage reads: "Hallose algunos años después, en este pueblo, después de bautizados, y que habían aprendido algunos a escribir, un libro de mano escrito en buen papel, con historias en su lengua como las del Génesis, empezando por la creación del mundo, y vidas de sus mayores como la de los patriarcas . . . y este libro fue tan secreto su autor, que no se pudo descubrir ni rastrear, diciendo el que lo tenía que lo había heredado, y lo peor fue, que guardado en la caja del depósito, debajo de dos llaves se desapareció, como si fuera de humo." Burgoa, *Geográfica descripción*, 135–136.

108. Map of Tepozcolula, 1590, AGN, no. 1711, Tierras, vol. 2696, exp. 21, f. 8.

109. In the region of Hidalgo, see Map of Tlilcuauhtla (1599), AGN, no. 589, Tierras, vol. 64, exp. 1, f. 21; and Map of Santa María Nativitas and San Antonio (1603), AGN, no. 646, Tierras, vol. 183, exp. 2, f. 190. For the Michoacán region, see Map of San Juan Tendecutiro (1593), AGN, no. 1040, Tierras, vol. 1465, exp. 1, f. 64. For a study of the *traza* and urban design, see Kagan, *Urban Images*. Matthew Restall examines the spread of Renaissance ideas in Spanish America, including Vitruvian principles of design that guided the layout of cities, in "The Renaissance World from the West: Spanish America and the 'Real' Renaissance," in *A Companion to the Worlds of the Renaissance*, ed. Guido Ruggiero.

110. Kirsten Weld, *Paper Cadavers: The Archives of Dictatorship in Guatemala*, 5–6.

111. The series has produced four volumes published by the University of Chicago Press from 1987 to 2015, one of them a three-volume series on non-Western societies, another a two-part series on the Renaissance. See *The History of Cartography*, vol. 1, "Cartography in Prehistoric, Ancient, and Medieval Europe and the Mediterranean," ed. J. B. Harley and David Woodward (1987); *The History of Cartography*, vol. 2, book 1, "Cartography in the Traditional Islamic and South Asian Societies," ed. Harley and Woodward (1992); *The History of Cartography*, vol. 2, book 2, "Cartography in the Traditional East and Southeast Asian Societies," ed. Harley and Woodward

(1994); *The History of Cartography*, vol. 2, book 3, "Cartographic in the Traditional African, American, Artic, Australian, and Pacific Societies," ed. Woodward and G. Malcolm Lewis (1998); *The History of Cartography*, vol. 3, "Cartography in the European Renaissance," part 1, ed. Woodward (2007); *The History of Cartography*, vol. 3, "Cartography in the European Renaissance," part 2, ed. Woodward (2007); and *The History of Cartography*, vol. 6, "Cartography in the Twentieth Century," ed. Mark Monmonier (2015).

112. Kathryn Burns, *Into the Archive: Writing and Power in Colonial Peru*, 3.

113. Joanne Rappaport and Tom Cummins, *Beyond the Lettered City: Indigenous Literacies in the Andes*, 5.

114. Map of Myltepec (1617), AGN, no. 1776, Tierras, vol. 2711, exp. 7, fs. 9v and 10.

115. Taylor, *Landlord and Peasant*, 99, 103.

116. Terraciano, *The Mixtecs*, 249; Gerhard, *A Guide*, 187.

117. "Demanda puesta por Doña Ana Velázquez, viuda del Capitán Martín de Arce, contra Juan Martínez por haberle robado ciertas mercancías," AGEO, Alcaldías Mayores, leg. 5, exp. 4.

118. Antonio Robles, *Diario de sucesos notables (1665–1703)*, vol. I, ed. Antonio Castro Leal, 220.

119. Robles, *Diario*, 228–229.

120. Michelle P. Brown, *Understanding Illuminated Manuscripts: A Guide to Technical Terms*, 96.

121. Diego Antonio Francés de Urrutigoyti, *Forum conscientiae sive pastorale internum ad Ioannem de Palafox et Mendoza*, BFB.

122. *The Afterlife of Used Things: Recycling in the Long Eighteenth Century*, ed. Ariane Fennetaux, Amélie Junqua, and Sophie Vasset, 1–2.

123. See note 17 in introduction; Terraciano, *The Mixtecs*, 19.

124. Alvarado, *Vocabulario en lengua mixteca*, 138.

125. See, for instance, Map of Xoxocotlán (1686), AGN, no. 0625; Map of San Pablo Mitla (1730), AGN, no. 0719, Tierras, vol. 489, 1ª. pte., exp. 1, f. 271; Map of San Juan Tabaa, AGN, no. 837, Tierras, vol. 759, exp. 1, f. 45; and Map of Nuestra Madre del Rosario, Santa María Atzompa, c. 1700s, Santa María Atzompa (map lost; author in possession of digital images). Also see Boone, *Stories in Red and Black*, chap. 6.

126. This map was held in the Municipality of Santa María Atzompa in the Valley of Oaxaca. Together with a book of land titles tracing the ownership of an estate belonging to the town during the seventeenth and eighteenth centuries, and another map painted in watercolor, they formed part of the town's historical records. Since 2008, the documents have disappeared. The author has digital copies of all three items.

127. Lockhart, *The Nahuas*, 208–210.

128. On the use of colors in Nahua society, see Burkhart, *The Slippery Earth*, 59.

129. Haude, "Identification of Colorants on Maps from the Early Colonial Period of New Spain (Mexico)," 250–251; and Richard Newman and Michelle Derrick, "Analytical Report of the Pigments

and Binding Materials Used in the Beinecke Map," in *Painting a Map*, 94–95.

130. Alicia del Carmen Contreras, *Capital comercial y colorantes en la Nueva España: Segunda mitad del siglo XVIII*, 43.

131. Contreras, *Capital comercial*, 123; Martínez, *Catálogo*, 33.

132. "Se echan las hojas despedazadas en un perol o caldera de agua hervida, pero ya quitada del fuego y tibia, o mejor (según afirman los peritos) fría y sin haber pasado por el fuego; se agitan fuertemente con una pala de madera, y se vacía poco a poco el agua ya teñida en una vasija de barro o tinaja, dejando después que se derrame el líquido por unos agujeros que tiene a cierta altura, y que se asiente lo que salió de las hojas. Este sedimento es el colorante; se seca al sol, se cuela en una bolsa de cáñamo, se le da luego la forma de ruedecillas que se endurecen poniéndolas en platos sobre las brasas, y se guarda por último para usarse durante el año." *HNNE* 2, 112.

133. "Xiuhquilitl," *Florentine Codex*, book 11, f. 219, Biblioteca Medicea Laurenziana via World Digital Library.

134. HGNE, 90, 1038.

135. HNNE 2, 113.

136. Manuel Rubio Sánchez, *Historia del añil o xiquilite en Centro América*, 67–74.

137. The work of archeologists has been instrumental to understand the way terrestrial roadways in the Americas fostered regional networks. See David Bolles and William Folan, "An Analysis of Roads Listed in Colonial Dictionaries and Their Relevance to Pre-Hispanic Linear Features in the Yucatan Peninsula"; Christian Strassning, "Rediscovering the *Camino Real* of Panama: Archaeology and Heritage Tourism Potentials"; and John Hyslop, *The Inka Road System*. For the colonial period, see Chantal Cramaussel, ed., *Rutas de la Nueva España*; Bruce Castleman, *Building the King's Highway: Labor, Society, and Family on Mexico's Caminos Reales, 1757–1804*; and Ross Hassig, *Trade, Tribute, and Transportation: The Sixteenth-Century Political Economy of the Valley of Mexico*. On the relationship between roads, ritual, and state building, see Jessica Joyce Christie, "Inka Roads, Lines, and Rock Shrines: A Discussion of the Context of Trail Markers."

138. David Ringrose, "Carting in the Hispanic World: An Example of Divergent Development."

139. Butzer, "The Roadside Inn or 'Venta.'" Also see map of Cuscatlan (1611), AGN, no. 1607, Tierras, vol. 2682, exp. 4, f. 9.

140. Russo, *El realismo circular*, 93–98.

141. Sellers-García, *Documents and Distance*, 19.

142. "Cuyos cien zurrones parece ser lo mismo que constan en el conocimiento de 6 de enero de 1756 . . . en cuanto a su número, y no en cuanto a su peso por la falla que se percibe del adjunto peso." AGEO, Alcaldías Mayores, leg. 29, exp. 17.

CHAPTER 4

1. Map of Myltepec (1617), AGN, no. 1776, Tierras, vol. 2711, exp. 7, fs. 9v. y 10.

2. AGN, Tierras, vol. 2711, exp. 7, f. 2.

3. AGN, Tierras, vol. 2711, exp. 7, f. 3.

4. AGN, Tierras, vol. 2711, exp. 7, f. 3.

5. See James C. Scott, *Seeing Like a State: How Certain Schemes to Improve the Human Condition Have Failed*, 2–3; and Daniel Lord Smail, *Imaginary Cartographies: Possession and Identity in Late Medieval Marseille*, 10.

6. Ann Laura Stoler, *Along the Archival Grain: Epistemic Anxieties and Colonial Common Sense*, 3.

7. See Yannakakis, "Witnesses, Spatial Practices," 166.

8. See Demetrio Ramos Pérez, "La junta magna de 1568. Planificación de una época nueva," in *La formación de las sociedades Iberoamericanas (1568–1700)*, ed. Demetrio Ramos Pérez.

9. Smail, *Imaginary Cartographies*; Raymond Craib, "Relocating Cartography"; and Kapil Raj, *Relocating Modern Science: Circulation and the Construction of Knowledge in South Asia and Europe, 1650–1900*, esp. ch. 2.

10. Smail, *Imaginary Cartographies*, 224.

11. Roberto González Echevarría, *Myth and Archive: A Theory of Latin American Narrative*; Mignolo, *The Darker Side*; Cummins, "From Lies to Truth"; Cañizares-Esguerra, *How to Write*; Padrón, *The Spacious Word*; and Burns, *Into the Archive*.

12. Daniela Bleichmar, "The Imperial Visual Archive: Images, Evidence, and Knowledge in the Early Modern Hispanic World"; Thomas B. F. Cummins et al., eds., *Manuscript Cultures of Colonial Mexico and Peru: New Questions and Approaches*; and Rappaport and Cummins, *Beyond the Lettered City*.

13. Ángel Rama, *The Lettered City*, trans. John Charles Chasteen, 16.

14. Rappaport and Cummins, *Beyond the Lettered City*.

15. See Burns, *Into the Archive*, 13; and Juan Ricardo Jiménez Gómez, *Un formulario notarial mexicano del siglo XVIII: La instrucción de escribanos de Juan Elías Ortiz de Logroño*, 18 (n. 17), 21.

16. "De los escribanos de gobernación, Título Ocho," in *Recopilación de leyes de los reinos de las Indias*, 179.

17. Kathryn Burns, "Notaries, Truth, and Consequences," 355.

18. Fernando Bouza, *Corre manuscrito: Una historia cultural del Siglo de Oro*, 31.

19. Burns, *Into the Archive*, 2–3.

20. See Bernardo Pérez Fernández del Castillo's useful catalog of handbooks in *Historia de la escribanía en la Nueva España y del notariado en México*, 49–52.

21. Map of Juxtlahuaca (1609), AGN, no. 1271, Tierras, vol. 1871, exp. 11, f. 11.

22. See Yannakakis, "Witnesses, Spatial Practices"; and Beyersdorff, "Covering the Earth."

23. Map of Juxtlahuaca (1609), AGN, no. 1271, Tierras, vol. 1871, exp. 11, f. 11.

24. Map of Tlaxiaco and Cuquila (1588), AGN, no. 1692.9, Tierras, vol. 2692, exp. 17, f. 8.

25. Map of Ahuehuetitlan and Suchi[te]petongo (1616), AGN, no. 2056, Tierras, vol. 2763, exp. 13, f. 9.

26. "Aquí el sitio que se pide llamado Ahuehuetitlan," Map of

Ahuehuetitlan and Suchi[te]petongo (1616), AGN, no. 2056, Tierras, vol. 2763, exp. 13, f. 9.

27. Map of Cuscatlan (1611), AGN, no. 1607, Tierras, vol. 2682, exp. 4, f. 9. This map still forms part of its original docket.

28. Gruzinski, "Colonial Indian Maps," 57.

29. AGN, Tierras, vol. 243, exp. 4, f. 17.

30. AGN, Tierras, vol. 243, exp. 4, f. 17.

31. On *tequitlato*, see Lockhart, *The Nahuas*, 44.

32. AGN, Tierras, vol. 243, exp. 4, f. 15–16.

33. AGN, Tierras, vol. 243, exp. 4, f. 15.

34. "Cédula," in Howard F. Cline, "The *Relaciones Geográficas* of the Spanish Indies, 1577–1648," *HMAI*, appendix A, 233.

35. English translation follows Mundy, *The Mapping of New Spain*, appendix B, 228.

36. English translation follows Mundy, *The Mapping of New Spain*, appendix B, 230.

37. Relación de Tehuantepec, BLAC, Folder XXV-4, f. 4v–6.

38. Smail, *Imaginary Cartographies*, 2.

39. Smail, *Imaginary Cartographies*, 1; Burns, *Into the Archive*, 68.

40. Yanna Yannakakis, "Making Law Intelligible: Networks of Translation in Mid-Colonial Oaxaca," in *Indigenous Intellectuals: Knowledge, Power, and Colonial Culture in Mexico and the Andes*, ed. Gabriela Ramos and Yanna Yannakakis.

41. Map of Tzanaltepec, Tonaltepec, and Oztutlán (1580), AGN, no. 1903, Tierras, vol. 2729, exp. 4, f. 107v and 108.

42. AGN, Tierras, vol. 2729, exp. 4.

43. See, for example, AGN, Indiferente Virreinal, exp. 030; AGN, Indios, vol. 25, exp. 289; AGN, Indios, vol. 4, exp. 517; and AGN, Indios, vol. 6, exp. 372.

44. Yannakakis, "Making Law Intelligible," 79.

45. Teozapotlán was commonly referred to as "Zaachila"; see Gerhard, *A Guide*, 52.

46. The original reads: "Que ha ejercido otra vez dicho oficio, y la buena cuenta que tienen experimentado los naturales a dado siempre y sus buenos procedimientos, y que es dócil y humilde y no les hace extorciones ni les quita nada." AGN, Indiferente Virreinal, exp. 007. Also see AGN, Indios, vol. 25, exp. 106.

47. Haskett, *Indigenous Rulers: An Ethnohistory of Town Government in Colonial Cuernavaca*, 82.

48. Rappaport and Cummins, *Beyond the Lettered City*, 18.

49. Yannakakis, "Making Law Intelligible," 84–85.

50. Yannakakis, "Making Law Intelligible," 87.

51. Herzog, "Colonial Law"; Taylor, *Landlord and Peasant*.

52. Map of Santa Ana and Santa Cruz (1591), AGN, no. 0581, Tierras, vol. 56, exp. 5, f. 16.

53. AGN, Tierras, vol. 58, exp. 5, n.p.

54. "Sin saber quien expuso fuego se quemó y que oyó decir este testigo que maliciosamente y por revolver pleito lo habían hecho[?] los dichos indios del pueblo de Santa Ana." AGN, Tierras, vol. 58, exp. 5.

55. Rappaport and Cummins, *Beyond the Lettered City*, 8.

56. Map of Simatlán and Ocotlán (1686 [1639]), AGN, no. 3009, Hospital de Jesús, leg. 85, exp. 4.

57. AGN, Hospital de Jesús, leg. 85, exp. 4, f. 117v.

58. AGN, Hospital de Jesús, leg. 85, exp. 4, f. 117v.

59. AGN, Hospital de Jesús, leg. 85, exp. 4, f. 118v and 119v.

60. A Spanish transcription of the inventory of manuscripts and maps handed over to López de Velasco in 1583 can be found in Cline, "The Relaciones Geográficas," appendix D, 237–240.

61. There is some debate about the identity of the cataloger. The two likely candidates include López de Velasco and Céspedes. Cline, "The Relaciones Geográficas," 196.

62. Cline, "The Relaciones Geográficas," 194 and appendix E, which includes a Spanish transcription of the manuscripts consulted by León Pinelo at 240–242.

63. Cline, "The Relaciones Geográficas," 194; Mundy, *The Mapping of New Spain*, 27.

64. Portuondo, *Secret Science*, 221–223.

65. AGN, Hospital de Jesús, leg. 85, exp. 4, f. 104.

66. AGN, Hospital de Jesús, leg. 85, exp. 4, f. 104.

67. Antonio de León y Gama, *Descripción histórica y cronológica de las dos piedras, que con ocasión del nuevo empedrado que se está formando en la plaza principal de México se hallaron en ella el año de 1790*, 5.

68. Dorothy Tanck de Estrada, "Trips by Indians Financed by Communal Funds in Colonial Mexico"; and José Carlos de la Puente Luna, *Andean Cosmopolitans: Seeking Justice and Reward at the Spanish Royal Court*.

69. Map of Tehuantepec, Juchitlán, Chicapa, Niltepec, Isguatán, San Francisco, and San Dionisio (1746), AGN, no. 0785, Tierras, vol. 584, exp. 1, cuad. 4, f. 26.

70. The original reads: "Hallará V.A. que el mapa formado por dichos indios de San Francisco de el Mar, ni está concordado con los autos, y no solo no está consono con ellos, sino totalmente disono y opuesto." AGN, Tierras, vol. 584, exp. 1, f. 138.

71. "Lo que hiso malicia y la impericia, fue amontonar diversidad de parajes, que ni se litigan, ni conduce a nada el delinearlos, y lo mejor de todo fue, que no se hallan figuarados, ni mapeados los parajes de el litigio." AGN, Tierras, vol. 584, exp. 1, f. 138.

72. Map of San Dionisio del Mar (1740), AGN, no. 0784, Tierras, vol. 584, exp. 1, cuad. 2, f. 55.

73. "La que comenzó en un portillo que está entre dos cerros pequeños, donde está una piedra de cuatro caras, la misma que se demarca en el mapa de f. 55, cuaderno no. 4., formado por mis partes." Tierras, vol. 584, exp. 1, f. 137v.

74. "Se certifíque por el presente escribano de cámara ser cierto, como lo es, no haber en todo el mapa presentado por los de San Francisco paraje ninguno de que intitule Colotepeque. Lo segundo, no haber figurada ni demarcada salina o laguna de sal ninguna con el nombre de Quespalapa. Lo tercero, no estar figurada ni demarcada la piedra de cuatro caras. Lo cuarto, certifiqué así mismo no estar figuradas ni delineadas en dicho mapa ninguna de las tres lagunetas o salinas que dicen los testigos de los indios de

San Francisco estan inmediatas a el pueblo de mis partes, y sea con citación de las contrarias, y rubriqué dicho mapa." AGN, Tierras, vol. 584, exp. 1, f. 138v.

75. The distinction carried with it an assortment of responsibilities. When viceregal authorities implemented a new policy in 1756 that required scribes attached to the Audiencia to report all cases of homicide and violent crime by January 8 of each new year, they requested the reports be deposited "en el Oficio de Cámara más antiguo de esta Real Sala." Eusebio Buenaventura Beleña, *Recopilación sumaria de los autos acordados de la Real Audiencia de esta Nueva España, que desde el año de 1677 hasta el de 1786 han podido recogerse*, 56.

76. "Y así [no] importa el que estos en su mapa no hagan constar figurado sitio alguno con este título de *Colotepec*, cuando estan allí constantes, y demarcados sus linderos; y por ellos manifiesto el mismo cuerpo de la cosa." AGN, Tierras, vol. 584, exp. 1, f. 141v–142.

77. See Lisa Sousa and Kevin Terraciano, "The 'Original Conquest,'" 356.

78. See Paula López Caballero, ed., *Los títulos primordiales del centro de México*; Florescano, *Historia de las historias* and "El canon memorioso forjado por los títulos primordiales"; Xavier Noguez and Stephanie Wood, eds., *De tlacuilos y escribanos: Estudios sobre documentos indígenas coloniales del centro de México*; Robert Haskett, "Paper Shields"; and Lockhart, *The Nahuas*, 357, 360–364, and 410–418. The case of San Juan Chapultepec is one of just a handful of primordial titles identified for the Oaxaca region. See Sousa and Terraciano, "The 'Original Conquest'"; and María de los Ángeles Romero Frizzi, "El título de San Mateo Capulalpan, Oaxaca. Actualidad y autenticidad de un título primordial." A subgenre of *títulos primordiales* includes the so-called Techialoyan manuscripts, which share similar characteristics. See Donald Robertson, "Techialoyan Manuscripts and Paintings with a Catalogue," in *HMAI*, vol. 14, ed. Robert Wauchope and Howard Cline; Stephanie Wood, "Pedro Villafranca y Juana Gertrudis Navarrete: falsificador de títulos y su viuda (Nueva España, siglo XVIII)," in *Lucha por la supervivencia en América colonial*, ed. David G. Sweet and Gary B. Nash; "Don Diego García de Mendoza Moctezuma: A Techialoyan Mastermind?"; "El problema de la historicidad de Títulos y los códices del grupo Techialoyan," in *De tlacuilos*; and "The Techialoyan Codices," in *Sources and Methods for the Study of Postconquest Mesoamerican Ethnohistory*.

79. Map of San Juan Chapultepec (1523?), AGN, no. 0660, Tierras, vol. 236, exp. 6, f. 2.

80. Sousa and Terraciano, "The 'Original Conquest,'" 369.

81. Sousa and Terraciano, "The 'Original Conquest,'" 368–369.

82. Sousa and Terraciano, "The 'Original Conquest,'" 374.

83. Sousa and Terraciano, "The 'Original Conquest,'" 381; Wood, "Pedro Villafranca," 477.

84. Wood, "Pedro Villafranca."

85. Wood, "Pedro Villafranca."

86. León y Gama, *Descripción histórica*, 5.

87. By his own account, León y Gama, an attorney by trade,

served over twenty years as a royal scribe at the Audiencia and another eleven as *oficial mayor*; AGN, Inquisición, vol. 1184, f. 49.

88. Cañizares-Esguerra, *How to Write*, 299.

EPILOGUE

1. Two recent studies on Boturini describe his experience in New Spain as a misadventure: Giorgio Antei, *El caballero andante: Vida, obra y desaventuras de Lorenzo Boturini Benaduci (1698–1755)*, and Guillermo González del Campo and José J. Hernández Palomo, "Boturini o las desaventuras de un devoto guadalupano (Seis cartas desde la cárcel)." Intellectual historians have situated Boturini within the Iberian Atlantic's burgeoning Enlightenment culture; see Cañizares-Esguerra, *How to Write*, and Álvaro Matute, *Lorenzo Boturini y el pensamiento histórico de Vico*. The critical bibliographic studies of John Glass reproduced the contents of the various inventories and legal papers associated with Boturini's collection prepared from the time of his arrest until the early nineteenth century. For an introduction to this subject, see Glass's entry titled "The Boturini Collection," in *Handbook of Middle American Indians*, vol. 15, part 4. Most recently, the work of Iván Escamilla has offered a much-needed analysis of the social dimensions that allowed Boturini to engage in his activities in Mexico City; see "Lorenzo Boturini y el entorno social de su empresa historiográfica," in *Memorias del coloquio, El caballero Lorenzo Boturini: Entre dos mundos y dos historias*; and "'Próvido y proporcionado' socorro: Lorenzo Boturini y sus patrocinadores novohispanos," in *Poder civil y catolicismo en México, siglos XVI al XIX*.

2. Ann Laura Stoler, "Colonial Archives and the Arts of Governance," 15.

3. Jessica Keating and Lia Markey observe that annotations in inventories translate material things into linguistic statements: "Introduction: Captured Objects: Inventories of Early Modern Collections," 209.

4. "Poner en pública custodia y en seguridad los instrumentos y papeles públicos," in *Diccionario de la lengua castellana en que se explica el verdadero sentido de las voces, su naturaleza y calidad, con las frases o modos de hablar, los proverbios o refranes, y otras cosas convenientes al uso de la lengua*, 379 (hereafter cited as RAE 1726).

5. Stoler, *Along the Archival Grain*, 9.

6. Stoler, *Along the Archival Grain*, 1.

7. See Markus Friedrich's recent work, *The Birth of the Archive: A History of Knowledge*, trans. John Noël Dillon. He examines the way multiple forms of archiving functioned in the context of late medieval and early modern Europe.

8. Iván Escamilla, "Lorenzo Boturini y el entorno social de su empresa historiográfica," in *Memorias del coloquio*, 75–77.

9. "No cansaré en referir los inmensos trabajos, y gastos, que me han cobrado estas preseas inestimables de la antigüedad indiana; solo si advierto, que como las tenían, y tienen otras los indios de aquella dilatada región, me fue preciso correr grandes tierras, adivinando y preguntando: Y aunque con notoria constancia, jamás

dejé de la mano las emprendidas diligencias. No obstante pasaron dos años sin que pudiese conseguir siquiera un mapa, ni ver la cara a manuscrito alguno, habiéndome sucedido muchas veces peregrinar muchas veces de unos lugares a otros los cinco, y seis meses continuos, y volverme a la ciudad." Lorenzo Boturini Benaduci, *Idea de una nueva historia general de la América septentrional fundada sobre material copioso de figuras, símbolos, caracteres, y jeroglíficos, cantares, y manuscritos de autores indios últimamente descubiertos*, 3.

10. The Republic of Indians from Tehuantepec to the Viceroy, Duque de Albuquerque, 1660, in María de los Ángeles Romero Frizzi, *El sol y la cruz: Los pueblos indios de Oaxaca colonial*, 256. Emphasis added.

11. Lorenzo Boturini to the Priests of the Province of Tepeaca, September 24, 1742, Archivo Histórico del Estado de Tlaxcala, Fondo Histórico, Sección Colonia, 1742.

12. López wrote an historic poem about the Zapotec nation in honor of the entry of New Spain's recently appointed viceroy, Pedro de Castro y Figueroa. He also wrote popular romances that used crime and social deviance to tell edifying tales. See Patricio Antonio López, *Mercurio yndiano: Un poema histórico*, ed. Beatriz Mariscal Hay.

13. Lorenzo Boturini to Indigenous Leaders in New Spain, in Giorgio Antei, *El caballero anadante*, 162. Antei does not provide date or location of the cited letter.

14. As Jorge Cañizares-Esguerra has aptly demonstrated, Boturini's proposal was not unique in New World historiography: *How to Write*, 135–148.

15. Boturini to Indigenous Leaders in New Spain, in Antei, *El caballero anadante*, 162.

16. Inventory by Antonio de Roxas y Abreu, February 5, 1743, in Causa de Boturini, no. 440, f. 27. The "Causa de Boturini" is a lengthy report of the criminal proceedings against Boturini that includes testimonies, correspondence, inventories, petitions, and mandates formulated during the investigation into the Italian's activities. The copy of the proceedings I consulted for this chapter forms part of the Joaquín García Icazbalceta Manuscript Collection [1500]–1887, BLAC. The manuscript is paginated up to f. 55, at which point page numbers disappear.

17. Inventory by Antonio de Roxas y Abreu, February 5, 1743, in Causa de Boturini, f. 27.

18. Inventory by Antonio de Roxas y Abreu, February 5, 1743, in Causa de Boturini, f. 27.

19. Stoler, *Along the Archival Grain*, 2.

20. See the essays in Daniela Bleichmar and Peter C. Mancall, eds., *Collecting Across Cultures: Material Exchanges in the Early Modern Atlantic World*.

21. Paula Findlen, "Introduction: Early Modern Things: Objects in Motion, 1500–1800," in *Early Modern Things: Objects and Their Histories, 1500–1800*, 6; and Fennetaux, Junqua, and Vasset, eds., *The Afterlife of Used Things*.

22. Peter Miller, "How Objects Speak," *The Chronicle of Higher Education*.

23. Keating and Markey, "Captured Objects," 211.

24. Lorenzo Boturini to the Viceroy, April 2, 1743, cited in Antei, *El caballero anadante*, 194.

25. Keating and Markey, "Captured Objects," 209.

26. James Delbourgo and Staffan Müller-Wille, "Introduction: Listmania," 713.

27. A *vara* was a unit of measure that equaled roughly 33 inches; see Table 1.2 in chapter 1.

28. Rublack, "Matter in the Material Renaissance," 43.

29. Lorenzo Boturini to the King, June 17, 1743, in Guillermo González del Campo and José J. Hernández Palomo, "Boturini o las desaventuras de un devoto guadalupano (Seis cartas desde la cárcel)," 171 (hereafter cited as "Seis Cartas").

30. Lorenzo Boturini to the King, June 17, 1743, in "Seis Cartas," 172.

31. Keating and Markey, "Captured Objects," 209.

32. Keating and Markey, "Captured Objects," 209.

33. According to Keating and Markey, "Disembodied teeth and bones of large animals were frequently recorded as the remnants of primordial giants"; "Captured Objects," 210. Boturini's catalog listed "un diente de gigante que dicho Don Lorenzo tiene en el estante de su archivo." Item no. 29, sixth inventory, September 26, 1743, in Causa de Boturini, n.p.

34. Balbuena certifications from August 9, 1743, and September 6, 1743, in Causa de Boturini, n.p.

35. Sabastián de Covarrubias, *Tesoro de la lengua española*, 90.

36. RAE 1726, 379.

37. RAE 1726, 379.

38. Boturini, "Catálogo del museo histórico indiano del caballero Lorenzo Boturini Benaduci, Señor de la Torre y de Hono," in *Idea de una nueva historia general*.

39. Besides the inherent prestige associated with the cabinet of curiosities during the early modern period, they also functioned as tools of politics, as spaces of technological innovation, and as a source of capital. See Mark Meadow, "Merchants and Marvels: Hans Jacob Fugger and the Origins of the Wunderkammer," in *Merchants and Marvels*, ed. Pamela H. Smith and Paula Findlen; Paula Findlen, "Possessing the Past: The Material World of the Italian Renaissance"; Daniela Bleichmar, "Seeing the World in a Room: Looking at Exotica in Early Modern Collections," in *Collecting Across Cultures*, ed. Bleichmar and Mancall; and Susan Pearce, *On Collecting*, 109–121.

40. RAE 1734, 636.

41. Constance Classen, "Museum Manners: The Sensory Life of the Early Museum," 897.

42. Mark Meadow, "Merchants and Marvels."

43. Boturini, "Catálogo del museo histórico indiano."

44. Anna More, *Baroque Sovereignty*.

45. A string of recent studies sheds light on the importance of this New World intellectual. See, for instance, Galen Brokaw and Jongsoon Lee's collection of essays titled *Fernando de Alva Ixtlilxochitl and His Legacy*; Amber Brian, *Alva Ixtlilxochitl's Native Archive and*

the Circulation of Knowledge in Colonial Mexico; and *Colonial Latin American Review* (Special Issue) 23:1 (2014).

46. More, *Baroque Sovereignty*, 13.

47. Lorenzo Boturini to the King, June 17, 1743, in "Seis cartas," 171.

48. Lorenzo Boturini to the King, August 3, 1743, 179, and September 29, 1743, in "Seis cartas," 180.

49. Jean Baudrillard, "The System of Collecting," in *The Cultures of Collecting*, ed. John Elsner and Roger Cardinal, 10.

50. *Papel de marquilla* refers to paper that is "quite larger than the common one." See Esteban de Terreros y Pando, *Diccionario castellano con las voces de ciencias y artes y sus correspondientes en las tres lenguas francesa, latina e italiana*, 534. The document in question is the Matrícula de tributos, c. sixteenth century, no. 35-52, Biblioteca Nacional de Antropología e Historia, Mexico City (hereafter cited as BNAH). See also *Matrícula de tributos (Códice de Moctezuma), Museo Nacional de Antropología, México (Cód. 35–52) (Codices selecti phototypice impressi)*, ed. Frances Berdan and Jacqueline de Durand-Forest. The entry corresponds to item no. 35, second inventory, September 17, 1743, in Causa de Boturini, n.p.

51. Tonalamatl Aubin, c. sixteenth century, manuscrit mexicaines 18-19, Bibliothèque Nacionale de France (on loan at BNAH). The entry corresponds to item no. 23, sixth inventory, September 26, 1743, in Causa de Boturini, n.p.

52. On calendar wheels, see John Glass, "A Survey of Native Middle American Pictorial Manuscripts," in *Handbook of Middle American Indians*, vol. 14, 30–31.

53. Stoler points out that archives and the documents they held were not static units filled with "dead matter." Authorities could, and did, requisition, reclassify, or reuse records to fit changing imperial needs. *Along the Archival Grain*, 3.

54. Item no. 3, second inventory, September 17, 1743, Causa de Boturini, f. 55v.

55. Published transcription in Joaquín García Icazbalceta, *Nueva colección de documentos para la historia de México*, vol. 3, xv. Boturini's annotated copy of Alonso de Zorita's *Breve y sumaria relación de los señores, y maneras, y diferencias que había de ellos en la Nueva España y en otras provincias, sus comarcas, de sus leyes, usos y costumbres* is currently listed in the bookseller's online catalog: Plaza Books, Port Townsend, Washington.

56. Iván Escamilla González, "Lorenzo Boturini y el entorno social de su empresa historiográfica," in *El caballero Lorenzo Boturini: Entre dos mundos y dos historia*, 71.

57. Besides the typical vows of chastity, poverty, and obedience, members of the Society of Jesus *professed* a fourth vow of obedience to the pope tied to missionary activities.

58. "Siete cuadernos de a folio, que dicho Don Lorenzo copió, y mandó copiar de sus originales de varios documentos que halló en el Archivo de la Santa Iglesia de México; y en el Oratorio de San Felipe Neri pertenecientes a probar de como la aparición de la Santísima Imagen de Guadalupe al Ilustrísimo Señor Obispo, Dr. Don Juan de Zumárraga, fue en las casas arzobispales de hoy día, y no en otro lugar, por haberlas su Ilustrísima comprado y habitádolas un año antes de dicha aparición, en fojas treinta y ocho." Item no. 31, eighth inventory, September 28, 1743, Causa de Boturini, n.p.

59. Items no. 37, 39, and 40, second inventory, September 17, 1743, Causa de Boturini, n.p.

60. Plano parcial de la Ciudad de México, c. sixteenth century, no. 35-3, BNAH. In Boturini's catalog, item no. 30, second inventory, September 17, 1743: "Un mapa grande muy maltratado; representa en pintura el plan de la ciudad de México en lo antiguo, y trata de las descendencias de los reyes, en varias figuritas, que es en papel de maguey." María Castañeda de la Paz has noted that, although the description of this map refers to maguey paper, the latest conservation efforts reveal this map was made of *amate*. "Sibling Maps, Spatial Rivalries: The Beinecke Map and the Plano Parcial de la Ciudad de México," in *Painting a Map of Sixteenth-Century Mexico City: Land, Writing, and Native Rule*, ed. Mary Miller and Barbara Mundy, 71, n. 18.

61. Item no. 13, third inventory, September 25, 1743, Causa de Boturini, n.p.

62. "Otro mapa de lienzo algo más del tamaño de una sábana; trata de diferentes pueblos, y guerras que hubo entre ellos, muy maltratado y comido de la humedad. Otro semejante en la misma lengua, papel, y del propio tamaño, muy maltratado de la humedad, trata una descripción general de otras cabeceras y provincias, y sirve a la Historia General, en fojas ciento ochenta y cuatro." Item no. 27, fourth inventory, September 24, 1743, Causa de Boturini, n.p.

63. "Un envoltorio de pedazos de mapas, muy maltratados, para ajustar los mapas antecedentes. Dos pedazos de mapa, papel de Castilla, muy maltratados, cosidos con un hilo, trata de unos pedazos de tierra." Item no. 20, fourth inventory, 24 September 1743, Causa de Boturini, n.p.

64. "Un mapa, papel de Castilla con toscas figuras, como de una vara de largo y media tercia de ancho, maltratado, no se ha inteligenciado Don Lorenzo de lo que trata." Item no. 39, fourth inventory, September 24, 1743, Causa de Boturini, n.p.

65. "Un mapa en una piel adobada, ancho de más una tercia y de largo como de dos varas y media; que a dicho Don Lorenzo le enviaron de Oaxaca y no ha reconocido lo que explica." Item no. 31, fourth inventory, September 24, 1743, Causa de Boturini, n.p.

66. "Con lo cual se concluyó dicho inventario, quedando todos los referidos papeles, mapas y libros dentro del referido estante que queda en el citado cuarto que llaman General Común de esta Real Caja; y cerrado dicho estante con su llave, se entregó esta al factor oficial real, Don Ignacio Josef de Miranda." Eighth inventory, September 28, 1743, Causa de Boturini, n.p.

67. Antei, *El caballero andante*, 203.

68. AGN, Reales Cédulas, exp. 95.

69. On López's appointments as translator, see AGN, Indiferente Virreinal, exp. 27; and AGN, Indios, vol. 55, exp. 49, 32–32v.

70. Cited in López, *Mercurio yndiano*, ed. Beatriz Mariscal Hay, 55–56.

71. Informe presentado al Consejo de Indias sobre la causa de Boturini, April 27, 1790, in Causa de Boturini, n.p.

72. Item no. 9, second inventory. Patricio Antonio López, "Inventario de los documentos recogidos a Don Lorenzo Boturini por orden del gobierno virreinal," in *Anales del Museo Nacional de Arqueología, Historia y Etnografía*, 9 (hereafter cited as "Inventario").

73. Item no. 5, second inventory, in "Inventario, 8."

74. Item no. 31, second inventory, September 17, 1743, in Causa de Boturini, n.p.

75. Item no. 31, second inventory, in "Inventario," 13.

76. Item no. 31, second inventory, in "Inventario," 13.

77. Item no. 31, second inventory, in "Inventario," 13. For a first-hand testimonial of the deadly epidemic, see Cayetano de Cabrera y Quintero, *Escudo de armas de México*.

78. Item no. 3, second inventory, in "Inventario," 7.

79. López, *Mercurio yndiano*, 66.

80. López, *Mercurio yndiano*, 81.

81. AGN, Indiferente Virreinal, exp. 027 (1737); Indiferente Virreinal, exp. 025 (no date); and Tierras, vol. 1799, exp. 7, f. 14–14v. Also see Glass, "A Census of Native Middle American Pictorial Manuscripts," 117–118.

82. Amos Megged, *Social Memory in Ancient and Colonial Meso-america*, 66–68.

83. Megged, *Social Memory*, 67. See also Byron McAfee and Robert Barlow, "Anales de San Gregorio Acapulco"; and Serge Gruzinski, *La colonización de lo imaginario*, 110–111.

84. Item no. 19, second inventory, in "Inventario," 11.

85. "Otro mapa en un pliego de papel de marca mayor de los famosos cerros de San Juan Teotihuacan, que dicho Don Lorenzo dijo mandó hacer para la Historia General." Item no. 19, second inventory, September 17, 1743, in Causa de Boturini, n.p.

86. Item no. 20, second inventory, in "Inventario," 11.

87. Item no. 21, second inventory, in "Inventario," 11.

88. "En este papel de Castilla antiguo figurado de diferentes caracteres, denota ser nombre de los ejidos y tierras que repartían los caciques a sus indios terrazgueros porque fue muy propio de todas estas gentes dar nombre a cada lugar y paraje, como se experimenta hoy, sirviendo de mojoneras y límites a los pueblos el nombre conocido que les daban." Item no. 39, fourth inventory, in "Inventario," 27.

89. Map of Cuauhtinchan no. 4, c. 1563, no. 35–31, BNAH.

90. "En este otro de papel vasto de Indias se describen los pueblos de la provincia de Tepeaca, Cuautinchan, Tetela, y otros; es muy antiguo [y] tiene algunas letras sobrepuestas que descifran estos parajes." Item no. 44, fourth inventory, in "Inventario," 28.

91. López, *Mercurio yndiano*, 76.

92. Joseph Whitecotton has cautioned against subsuming dozens of independent Zapotec and Mixtec nation-states who regularly warred with each other within ethnic characterizations based on language and culture that broadly describe Mixtec and Zapotec peoples. Despite the conflict, he notes, stable alliances did exist prior to Spanish contact. See "Las genealogías del valle de Oaxaca: Época colonial," in *Escritura zapoteca: 2500 años de historia*, ed. María de los Ángeles Romero Frizzi, 318–319. The original passage reads: "En esta piel adobada se representa por sus cuarteles las familias de los indios nobles de la nación zapoteca de los valles de Oaxaca confederados de los Mixtecas, fueron imperios separados y muy temibles al imperio Mexica;" Item no. 31, fourth inventory, in "Inventario," 25.

93. "Hallase figurado cara a cara con dicho Cortés en medio de este mapa, echándose al cuello uno y otro, una cadena en demostración de paz; el caballo ensillado que se mira tras de él, y la escopeta tendida en el suelo vuelta la coz hacia donde está el príncipe, denota que aquellas tierras y gente no fueron conquistadas, ni se ganó con el estruendo de estas armas, ni caballería." Item no. 31, fourth inventory, in "Inventario," 26.

94. On Herrera, see items no. 31 and 51, fourth inventory; and item no. 6, sixth inventory, in "Inventario," 25–26, 36. On Torquemada, see item no. 3, third inventory, and item no. 31, fourth inventory, in "Inventario," 17, 25.

95. López also cites Burgoa in the preface to *Mercurio yndiano*, 75.

96. Cañizares-Esguerra, *How to Write*, 300.

97. AGN, Indiferente Virreinal, exp. 15. See also Cañizares-Esguerra, *How to Write*, 301–302.

98. AGN, Indiferente Virreinal, exp. 15. On the birth of the National Museum, see Miruna Achim, *From Idols to Antiquity: Forging the National Museum of Mexico*.

99. Antoinette Burton, "Thinking Beyond the Boundaries: Empire, Feminism, and the Domains of History," 66.

BIBLIOGRAPHY

ARCHIVES AND LIBRARIES

Archivo General de la Nación, Mexico City
> Hospital de Jesús
> Indiferente Virreinal
> Indios
> Mapoteca
> Reales Cédulas
> Tierras

Archivo General del Estado de Oaxaca, Oaxaca City
> Alcaldías Mayores

Archivo Histórico de Notarías, Oaxaca City

Archívo Histórico del Estado de Tlaxcala, Tlaxcala City

Benson Latin American Collection, University of Texas at Austin
> Joaquín García Icazbalceta Manuscript Collection, [1500]–1887
> Relaciones Geográficas of Mexico and Guatemala, 1577–1585

Biblioteca Nacional de Antropología e Historia, Mexico City
> Códices

Biblioteca Francisco de Burgoa, Oaxaca City

Library of Congress, Washington, DC
> Jay I. Kislak Collection
> Geography and Map Division
> Rare Books and Manuscripts

Mapoteca Orozco y Berra, Mexico City

Texas Christian University Special Collections

University of Arizona Special Collections

PRINTED PRIMARY SOURCES

Acosta, José de. *Historia natural y moral de las Indias, en que se tratan las cosas notables del cielo, y elementos, metales, plantas, y animales dellas: y los ritos, y ceremonias, leyes, y gobierno, y guerras de los indios.* Sevilla: Juan de León, 1590.

Alvarado, Francisco de. *Vocabulario en lengua mixteca.* Mexico City: Instituto Nacional Indigenista and Instituto Nacional de Antropología e Historia, 1962 [1593].

Bautista, Juan. *¿Cómo te confundes? ¿Acaso no somos conquistados? Anales de Juan Bautista.* Edited by Luis Reyes García. Mexico City: Centro de Investigaciones y Estudios Superiores en Antropología Social and Biblioteca Lorenzo Boturini, 2001.

Blagden, Charles. *Some Observations on Ancient Inks, with the Proposal of a New Method of Recovering the Legibility of Decayed Writings.* London: n.p., 1787.

Boturini Benaduci, Lorenzo. *Idea de una nueva historia general de la América septentrional fundada sobre material copioso de figuras, símbolos, caracteres, y jeroglíficos, cantares, y manuscritos de autores indios últimamente descubiertos.* Madrid: Juan de Zuñiga, 1746.

Buenaventura Beleña, Eusebio. *Recopilación sumaria de los autos acordados de la Real Audiencia de esta Nueva España, que desde el año de 1677 hasta el de 1786 han podido recogerse.* Mexico City: Felipe de Zúñiga y Ontiveros, 1787.

Bueno, Diego. *Arte nuevo de enseñar a leer, escribir, y contar príncipes y señores.* Zaragoza: Domingo Gascón, 1690.

Burgoa, Francisco de. *Geográfica descripción de la parte septentrional del polo ártico de la América, y nueva iglesia de las Indias occidentales, y sitio astronómico de esta provincia de predicadores de Antequera Valle de Oaxaca*. Mexico City: Juan Ruiz, 1674.

Cabrera y Quintero, Cayetano de. *Escudo de armas de México: Celestial protección de esta nobilísima ciudad, de la Nueva España y de casi todo el Nuevo Mundo, María santísima, en su portentosa imagen del mexicano Guadalupe, milagrosamente aparecida en el palacio arzobispal el año de 1531. Y jurada su principal patrona el pasado de 1737. En la angustia que ocasionó la pestilencia, que cebada con mayor rigor en los indios, mitigó sus ardores al abrigo de tanta sombra*. Mexico City: Viuda de D. Joseph Bernardo de Hogal, 1746.

Cartas de Indias. Madrid: Ministerio de Fomento and Imprenta de Manuel G. Hernández, 1877.

Casanova, José de. *Primera parte del arte de escribir todas formas de letras*. Madrid: Diego Díaz de la Carrera, 1650.

Cerda Sandoval Silva y Mendoza, Gaspar de la. *Orden para la correspondencia de pesos, varas, y medidas*. Mexico City, 1692.

Clavijero, Francisco Javier. *Historia antigua de México sacada de los mejores historiadores españoles, y de los manuscritos de los indios*. Mexico City: Imprenta de Juan Navarro, 1853.

Codex Fejérváry-Mayer: M 12014 City of Liverpool Museums. Edited by C. A. Burland. Codices selecti, vol. 26. Graz: Akademische Druck- u. Verlagsanstalt, 1971.

The Codex Mendoza, vol. 1–4. Edited by Frances Berdan and Patricia Anawalt. Berkeley: University of California Press, 1992.

The Codex Nuttall: A Picture Manuscript from Ancient Mexico. Edited by Zelia Nuttall. New York: Dover Publications, 1975.

Códice Baranda. Edited by René Acuña. Mexico City: Ediciones Toledo, 1989.

Códice Colombino: Interpretación del Códice Colombino por Alfonso Caso. Las glosas del Códice Colombino por Mary Elizabeth Smith. Mexico City: Sociedad Mexicana de Antropología, 1966.

Códice Dehesa, largo: 5 metros 20 centímetros; ancho: 17 centímetros; pintado por ambos lados; existente en el Museo Nacional de México. Mexico City, 1892.

Códice de Yucunama: Edición facsimilar, interpretación y análisis. Edited by Manuel Hermann Lejarazu. Mexico City: Centro de Investigaciones y Estudios Superiores en Antropología Social, 2009.

Códices cuicatecos Porfirio Díaz y Fernández Leal: edición facsimilar, contexto histórico e interpretación. Edited by Sebastián van Doesburg. Mexico City: Miguel Ángel Porrúa, 2001.

Códice Yanhuitlán. Edited by Wigberto Jiménez Moreno and Salvador Mateos Higuera. Mexico City: Instituto Nacional de Antropología e Historia and Museo Nacional, 1940.

Córdova, Juan de. *Vocabulario en lengua zapoteca*. Mexico City: Secretaría de Educación Pública and Ediciones Toledo, 1987 [1578].

Covarrubias, Sebastián de. *Tesoro de la lengua castellana o española*. Edited by Ignacio Arellano y Rafael Zafra. Madrid: Iberoamericana and Frankfurt am Main: Vervuert, 2006 [1611].

Cruz, Martín de la. *The Badianus Manuscript (Codex Barberini, Latin 241) Vatican Library: An Aztec Herbal of 1552*. Edited by Emily Walcott Emmart. Baltimore: Johns Hopkins University Press, 1940.

Diccionario de la lengua castellana, en que se explica el verdadero sentido de las voces, su naturaleza y calidad, con las phrases o modos de hablar, los proverbios o refranes, y otras cosas convenientes al uso de la lengua. Madrid: Imprenta de la Real Academia Española, por los herederos de Francisco del Hierro, 1726.

Diccionario de la lengua castellana, en que se explica el verdadero sentido de las voces, su naturaleza y calidad, con las frases o modos de hablar, los proverbios o refranes, y otras cosas convenientes al uso de la lengua. Madrid: Imprenta de la Real Academia Española, por los herederos de Francisco del Hierro, 1734.

Flórez, Andrés. *Doctrina cristiana del ermitaño y el niño*. Valladolid: Sebastián Martínez, 1552.

Francés de Urrutigoyti, Diego Antonio. *Forum conscientiae sive pastorale internum ad Ioannem de Palafox et Mendoza*. Zaragoza: Tip. Generalis Regij Xenodochii imp., 1651.

Gutiérrez de los Ríos, Gaspar. *Noticia general para la estimación de las artes, y de la manera en que se conocen las liberales de las que son mecánicas y serviles, con una exhortación a la honra de la virtud y del trabajo contra los ociosos, y otras particulares para las personas de todos estados*. Madrid: Pedro Madrigal, 1600.

Hernández, Francisco. *Historia natural de Nueva España*, vol. 1–2. In *Obras Completas*, vol. 2–3. Mexico City: Universidad Nacional Autónoma de México, 1959.

Icíar, Juan de. *Arte sutilísima, por la cual se enseña a escribir perfectamente*. Zaragoza: Miguel de Çapila, 1553.

Interpretación del Códice Bodley 2858. Edited by Alfonso Caso. Mexico City: Sociedad Mexicana de Antropología, 1960.

Interpretación del Códice Selden 3135 (A.2). Edited by Alfonso Caso. Mexico City: Sociedad Mexicana de Antropología, 1964.

Laguna, Andrés. *Pedacio Dioscorides Anazarbeo, acerca de la materia medicinalrecogidos y de los venenos mortíferos*. Antwerp: Juan Latio, 1555.

León y Gama, Antonio de. *Descripción histórica y cronológica de las dos piedras, que con ocasión del nuevo empedrado que se esta formando en la plaza principal de México se hallaron en ella el año de 1790*. Mexico City: Alejandro Valdés, 1822.

López, Patricio Antonio. "Inventario de los documentos recogidos a Don Lorenzo Boturini por orden del gobierno virreinal." *Anales del Museo Nacional de Arqueología, Historia y Etnografía* 3 (1925): 1–55.

———. *Mercurio Yndiano: Un poema histórico*. Edited by Beatriz Mariscal Hay. Mexico City: El Colegio de México, 2014.

Manuscritos del Concilio Tercero Provincial Mexicano (1585), vol. 1–2. Edited by Alberto Carrillo Cázares. Zamora: El Colegio de Michoacán and Universidad Pontificia de México, 2006.

Matrícula de tributos (Códice de Moctezuma), Museo Nacional de Antropología, México (Cód. 35-52) (Codices selecti phototypice impressi). Edited by Frances Berdan and Jacqueline de Durand-Forest. Graz, Austria: Akademische Druck- u. Verlagsanstalt, 1980.

Molina, Alonso de. *Vocabulario en lengua castellana y mexicana.* Madrid: Ediciones Cultura Hispánica, 1944 [1571].

Monardes, Nicolás. *Primera y segunda y tercera parte de la historia medicinal de las cosas que traen de nuestras Indias occidentales que sirven en medicina.* Madrid: En casa de Alonso Escribano, 1574.

Moxon, Joseph. *Mechanic Exercises, or, the Doctrine of Handy-Works.* London: Printed for Joseph Moxon, 1677.

Navarro, Juan. *Historia natural o jardín americano.* Mexico City: Universidad Nacional Autónoma de México, Instituto Mexicano del Seguro Social, and Instituto de Seguridad y Servicios Sociales de los Trabajadores del Estado, 1992.

Ortiz de Logroño, Juan Elías. *Un formulario notarial mexicano del siglo XVIII: La instrucción de escribanos de Juan Elías Ortiz de Logroño.* Edited by Juan Ricardo Jiménez Gómez. Mexico City: Universidad Autónoma de Querétaro and Miguel Ángel Porrúa, 2005.

Pask, Robert. Advertisement. Robert Pask stationer, at the Stationer's Arms and Inck-Bottle on the north side of the Royal Exchange, London: Hath made a choice sort of black inck in hard balls, with that conveniency, that you may wear them about you, without any damage to the inck or your linnen; . . . Sold only at his own shop. London, 16[7–?]. Early English Books Online, Record No. E4:2[18b]; original in the British Library.

Pérez, Ignacio. *Arte de escribir.* Madrid: En la Imprenta Real, 1599.

Recopilación de leyes de los reinos de las Indias. Madrid: Boiz, 1841.

Reyes, Antonio de los. *Arte en lengua mixteca.* Nashville, TN: Vanderbilt University, 1976 [1593].

Robles, Antonio. *Diario de sucesos notables (1665–1703),* vol. 1. Edited by Antonio Castro Leal. Mexico City: Editorial Porrúa, 1946.

Sahagún, Bernardino de. *Historia general de las cosas de Nueva España,* vol. 3. Edited by Ángel María Garibay. Mexico City: Editorial Porrúa, 1977.

———. *Historia general de las cosas de la Nueva España,* vol. 2. Edited by Juan Carlos Temprano. Madrid: Dastin, 2001.

———. *Historia general de las cosas de la Nueva España,* Books I–XII. Biblioteca Medicea Laurenziana. www.wdl.org/en/search/?collection=florentine-codex#10096.

Terreros y Pando, Esteban de. *Diccionario castellano con las voces de ciencias y artes y sus correspondientes en las tres lenguas francesa, latina e italiana.* Madrid: Viuda de Ibarra, 1787.

Transcripción de las Ordenanzas de descubrimiento, nueva población y pacificación de las Indias dadas por Felipe II, el 13 de julio de 1573, en el Bosque de Segovia, según el original que se conserva en el Archivo General de Indias de Sevilla. Madrid: Ministerio de la Vivienda, 1973.

Ximénez, Francisco. *Historia natural del reino de Guatemala.* Guatemala: Editorial José de Pineda Ibarra, 1967 [1722].

Zorita, Alonso de. *Breve y sumaria relación de los señores, y maneras, y diferencias que había de ellos en la Nueva España y en otras provincias, sus comarcas, de sus leyes, usos y costumbres.* Copied by Lorenzo Boturini, Mexico City, 1738 [c. 1570].

SECONDARY SOURCES

Achim, Miruna. *From Idols to Antiquity: Forging the National Museum of Mexico.* Lincoln: University of Nebraska Press, 2017.

Acuña, René. *Relaciones geográficas del siglo XVI: Antequera,* vol. 2. Mexico City: Universidad Autónoma de México, 1986.

Aguilar-Robledo, Miguel. "Contested Terrain: The Rise and Decline of Surveying in New Spain, 1500–1800." *Journal of Latin American Geography* 8:2 (2009): 23–47.

Albro, Sylvia Rodgers, and Thomas C. Albro II. "The Examination and Conservation Treatment of the Library of Congress Harkness 1531 Huejotzingo Codex." *Journal of the American Institute for Conservation* 29:2 (1990): 97–115.

Anderson, Arthur. "Materiales colorantes prehispánicos." *Estudios de Cultura Náhuatl* 4 (1963): 73–83.

Anderson, Arthur, Frances Berdan, and James Lockhart, eds. *Beyond the Codices: The Nahua View of Colonial Mexico.* Berkeley: University of California Press, 1976.

Antei, Giorgio. *El caballero anadante: Vida, obra y desaventuras de Lorenzo Boturini Benaduci (1698–1755).* Mexico City: Museo de la Basílica de Guadalupe, 2007.

Archivo General de la Nación. "Sixteenth to Eighteenth-Century Pictographs from the Record Group 'Maps, Drawings, and Illustrations' of the National General Archives of Mexico." Reference No. 2010-41. Documentary Heritage Proposal Accepted by UNESCO for Memory of the World Program. Inscribed in 2011.

Arellano Hoffmann, Carmen. "El escriba mesoamericano y sus utensilios de trabajo. La posición social del escriba antes y después de la conquista española." In *Libros y escritura de tradición indígena: Ensayos sobre los códices prehispánicos y coloniales de México.* Edited by Carmen Arellano Hoffmann, Peer Schmidt, and Xavier Noguez. Toluca and Eichstätt: El Colegio Mexiquense and Katholische Universität, 2002.

Arellano Hoffmann, Carmen, Peer Schmidt, and Xavier Noguez, eds. *Libros y escritura de tradición indígena: Ensayos sobre los códices prehispánicos y coloniales de México.* Toluca and Eichstätt: El Colegio Mexiquense and Katholische Universität, 2002.

Ares Queija, Berta, and Serge Gruzinski, eds. *Entre dos mundos: fronteras culturales y agentes mediadores.* Sevilla: Consejo Superior de Investigaciones Científicas, 1997.

Arnold, Philip. "Paper Ties to Land: Indigenous and Colonial Material Orientations to the Valley of Mexico." *History of Religions* 35:1 (1995): 27–60.

Arroyo Ortiz, Laura. *Tintes naturales mexicanos: Su aplicación en algodón, henequén y lana.* Mexico City: Comisión Nacional para el Conocimiento y Uso de la Biodiversidad and Universidad Nacional Autónoma de México, 2008.

Asselbergs, Florine. *Conquered Conquistadors: The Lienzo de Quauhquechollan, A Nahua Vision of the Conquest of Guatemala.* Boulder: University Press of Colorado, 2008.

Baird, Ellen T. "The Artists of Sahagún's *Primeros Memoriales*: A Question of Identity." In *The Work of Bernardino de Sahagún: Pioneer Ethnographer of Sixteenth-Century Aztec Mexico.* Edited by

Jorge Klor de Alva, H. B. Nicholson, and Eloise Quiñones Keber. Albany: Institute for Mesoamerican Studies, SUNY–Albany; Austin: University of Texas Press, 1988.

Bargellini, Clara. "Originality and Invention in the Painting of New Spain." In *Painting a New World: Mexican Art and Life, 1521–1821*. Denver: Denver Art Museum, 2004.

Barickman, Bert J. "'Tame Indians,' 'Wild Heathens,' and Settlers in Southern Bahia in the Late Eighteenth and Early Nineteenth Centuries." *The Americas* 51:3 (1995): 325–368.

Barrera-Osorio, Antonio. *Experiencing Nature: The Spanish American Empire and the Early Scientific Revolution*. Austin: University of Texas Press, 2006.

Baudot, Georges. *Utopia and History in Mexico: The First Chroniclers of Mexican Civilization (1520–1569)*. Translated by Bernard R. Ortiz de Montellano and Thelma Ortiz de Montellano. Niwot: University Press of Colorado, 1995.

Baudrillard, Jean. "The System of Collecting." In *The Cultures of Collecting*. Edited by John Elsner and Roger Cardinal. London: Reaktion Books, 1994.

Bauer, Arnold. *Goods, Power, History: Latin America's Material Culture*. Cambridge: Cambridge University Press, 2001.

———. *Search for the Codex Cardona: On the Trail of a Sixteenth-Century Mexican Treasure*. Durham: Duke University Press, 2009.

Baxandall, Michael. *Painting and Experience in Fifteenth-Century Italy*. Oxford: Oxford University Press, 1988.

Beyersdorff, Margot. "Covering the Earth: Mapping the Walkabout in Andean *Pueblos de Indios*." *Latin American Research Review* 42 (2007): 129–160.

Bleichmar, Daniela. "Seeing the World in a Room: Looking at Exotica in Early Modern Collections." In *Collecting Across Cultures: Material Exchanges in the Early Modern Atlantic World*. Edited by Daniela Bleichmar and Peter C. Mancall. Philadelphia: University of Pennsylvania Press, 2011.

———. *Visible Empire: Botanical Expeditions and Visual Culture in the Hispanic Enlightenment*. Chicago: University of Chicago Press, 2012.

"History in Pictures: Translating the *Codex Mendoza*." *Art History* 38:4 (2015): 682–701.

———. "The Imperial Visual Archive: Images, Evidence, and Knowledge in the Early Modern Hispanic World." *Colonial Latin American Review* 24:2 (2015): 236–266.

Bleichmar, Daniela, Paula de Vos, Kristin Huffine, and Kevin Sheehan, eds. *Science in the Spanish and Portuguese Empires, 1500–1800*. Stanford: Stanford University Press, 2009.

———. "The Imperial Visual Archive: Images, Evidence, and Knowledge in the Early Modern Hispanic World." *Colonial Latin American Review* 24:2 (2015): 236–266.

Bleichmar, Daniela, and Peter C. Mancall, eds. *Collecting Across Cultures: Material Exchanges in the Early Modern Atlantic World*. Philadelphia: University of Pennsylvania Press, 2011.

Bolles, David, and William Folan. "An Analysis of Roads Listed in Colonial Dictionaries and Their Relevance to Pre-Hispanic Linear Features in the Yucatan Peninsula." *Ancient Mesoamerica* 12:2 (2001): 299–314.

Boone, Elizabeth H. "Aztec Pictorial Histories: Records without Words." In *Writing without Words: Alternative Literacies in Mesoamerica and the Andes*. Edited by Elizabeth H. Boone and Walter Mignolo. Durham: Duke University Press, 1994.

———. "Pictorial Documents and Visual Thinking in Postconquest Mexico." In *Native Traditions in the Postconquest World*. Edited by Elizabeth H. Boone and Thomas Cummins. Washington, DC: Dumbarton Oaks, 1998.

———. *Stories in Red and Black: Pictorial Histories of the Aztecs and Mixtecs*. Austin: University of Texas Press, 2000.

———. *Cycles of Time and Meaning in the Mexican Books of Fate*. Austin: University of Texas Press, 2007.

Boone, Elizabeth H., ed. *The Art and Iconography of Late Post-Classic Central Mexico*. Washington, DC: Dumbarton Oaks, 1982.

Boone, Elizabeth H., and Thomas Cummins, eds. *Native Traditions in the Postcoquest World*. Washington, DC: Dumbarton Oaks, 1998.

Boone, Elizabeth H., and Walter D. Mignolo, eds. *Writing without Words: Alternative Literacies in Mesoamerica and the Andes*. Durham: Duke University Press, 1994.

Borah, Woodrow. *Justice by Insurance: The General Indian Court of Colonial Mexico and the Legal Aides of the Half-Real*. Berkeley: University of California Press, 1983.

Bouza, Fernando. *Corre manuscrito: Una historia cultural del Siglo de Oro*. Madrid: Marcial Pons, 2001.

———. *Communication, Knowledge, and Memory in Early Modern Spain*. Translated by Sonia López and Michael Agnew. Philadelphia: University of Pennsylvania Press, 2004.

Boyd-Bowman, Peter. "Otro inventario de mercancías del siglo XVI." *Historia Mexicana* 20 (1970): 92–118.

———. "Two Country Stores in XVIIth Century Mexico." *The Americas* 28 (1972): 237–251.

———. "Spanish and European Textiles in Sixteenth-Century Mexico." *The Americas* 29 (1973): 334–358.

Brian, Amber. *Alva Ixtlilxochitl's Native Archive and the Circulation of Knowledge in Colonial Mexico*. Nashville, TN: Vanderbilt University Press, 2016.

Brockington, Lolita G. *The Leverage of Labor: Managing the Cortés Haciendas in Tehuantepec, 1588–1688*. Durham: Duke University Press, 1989.

Brokaw, Galen, and Jongsoon Lee, ed. *Fernando de Alva Ixtlilxochitl and His Legacy*. Tucson: University of Arizona Press, 2016.

Brown, Michelle P. *Understanding Illuminated Manuscripts: A Guide to Technical Terms*. Los Angeles: The J. Paul Getty Museum and the British Library, 1994.

Brownstone, Arni, ed. *The Lienzo of Tlapiltepec: A Painted History from the Northern Mixteca*. Norman: University of Oklahoma Press, 2015.

Buisseret, David. *The Mapmakers' Quest: Depicting New Worlds in Renaissance Europe*. Oxford: Oxford University Press, 2003.

Buisseret, David, ed. *Monarchs, Ministers, and Maps: The Emergence of Cartography as a Tool of Government in Early Modern Europe*. Chicago: University of Chicago Press, 1992.

Burkhart, Louise M. *The Slippery Earth: Nahua-Christian Moral Dialogue in Sixteenth-Century Mexico*. Tucson: University of Arizona Press, 1989.

Burnett, Graham D. *Masters of All They Surveyed: Exploration, Geography, and a British El Dorado*. Chicago: University of Chicago Press, 2000.

Burns, Kathryn. "Notaries, Truth, and Consequences." *American Historical Review* 110 (2005): 350–379.

———. *Into the Archive: Writing and Power in Colonial Peru*. Durham: Duke University Press, 2010.

Burton, Antoinette. "Thinking Beyond the Boundaries: Empire, Feminism, and the Domains of History." *Journal of Social History* 26:1 (2001): 60–71.

Butzer, Elisabeth. "The Roadside Inn or 'Venta': Origins and Early Development in New Spain." *Yearbook: Conference of Latin Americanist Geographers* 23 (1997): 1–15.

Butzer, Karl W. "From Columbus to Acosta: Science, Geography, and the New World." *Annals of the Association of American Geographers* 82:3 (1992): 543–565.

Cañizares-Esguerra, Jorge. *How to Write the History of the New World: Histories, Epistemologies, and Identities in the Eighteenth-Century Atlantic World*. Stanford: Stanford University Press, 2002.

———. "Renaissance Mess(tizaje): What Mexican Indians Did to Titian and Ovid." *New Centennial Review* 2 (2002): 267–276.

———. *Nature, Empire, and Nation: Explorations of the History of Science in the Iberian World*. Stanford: Stanford University Press, 2006.

Carmagnani, Marcello. *El regreso de los dioses: El proceso de reconstitución de la identidad étnica en Oaxaca. Siglos XVII y XVIII*. Mexico City: Fondo de Cultura Económica, 1988.

Carrera Stampa, Manuel. "*El sistema de pesos y medidas colonial*." *Memorias de la Academia Mexicana de la Historia* 26:1 (1967): 1–37.

Carvalho, David. *Forty Centuries of Ink, or A Chronological Narrative Concerning Ink and Its Backgrounds*. New York: The Banks Law Publishing Company, 1904.

Caso, Alfonso. "El mapa de Teozacoalco." In *Obras: El México antiguo*, vol. 8: "Calendarios, códices, y manuscritos antiguos." Mexico City: El Colegio Nacional, 2007.

Castañeda, Carmen, ed. *Del autor al lector: Libros y libreros en la historia*. Mexico City: Centro de Investigaciones y Estudios Superiores en Antropología Social, 2002.

Castañeda de la Paz, María. "Sibling Maps, Spatial Rivalries: The Beinecke Map and the Plano Parcial de la Ciudad de México." In *Painting a Map of Sixteenth-Century Mexico City: Land, Writing, and Native Rule*. Edited by Mary Miller and Barbara Mundy. New Haven: Yale University Press, 2012.

Castelló Yturbide, Teresa. *Colorantes naturales de México*. Mexico City: Industrias Resistol, 1988.

Castleman, Bruce. *Building the King's Highway: Labor, Society, and Family on Mexico's Caminos Reales, 1757–1804*. Tucson: University of Arizona Press, 2005.

Castro Pérez, Candelaria, Mercedes Calvo Cruz, and Sonia Granado Suárez. "Las capellanías en los siglos XVII–XVIII a través del estudio de escritura de fundación." *Anuario de Historia de la Iglesia* 16 (2007): 335–348.

Catálogo de ilustraciones, vol. 1–14. Mexico City: Archivo General de la Nación, 1979–1984.

Cervantes, Fernando. *The Devil in the New World: The Impact of Diabolism in New Spain*. New Haven: Yale University Press, 1994.

Chance, John K. *Race and Class in Colonial Oaxaca*. Stanford: Stanford University Press, 1978.

Chevalier, François. *Land and Society in Colonial Mexico: The Great Hacienda*. Translated by Alvis Eustis. Berkeley: University of California Press, 1970.

Christensen, Bodil. "Bark Paper and Witchcraft in Indian Mexico." *Economic Botany* 17:4 (1963): 360–367.

Christian, William. *Local Religion in Sixteenth-Century Spain*. Princeton: Princeton University Press, 1981.

Christie, Jessica Joyce. "Inka Roads, Lines, and Rock Shrines: A Discussion of the Contexts of Trail Markers." *Journal of Anthropological Research* 64:1 (2008): 41–66.

Classen, Constance. "Museum Manners: The Sensory Life of the Early Museum." *Journal of Social History* 40:4 (2007): 895–914.

Clendinnen, Inga. *Ambivalent Conquests: Maya and Spaniard in Yucatan, 1517–1570*. Cambridge: Cambridge University Press, 2003.

Cline, Howard F. "The *Relaciones Geográficas* of the Spanish Indies, 1577–1648." In *Handbook of Middle American Indians*, vol. 12. Edited by Robert Wauchope and Howard F. Cline. Austin: University of Texas Press, 1972.

Cline, Sarah. "The Spiritual Conquest Reexamined: Baptism and Christian Marriage in Early Sixteenth-Century Mexico." *Hispanic American Historical Review* 73:3 (1993): 453–480.

Confino, Alon. "Collective Memory and Cultural History: Problems of Method." *American Historical Review* 102 (1997): 1386–1403.

Contreras Sánchez, Alicia del Carmen. *Capital comercial y colorantes en la Nueva España: Segunda mitad del S. XVIII*. Zamora: El Colegio de Michoacán, 1996.

Craib, Raymond. "Cartography and Power in the Conquest and Creation of New Spain." *Latin American Research Review* 35:1 (2000): 7–36.

———. *Cartographic Mexico: A History of State Fixations and Fugitive Landscapes*. Durham: Duke University Press, 2004.

———. "Relocating Cartography." *Postcolonial Studies* 12:4 (2009): 481–490.

Cramaussel, Chantal, ed. *Rutas de la Nueva España*. Zamora: El Colegio de Michoacán, 2006.

Crane, Susan. "Writing the Individual Back Into Collective Memory." *American Historical Review* 102 (1997): 1372–1385.

Cummins, Thomas B. F. "From Lies to Truth: Colonial Ekphrasis and the Act of Crosscultural Translation." In *Reframing the Renaissance: Visual Culture in Europe and Latin America, 1450–1650.* Edited by Claire Farago. New Haven: Yale University Press, 1995.

Cummins, Thomas B. F., Emily A. Engel, Barbara Anderson, and Juan M. Ossio A., eds. *Manuscript Cultures of Colonial Mexico and Peru: New Questions and Approaches.* Los Angeles: The Getty Research Institute, 2014.

Darnton, Robert. "The Library in the New Age." *The New York Review of Books,* June 12, 2008, 72–80.

De Vos, Paula. "The Science of Spices: Empiricism and Economic Botany in the Early Spanish Empire." *Journal of World History* 17:4 (2006): 399–427.

———. "Natural History and the Pursuit of Empire in Eighteenth-Century Spain." *Eighteenth-Century Studies* 40:2 (2007): 209–239.

———. "Apothecaries, Artists, and Artisans: Early Industrial Material Culture in the Biological Old Regime." *Journal of Interdisciplinary History* 45:3 (2015): 277–336.

Dean, Carolyn, and Dana Leibsohn. "Hybridity and Its Discontents: Considering Visual Culture in Colonial Spanish America." *Colonial Latin American Review* 12 (2003): 5–35.

Delbourgo, James, and Staffan Müller-Wille. Introduction to Focus Section: "Listmania." *Isis* 103:4 (2012): 710–715.

Díaz Álvarez, Ana G. "El *Códice Dehesa*: Reflexiones en torno a un documento mixteco colonial a partir de su análisis codicológico." *Revista Española de Antropología Americana* 40:2 (2010): 149–165.

DiCesare, Catherine. *Sweeping the Way: Divine Transformation in the Aztec Festival of Ochpaniztli.* Boulder: University Press of Colorado, 2009.

Doesburg, Sebastián van. "Documentos pictográficos de la Mixteca Baja." *Arqueología Mexicana* 90 (2008): 53–57.

Donahue-Wallace, Kelly. "Picturing Prints in Early Modern New Spain." *The Americas* 64:3 (2008): 325–349.

Donkin, R. A. "Spanish Red: An Ethnogeographical Study of Cochineal and the Opuntia Cactus." *Transactions of the American Philosophical Society* 67 (1977): 1–84.

Douglas, Eduardo de Jesús. *In the Palace of Nezahualcoyotl: Painting Manuscripts, Writing the Pre-Hispanic Past in Early Colonial Period Tetzcoco, Mexico.* Austin: University of Texas Press, 2010.

Dunmire, William. *Gardens of New Spain: How Mediterranean Plants and Foods Changed America.* Austin: University of Texas Press, 2004.

Earle, Rebecca. "'Two Pairs of Pink Satin Shoes!!': Race, Clothing, and Identity in the Americas (17th–19th Centuries)." *History Workshop Journal* 52 (2001): 175–195.

———. "Luxury, Clothing, and Race in Colonial Spanish America." In *Luxury in the Eighteenth Century: Debates, Desires, and Delectable Goods.* Edited by Maxine Berg and Elizabeth Eger. New York: Palgrave, 2003.

———. "Letters and Love in Colonial Spanish America." *The Americas* 62 (2005): 17–46.

Edgerton, Samuel Y. *Theatres of Conversion: Religious Architecture and Indian Artisans in Colonial Mexico.* Albuquerque: University of New Mexico Press, 2001.

Edney, Matthew H. "Theory and the History of Cartography." *Imago Mundi* 48 (1996): 185–191.

———. *Mapping an Empire: The Geographical Construction of British India, 1765–1843.* Chicago: University of Chicago Press, 1997.

Eisenstein, Elizabeth. *The Printing Press as an Agent of Change,* vol. 1–2. Cambridge: Cambridge University Press, 1979.

———. "An Unacknowledged Revolution Revisited." *American Historical Review* 107:1 (2002): 87–105.

El papel y las tintas en la transmisión de la información. Primeras jornadas archivísticas del 12 al 16 de mayo de 1992. Huelva: Diputación Provincial, 1994.

Enfeld, Georgina H. "'Pinturas,' Land, and Lawsuits: Maps in Colonial Mexican Legal Documents." *Imago Mundi* 53 (2001): 7–27.

Erickson, Peter, and Clark Hulse, eds. *Early Modern Visual Culture: Representation, Race, and Empire in Renaissance England.* Philadelphia: University of Pennsylvania Press, 2000.

Escamilla, Iván. "'Próvido y proporcionado' socorro: Lorenzo Boturini y sus patrocinadores novohispanos." In *Poder civil y catolicismo en México, siglos XVI al XIX.* Edited by Francisco Javier Cervantes Bello, Alicia Tecuanhuey Sandoval, and María del Pilar Martínez López-Cano. Puebla: Benemérita Universidad Autónoma de Puebla and Universidad Nacional Autónoma de México, 2008.

———. "Lorenzo Boturini y el entorno social de su empresa historiográfica." In *Memorias del coloquio, El caballero Lorenzo Boturini: Entre dos mundos y dos historias.* Mexico City: Museo de la Basílica de Guadalupe, 2010.

Farago, Claire, ed. *Reframing the Renaissance: Visual Culture in Europe and Latin America, 1450–1650.* New Haven: Yale University Press, 1995.

Farriss, Nancy. *Maya Society under Colonial Rule: The Collective Enterprise of Survival.* Princeton: Princeton University Press, 1984.

———. "Introductory Essay: The Power of Images." *Colonial Latin American Review* 19:1 (2010): 5–28.

Fennetaux, Ariane, Amélie Junqua, and Sophie Vasset, eds. *The Afterlife of Used Things: Recycling in the Long Eighteenth Century.* New York: Routledge, 2015.

Few, Martha. *Women Who Live Evil Lives: Gender, Religion, and the Politics of Power in Colonial Guatemala, 1650–1750.* Austin: University of Texas Press, 2002.

———. "Indian Autopsy and Epidemic Disease in Early Colonial Mexico." In *Invasion and Transformation: Interdisciplinary Perspectives on the Conquest of Mexico.* Edited by Rebecca Brienen and Margaret Jackson. Boulder: University Press of Colorado, 2007.

———. *For All of Humanity: Mesoamerican and Colonial Medicine in*

Enlightenment Guatemala. Tucson: University of Arizona Press, 2015.

Findlen, Paula. "Possessing the Past: The Material World of the Italian Renaissance." *American Historical Review* 103:1 (1998): 83–114.

Findlen, Paula, ed. *Early Modern Things: Objects and Their Histories, 1500–1800*. London and New York: Routledge, 2013.

Florescano, Enrique. *Historia de las historias de la nación mexicana*. Mexico City: Taurus, 2002.

———. "El canon memorioso forjado por los títulos primordiales." *Colonial Latin American Review* 11:2 (2002): 183–230.

Friedrich, Markus. *The Birth of the Archive: A History of Knowledge*. Translated by John Noël Dillon. Ann Arbor: University of Michigan Press, 2018.

Galarza, Joaquín. *Códices y pinturas tradicionales indígenas en el Archivo General de la Nación. Estudio y catálogo*. Mexico City: Amatl and Librería Madero, 1996.

García Icazbalceta, Joaquín. *Nueva colección de documentos para la historia de México*, vol. 3. Mexico City: Francisco Díaz de León, 1891.

Geertz, Clifford. *The Interpretation of Cultures: Selected Essays*. New York: Basic Books, 1973.

Gerhard, Peter. *A Guide to the Historical Geography of New Spain*. Norman: University of Oklahoma Press, 1993 [1972].

Gibson, Charles. *The Aztecs under Spanish Rule: A History of the Indians of the Valley of Mexico, 1519–1810*. Stanford: Stanford University Press, 1964.

Glass, John. "A Survey of Native Middle American Pictorial Manuscripts." In *Handbook of Middle American Indians*, vol. 14. Austin: University of Texas Press, 1975.

———. "The Boturini Collection." In *Handbook of Middle American Indians*, vol. 15. Austin: University of Texas Press, 1975.

Glass, John, and Donald Robertson. "A Census of Native Middle American Pictorial Manuscripts." In *Handbook of Middle American Indians*, vol. 14. Austin: University of Texas Press, 1975.

González del Campo, Guillermo, and José J. Hernández Palomo. "Boturini o las desaventuras de un devoto guadalupano (seis cartas desde la cárcel)." *Estudios de Historia Novohispana* 42 (2010): 151–205.

González Echevarría, Roberto. *Myth and Archive: A Theory of Latin American Narrative*. Cambridge: Cambridge University Press, 1990.

González Salgado, José Antonio. "Contribución al estudio de la ortografía en el siglo XVI: La reforma del padre Flórez." *Dicenda: Cuadernos de filología hispánica* 14 (1996): 149–158.

Gosner, Kevin. *Soldiers of the Virgin: The Moral Economy of a Colonial Maya Rebellion*. Tucson: University of Arizona Press, 1992.

Grafton, Anthony. *New Worlds, Ancient Texts: The Power of Tradition and the Shock of Discovery*. Cambridge, MA: Harvard University Press, 1992.

Granziera, Patrizia. "Concept of the Garden in Pre-Hispanic Mexico." *Garden History* 29:2 (2001): 185–213.

———. "Huaxtepec: The Sacred Garden of an Aztec Emperor." *Landscape Research* 30:1 (2005): 81–107.

Gruzinski, Serge. "Colonial Indian Maps in Sixteenth-Century Mexico: An Essay in Mixed Cartography." *Res: Anthropology and Aesthetics* 13 (1987): 46–61.

———. *Man-Gods in the Mexican Highlands: Indian Power and Colonial Society, 1550–1580*. Translated by Eileen Corrigan. Stanford: Stanford University Press, 1989.

———. *La colonización de lo imaginario: Sociedades indígenas y occidentalización en el México español, siglos XVI–XVIII*. Mexico City: Fondo de Cultura Económica, 1991.

———. *Images at War: Mexico from Columbus to Blade Runner (1492–2019)*. Translated by Heather MacLean. Durham: Duke University Press, 2001.

———. *The Mestizo Mind: The Intellectual Dynamics of Colonization and Globalization*. New York: Routledge, 2002.

Gutiérrez, Ramón. *When Jesus Came, the Corn Mothers Went Away: Marriage, Sexuality, and Power in New Mexico, 1500–1846*. Stanford: Stanford University Press, 1991.

Hamman, Byron. "Object, Image, Cleverness: The Lienzo de Tlaxcala." *Art History* 36:3 (2013): 518–545.

Harley, J. B. "Rereading the Maps of the Colombian Encounter." *Annals of the Association of American Geographers* 82:3 (1992): 522–536.

———. *The New Nature of Maps: Essays in the History of Cartography*. Edited by Paul Laxton. Baltimore: Johns Hopkins University Press, 2001.

Haskett, Robert. *Indigenous Rulers: An Ethnohistory of Town Government in Colonial Cuernavaca*. Albuquerque: University of New Mexico Press, 1991.

———. "Paper Shields: The Ideology of Coats of Arms in Colonial Mexican Primordial Titles." *Ethnohistory* 43 (1996): 99–126.

Hassig, Ross. *Trade, Tribute, and Transportation: The Sixteenth-Century Political Economy of the Valley of Mexico*. Norman: University of Oklahoma Press, 1985.

Haude, Mary Elizabeth. "Identification of Colorants on Maps from the Early Colonial Period of New Spain (Mexico)." *Journal of the American Institute for Conservation* 37 (1996): 240–270.

Herrera, Marta, Santiago Muñoz, and Santiago Paredes. "Geographies of the Name: Naming Practices among the Muisca and Páez in the Audiencias of Santafé and Quito, Sixteenth and Seventeenth Centuries." *Journal of Latin American Geography* 11 (Special Issue) (2012): 91–115.

Herzog, Tamar. *Defining Nations: Immigrants and Citizens in Early Modern Spain and Spanish America*. New Haven: Yale University Press, 2003.

———. "Colonial Law and 'Native Customs': Indigenous Land Rights in Colonial Spanish America." *The Americas* 69:3 (2013): 303–321.

Hidalgo, Alex. "A True and Faithful Copy: Reproducing Indian Maps in the Seventeenth-Century Valley of Oaxaca." *Journal of Latin American Geography* 11 (Special Issue) (2012): 117–144.

———. "How to Map with Ink: Cartographic Materials from Colonial Oaxaca." *Ethnohistory* 61:2 (2014): 277–299.

Hidalgo, Alex, and John F. López, eds. "The Ethnohistorical Map in New Spain." Special issue, *Ethnohistory* 61: 2 (2014).

Hyslop, John. *The Inka Road System*. Orlando: Academic Press, 1984.

Jacob, Christian. "Toward a Cultural History of Cartography." *Imago Mundi* 48 (1996): 191–198.

Jansen, Maarten. "Monte Albán y Zaachila en los códices mixtecos." In *The Shadow of Monte Alban: Politics and historiography in postclassic Oaxaca, Mexico*. Edited by Maarten Jansen, Peter Kröfges, and Michel Oudijk. Leiden: Research School CNWS, School of Asian, African, and Amerindian Studies, 1998.

Jansen, Maarten, Dante García Ríos, and Ángel Rivera Guzmán. "La identificación de Monte Albán en los códices mixtecos: Nueva evidencia." Paper presented at the VI Monte Albán Roundtable Conference, Oaxaca, Mexico, 2011.

Jansen, Maarten, and Gabina A. Pérez Jiménez. *Voces del Dzaha Zdavui: Análisis y conversión del* Vocabulario *de Fray Francisco de Alvarado (1593)*. Oaxaca City: Colegio Superior para la Educación Integral Intercultural de Oaxaca, 2009.

Jansen, Maarten, Peter Kröfges, and Michel Oudijk, eds. *The Shadow of Monte Alban: Politics and historiography in postclassic Oaxaca, Mexico*. Leiden: Research School CNWS, School of Asian, African, and Amerindian Studies, 1998.

Johns, Adrian. *The Nature of the Book: Print and Knowledge in the Making*. Chicago: University of Chicago Press, 1998.

———. "How to Acknowledge a Revolution." *American Historical Review* 107:1 (2002): 106–125.

———. "Ink." In *Materials and Expertise in Early Modern Europe: Between Market and Laboratory*. Edited by Ursula Klein and E. C. Spary. Chicago: University of Chicago Press, 2010.

Kagan, Richard. *Lawsuits and Litigants in Castile, 1500–1700*. Chapel Hill: University of North Carolina Press, 1981.

———. *Urban Images of the Hispanic World, 1493–1793*. New Haven: Yale University Press, 2000.

Karttunen, Frances. "After the Conquest: The Survival of Indigenous Patterns of Life and Belief." *Journal of World History* 3 (1992): 239–256.

Kashanipour, Ryan. "A World of Cures: Magic and Medicine in Colonial Yucatán." PhD diss., University of Arizona, 2012.

Keating, Jessica, and Lia Markey. "Introduction: Captured Objects: Inventories of Early Modern Collections." *Journal of History of Collections* 23:2 (2011): 209–213.

Kiracofe, James. "Architectural Fusion and Indigenous Ideology in Early Colonial Teposcolula: La Casa de la Cacica: A Building at the Edge of Oblivion." *Anales del Instituto de Investigaciones Estéticas* 17:66 (1995): 45–84.

Klein, Ursula, and E. C. Spary, eds. *Materials and Expertise in Early Modern Europe: Between Market and Laboratory*. Chicago: University of Chicago Press, 2010.

Klor de Alva, Jorge. H. B. Nicholson, and Eloise Quiñones Keber, eds. *The Work of Bernardino de Sahagún: Pioneer Ethnographer of Sixteenth-Century Aztec Mexico*. Albany: Institute for Mesoamerican Studies, SUNY–Albany; Austin: University of Texas Press.

Kranz, Travis. "Visual Persuasion: Sixteenth-Century Tlaxcalan Pictorials in Response to the Conquest of Mexico." In *The Conquest All Over Again: Nahuas and Zapotecs Thinking, Writing, and Painting Spanish Colonialism*. Edited by Susan Schroeder. Eastbourne: Sussex Academic Press, 2010.

Kubler, George. "On the Colonial Extinction of the Motifs of Pre-Colombian Art." *Essays in Pre-Colombian Art and Archaeology*. Edited by Samuel Lothrop. Cambridge, MA: Harvard University Press, 1961.

Langfur, Hal. "Uncertain Refuge: Frontier Formation and the Origins of the Botocudo War in Late Colonial Brazil." *Hispanic American Historical Review* 82:2 (2002): 215–256.

Lara, Jaime. *City, Temple, Stage: Eschatological Architecture and Liturgical Theatrics in New Spain*. South Bend, IN: University of Notre Dame Press, 2005.

Lechuga, Ruth. *El traje indígena de México: su evolución, desde la época Prehispánica hasta la actualidad*. Mexico City: Panorama, 1982.

Lefebvre, Henri. *The Production of Space*. Translated by Donald Nicholson-Smith. Oxford: Blackwell Publishing, 1991.

Leibsohn, Dana. "Primers for Memory: Cartographic Histories and Nahua Identity." In *Writing Without Words: Alternative Literacies in Mesoamerican and the Andes*. Edited by Elizabeth H. Boone and Walter D. Mignolo. Durham: Duke University Press, 1994.

———. "Colony and Cartography: Shifting Signs on Indigenous Maps of New Spain." In *Reframing the Renaissance: Visual Culture in Europe and Latin America, 1450–1650*. Edited by Claire Farago. New Haven: Yale University Press, 1995.

———. *Script and Glyph: Pre-Hispanic History, Colonial Bookmaking and the* Historia Tolteca-Chichimeca. Washington, DC: Dumbarton Oaks Research Library and Collection, 2009.

Lenz, Hans. *El papel indígena mexicano*. Mexico City: SEP-Setentas, 1973 [1948].

———. "Paper and Superstitions." *Artes de México* 124 (1969): 93–98.

———. *Historia del papel en México y cosas relacionadas (1525–1950)*. Mexico City: Miguel Ángel Porrúa, 1990.

Lockhart, James. *The Nahuas after the Conquest: A Social and Cultural History of the Indians of Central Mexico, Sixteenth through Eighteenth Centuries*. Stanford: Stanford University Press, 1992.

———. "Encomienda and Hacienda." In *Of Things of the Indies: Essays Old and New in Early Latin American History*. Edited by James Lockhart. Stanford: Stanford University Press, 1999.

Lockhart, James, Lisa Sousa, and Stephanie Wood, eds. *Sources and Methods for the Study of Postconquest Mesoamerican Ethnohistory*. Provisional Version (e-book). Eugene: Wired Humanities Project, University of Oregon, 2007.

Long, Pamela O. *Openness, Secrecy, Authorship: Technical Arts and the Culture of Knowledge from Antiquity to the Renaissance*. Baltimore: Johns Hopkins University Press, 2001.

López, John F. "'In the Art of My Profession': Adrian Boot and Dutch Water Management in Colonial Mexico City." *Journal of Latin American Geography* 11 (Special Issue) (2012): 35–60.

———. "Indigenous Commentary on Sixteenth-Century Mexico." *Ethnohistory* 61:2 (2014): 253–275.

López Caballero, Paula, ed. *Los títulos primordiales del centro de México*. Mexico City: Consejo Nacional para la Cultura y las Artes and Fondo Editorial Tierra Adentro, 2003.

López Piñero, José María. "Las 'Nuevas Medicinas' Americanas en la Obra (1565–1574) de Nicolás Monardes." *Asclepio* 42:1 (1990): 3–67.

———. *El Códice Pomar (ca. 1590): El interés de Felipe II por la historia natural y la expedición Hernández a América*. Valencia: Universitat de València, 1991.

López Piñero, José M., and José Pardo Tomás. *La influencia de Francisco Hernández (1515–1587) en la constitución de la botánica y la materia médica modernas*. Valencia: Universitat de València, 1996.

———. "The Contribution of Hernández to European Botany and Materia Medica." In *Searching for the Secrets of Nature: The Life and Works of Dr. Francisco Hernández*. Edited by Simon Varey, Rafael Chabrán, and Dora B. Weiner. Stanford: Stanford University Press, 2000.

Los códices de México. Mexico City: Instituto Nacional de Antropología e Historia and Secretaría de Educación Pública, 1979.

Love, Harold. *The Culture and Commerce of Texts: Scribal Publication in Seventeenth-Century England*. Amherst: University of Massachusetts Press, 1993.

Luján Muñoz, Jorge. "La literatura notarial en España e Hispanoamérica, 1500–1820." *Anuario de Estudios Americanos* 38 (1981): 101–116.

Magaloni Kerpel, Diana. "Painters of the New World: The Process of Making the *Florentine Codex*." In *Colors between Two Worlds: The Florentine Codex of Bernardino de Sahagún*. Edited by Gerhard Wolf, Joseph Connors, and Louis Waldman. Cambridge: Harvard University Press, 2012.

———. "The Traces of the Creative Process: Pictorial Materials and Techniques in the Beinecke Map." In *Painting a Map of Sixteenth-Century Mexico City: Land, Writing, and Native Rule*. Edited by Mary Miller and Barbara Mundy. New Haven: Yale University Press, 2012.

———. *The Colors of the New World: Artists, Materials, and the Creation of the Florentine Codex* (Los Angeles: The Getty Research Institute, 2014).

Mallon, Florencia. *Peasant and Nation: The Making of Postcolonial Mexico and Peru*. Berkeley: University of California, 1995.

Marcus, Joyce. *Mesoamerican Writing Systems: Propaganda, Myth, and History in Four Ancient Civilizations*. Princeton: Princeton University Press, 1992.

Martínez, Ignacio. "The Paradox of Friendship: Loyalty and Betrayal on the Sonoran Frontier." *Journal of the Southwest* 56:2 (2014): 319–344.

Martínez, Maximino. *Catálogo de nombres vulgares y científicos de plantas mexicanas*. Mexico City: Ediciones Botas, 1937.

Martínez, Oscar. *Border People: Life and Society in the U.S.-Mexico Borderlands*. Tucson: University of Arizona Press, 1994.

Martínez Cortés, Fernando. *Pegamentos, gomas y resinas en el México Prehispánico*. Mexico City: Secretaría de Educación Pública, 1974.

Matías Alonso, Marcos. *Medidas indígenas de longitud, en documentos de la Ciudad de México del siglo XVI*. Mexico City: Centro de Investigaciones y Estudios Superiores en Antropología Social, 1984.

Matute, Álvaro. *Lorenzo Boturini y el pensamiento histórico de Vico*. Mexico City: Universidad Nacional Autónoma de México, 1976.

Mayer, Karl. "Cover: Amate Manuscripts of the Otomí of San Pablito, Puebla." *Mexicon* 34:6 (2012): 129–135.

McAfee, Byron, and Robert Barlow. "Anales de San Gregorio Acapulco." *Tlalocan* 3:2 (1952): 103–141.

Meadow, Mark. "Merchants and Marvels: Hans Jacob Fugger and the Origins of the Wunderkammer." In *Merchants and Marvels: Commerce, Science, and Art in Early Modern Europe*. Edited by Pamela H. Smith and Paula Findlen. New York and London: Routledge, 2002.

Megged, Amos. *Social Memory in Ancient and Colonial Mesoamerica*. New York: Cambridge University Press, 2010.

Melville, Elinor. *A Plague of Sheep: Environmental Consequences of the Conquest of Mexico*. Cambridge: Cambridge University Press, 1997.

Méndez Martínez, Enrique. *Índice de documentos relativos a los pueblos del estado de Oaxaca: Ramo Tierras del Archivo General de la Nación*. Mexico City: Instituto Nacional de Antropología e Historia, 1979.

Méndez Martínez, Enrique, and Enrique Méndez Torres, eds. *Límites, mapas y títulos primordiales de los pueblos del estado de Oaxaca: Índice del Ramo de Tierras*. Mexico City: Archivo General de la Nación, 1999.

———. *Historia de Zaachila, Cuilapan y Xoxocotlan: Tres pueblos unidos por sus orígines*. Oaxaca City: Instituto Cultural Oaxaqueño F.O.R.O., 2007.

Metcalf, Alida. *Go-Betweens and the Colonization of Brazil, 1500–1600*. Austin: University of Texas Press, 2005.

Mignolo, Walter D. *The Darker Side of the Renaissance: Literacy, Territoriality, and Colonization*. Ann Arbor: University of Michigan Press, 1995.

Miller, Mary, and Barbara Mundy, eds. *Painting a Map of Sixteenth-Century Mexico City: Land, Writing, and Native Rule*. New Haven: Yale University Press, 2012.

Miller, Peter. "How Objects Speak." *The Chronicle of Higher Education*, August 11, 2014.

Monaghan, John. "The Text in the Body, the Body in the Text: The Embodied Sign in Mixtec Writing." In *Writing without Words: Alternative Literacies in Mesoamerica and the Andes*. Edited by Elizabeth H. Boone and Walter D. Mignolo. Durham: Duke University Press, 1994.

Monmonier, Mark. *How to Lie with Maps*. Chicago: University of Chicago Press, 1996.

Montes de Oca Vega, Mercedes, Dominique Raby, Salvador Reyes Equiguas, and Adam Sellen. *Cartografía de tradición hispano-indígena: Mapas de mercedes de tierras, siglos XVI y XVII*, vol. 1–2. Mexico City: Universidad Nacional Autónoma de México, Instituto de Investigaciones Históricas, and Archivo General de la Nación, 2003.

More, Anna. *Baroque Sovereignty: Carlos de Sigüenza y Góngora and the Creole Archive of Colonial Mexico*. Philadelphia: University of Pennsylvania Press, 2013.

Mullen, Robert. *Dominican Architecture in Sixteenth-Century Oaxaca*. Tempe: Center for Latin American Studies, Arizona State University, 1975.

Mundy, Barbara. *The Mapping of New Spain: Indigenous Cartography and the Maps of the Relaciones Geográficas*. Chicago: University of Chicago Press, 1996.

———. "Mesoamerican Cartography." In *The History of Cartography*, vol. 2, book 3. Cartography in the Traditional African, American, Artic, Australian, and Pacific Societies. Edited by David Woodward and G. Malcolm Lewis. Chicago: University of Chicago Press, 1998.

———. "Pictography, Writing, and Mapping in the Valley of Mexico and the Beinecke Map." *Painting a Map of Sixteenth-Century Mexico City: Land, Writing, and Native Rule*. Edited by Mary Miller and Barbara Mundy. New Haven: Yale University Press, 2012.

Mundy, Barbara, and Dana Leibsohn. "Of Copies, Casts, and Codices: Mexico on Display in 1892." *Res* 29:30 (1996): 326–343.

Mut Calafell, Antonio. "Fórmulas españolas de la tinta caligráfica negra de los siglos XIII a XIX y otras relacionadas con la tinta (reavivar escritos, contra las manchas y goma glasa)." In *El papel y las tintas en la transmisión de la información*. Primeras jornadas archivísticas del 12 al 16 de mayo de 1992. Huelva: Diputación Provincial, 1994.

Nader, Helen. *Liberty in Absolutist Spain: The Habsburg Sale of Towns, 1516–1700*. Baltimore: Johns Hopkins University Press, 1990.

Neumann, Franke. "Paper: A Sacred Material in Aztec Ritual." *History of Religions* 13:2 (1973): 149–159.

Newman, Richard, and Michelle Derrick. "Analytical Report of the Pigments and Binding Materials Used in the Beinecke Map." In *Painting a Map of Sixteenth-Century Mexico City: Land, Writing, and Native Rule*. Edited by Mary Miller and Barbara Mundy. New Haven: Yale University Press, 2012.

Nicholson, H. B. "The Temalacatl of Tehuacan." *El México Antiguo* 8 (1955): 95–134.

———. "The Mixteca-Puebla Concept in Mesoamerican Archeology: A Re-examination." In *Men and Cultures: Selected Papers from the Fifth International Congress of Anthropological and Ethnological Sciences*. Edited by Anthony F. C. Wallace. Philadelphia: University of Pennsylvania Press, 1960.

———. "The Mixteca-Puebla Concept Re-visited." In *The Art and Iconography of Late Post-Classic Central Mexico*. Edited by Elizabeth H. Boone. Washington, DC: Dumbarton Oaks, 1982.

Noguez, Xavier, and Stephanie Wood, eds. *De tlacuilos y escribanos: Estudios sobre documentos indígenas coloniales del centro de México*. Zamora: El Colegio de Michoacán, 1998.

Nora, Pierre. "Between Memory and History: Les Lieux de Mémoir." *Representations* 26 (1989): 7–24.

Nussdorfer, Laurie. "Writing and the Power of Speech: Notaries and Artisans in Baroque Rome." In *Culture and Identity in Early Modern Europe (1500–1800): Essays in Honor of Natalie Zemon Davis*. Edited by Barbara B. Diefendorf and Carla Hesse. Ann Arbor: University of Michigan Press, 1993.

Olko, Justina. *Insignia of Rank in the Nahua World: From the Fifteenth to the Seventeenth Century*. Boulder: University Press of Colorado, 2014.

Olson, Todd. "Clouds and Rain." *Representations* 104:1 (2008): 102–115.

Ortiz de Montellano, Bernard. "Empirical Aztec Medicine." *Science* 188 (1975): 215–220.

Oudijk, Michel, and Maarten Jansen. "Changing History in the Lienzos de Guevea and Santo Domingo Petapa." *Ethnohistory* 47:2 (2000): 281–331.

Oudijk, Michel, and Sebastián van Doesberg. *Los lienzos pictográficos de Santa Cruz Papalutla, Oaxaca*. Mexico City and Oaxaca: Universidad Nacional Autónoma de México and Fundación Harp Helú, 2010.

Owensby, Brian. *Empire of Law and Indian Justice in Colonial Mexico*. Stanford: Stanford University Press, 2008.

Padrón, Ricardo. *The Spacious Word: Cartography, Literature, and Empire in Early Modern Spain*. Chicago: University of Chicago Press, 2004.

Painting a New World: Mexican Art and Life, 1521–1821. Denver: Denver Art Museum, 2004.

Parmenter, Ross. "The Lienzo of Tulancingo, Oaxaca: An Introductory Study of a Ninth Painted Sheet from the Coixtlahuaca Valley." *Transactions of the American Philosophical Society* 83:7 (1993): 1–86.

Pearce, Susan. *On Collecting: An Investigation of Collecting in the European Tradition*. London: Routledge, 1995.

Pedley, Mary Sponberg. *The Commerce of Cartography: Making and Marketing Maps in Eighteenth-Century France and England*. Chicago: Chicago University Press, 2005.

Pérez Fernández del Castillo, Bernardo. *Historia de la escribanía en la Nueva España y del notariado en México*. Mexico City: Colegio de Notarios del Distrito Federal and Editorial Porrúa, 1988.

Perry, Mary Elizabeth, and Anne J. Cruz, eds. *Cultural Encounters: The Impact of the Inquisition in Spain and the New World*. Berkeley and Los Angeles: University of California Press, 1991.

Peterson, Jeanette F. *Paradise Murals of Malinalco: Utopia and Empire in Sixteenth-Century Mexico*. Austin: University of Texas Press, 1992.

———. "Synthesis and Survival: The Native Presence in Sixteenth-Century Murals of New Spain." Special issue on "Native Artisans and Patrons in Colonial Latin America." *Phoebus* 7 (1995): 14–35.

Pettas, William. "A Sixteenth-Century Spanish Bookstore: The

Inventory of Juan de Junta." *Transactions of the American Philosophical Society* 95 (1995): 29–188.

Piedra, José. "The Value of Paper." *Res* 16 (1988): 85–104.

Pohl, John M. D. "Mexican Codices, Maps, and Lienzos as Social Contracts." In *Writing without Words: Alternative Literacies in Mesoamerican and the Andes*. Edited by Elizabeth H. Boone and Walter D. Mignolo. Durham: Duke University Press, 1994.

Portuondo, María. *Secret Science: Spanish Cosmography and the New World*. Chicago: Chicago University Press, 2009.

Presta, Ana María. "Undressing the *Coya* and Dressing the Indian Woman: Market Economy, Clothing, and Identities in the Colonial Andes, La Plata (Charcas), Late Sixteenth and Early Seventeenth Centuries." *Hispanic American Historical Review* 90:1 (2010): 41–74.

Puente Luna, José Carlos de la. *Andean Cosmopolitans: Seeking Justice and Reward at the Spanish Royal Court*. Austin: University of Texas Press, 2018.

Pulido Rull, Ana. "Land Grant Painted Maps: Native Artists and the Power of Visual Persuasion in Colonial New Spain." PhD diss., Harvard University, 2012.

Quezada, Noemí. "The Inquisition's Repression of *Curanderos*." In *Cultural Encounters: The Impact of the Inquisition in Spain and the New World*. Edited by Mary Elizabeth Perry and Anne J. Cruz. Berkeley and Los Angeles: University of California Press, 1991.

Quiñones Keber, Eloise. "Collecting Cultures: A Mexican Manuscript in the Vatican Library." In *Reframing the Renaissance: Visual Culture in Europe and Latin America, 1450–1650*. Edited by Claire Farago. New Haven: Yale University Press, 1995.

Raj, Kapil. *Relocating Modern Science: Circulation and the Construction of Knowledge in South Asia and Europe, 1650–1900*. London: Palgrave, 2007.

Rama, Ángel. *The Lettered City*. Edited and translated by John Charles Chasteen. Durham: Duke University Press, 1996.

Ramos, Gabriela, and Yanna Yannakakis, eds. *Indigenous Intellectuals: Knowledge, Power, and Colonial Culture in Mexico and the Andes*. Durham: Duke University Press, 2014.

Ramos Pérez, Demetrio. "La crisis indiana y la Junta Magna de 1568." *Jahrbuch für Geschichte Lateinamerikas* 23 (1986): 1–61.

———. "La junta magna de 1568. Planificación de una época nueva." In *La formación de las sociedades Iberoamericanas (1568–1700)*. Edited by Demetrio Ramos. Madrid: Espasa Calpe, 1999.

Rappaport, Joanne, and Tom Cummins, eds. *Beyond the Lettered City: Indigenous Literacies in the Andes*. Durham: Duke University Press, 2012.

Reko, Blas Pablo. *Mitobotánica zapoteca*. Mexico City: General León 9, 1945.

Reséndez, Andrés. *Changing National Identities at the Frontier: Texas and New Mexico, 1800–1850*. Cambridge: Cambridge University Press, 2005.

Restall, Matthew. *The Maya World: Yucatec Culture and Society, 1550–1850*. Stanford: Stanford University Press, 1997.

———. "Heirs to the Hieroglyphs: Indigenous Writing in Colonial Mesoamerica." *The Americas* 54 (1997): 239–267.

———. "The Renaissance World from the West: Spanish America and the 'Real' Renaissance." In *A Companion to the Worlds of the Renaissance*. Edited by Guido Ruggiero. Oxford: Blackwell, 2002.

———. "A History of the New Philology and the New Philology in History." *Latin American Research Review* 38 (2003): 113–134.

Ringrose, David. "Carting in the Hispanic World: An Example of Divergent Development." *Hispanic American Historical Review* 50:1 (1970): 30–51.

Rivas Mata, Emma. "Impresores y mercaderes de libros en la ciudad de México, siglo XVII." In *Del autor al lector: Libros y libreros en la historia*. Edited by Carmen Castañeda. Mexico City: Centro de Investigaciones y Estudios Superiores en Antropología Social, 2002.

Robelo, Cecilio Agustín. *Diccionario de pesas y medidas mexicanas, antiguas y modernas y de su conversión. Para uso de los comerciantes y las familias*. Cuernavaca: Imprenta Cuauhnahuac, 1908.

Robertson, Donald. *Mexican Manuscript Painting of the Early Colonial Period: The Metropolitan Schools*. Norman: University of Oklahoma Press, 1994 [1959].

———. "The Pinturas (Maps) of the Relaciones Geográficas, with a Catalog." In *Handbook of Middle American Indians*, vol. 12. Edited by Robert Wauchope and Howard F. Cline. Austin: University of Texas Press, 1972.

———. "Techialoyan Manuscripts and Paintings, with a Catalog." In *Handbook of Middle American Indians*, vol. 14. Edited by Robert Wauchope and Howard F. Cline. Austin: University of Texas Press, 1975.

Romero Frizzi, María de los Ángeles. *El sol y la cruz: Los pueblos indios de Oaxaca colonial*. Mexico City: Centro de Investigaciones y Estudios Superiores en Antropología Social, 1996.

———. "Los caminos de Oaxaca." In *Rutas de la Nueva España*. Edited by Chantal Cramaussel. Zamora: El Colegio de Michoacán, 2006.

———. "El título de San Mateo Capulalpan, Oaxaca. Actualidad y autenticidad de un título primordial." *Relaciones: Estudios de Historia y Sociedad* 122 (2010): 21–54.

Romero Frizzi, María de los Ángeles, ed. *Escritura zapoteca: 2,500 años de historia*. Mexico City: Centro de Investigaciones y Estudios Superiores en Antropología Social, Instituto Nacional de Antropología e Historia, and Miguel Ángel Porrúa, 2003.

Rubio Sánchez, Manuel. *Historia del añil o xiquilite en Centro América*. San Salvador: Ministerio de Educación, 1976.

Rublack, Ulinka. "Matter in the Material Renaissance." *Past and Present* 219 (2013): 41–85.

Ruggiero, Guido, ed. *A Companion to the Worlds of the Renaissance*. Oxford: Blackwell, 2002.

Ruiz Medrano, Ethelia. *Mexico's Indigenous Communities: Their Lands and Histories, 1500–2010*. Boulder: University Press of Colorado, 2010.

Russo, Alessandra. *El realismo circular: Tierras, espacios y paisajes de la cartografía novohispana, siglos XVI y XVII*. Mexico City: Universidad Nacional Autónoma de México and Instituto de Investigaciones Estéticas, 2005.

———. *The Untranslatable Image: A Mestizo History of the Arts in New Spain, 1500–1600*. Austin: University of Texas Press, 2014.

Sánchez Bueno de Bonfil, María Cristina. *El papel del papel en la Nueva España*. Mexico City: Instituto Nacional de Antropología e Historia, 1993.

Schama, Simon. *Landscape and Memory*. New York: Alfred Knopf, 1995.

Schiebinger, Londa. "Feminine Icons: The Face of Early Modern Science." *Critical Inquiry* 14:4 (1988): 661–691.

Schroeder, Susan, ed. *The Conquest All Over Again: Nahuas and Zapotecs Thinking, Writing, and Painting Spanish Colonialism*. Eastbourne: Sussex Academic Press, 2010.

Schroeder, Susan, Stephanie Wood, and Robert Haskett, eds. *Indian Women of Early Mexico*. Norman: University of Oklahoma Press, 1997.

Scott, James C. *Weapons of the Weak: Everyday Forms of Peasant Resistance*. New Haven: Yale University Press, 1985.

———. *Domination and the Arts of Resistance: Hidden Transcripts*. New Haven: Yale University Press, 1990.

———. *Seeing Like a State: How Certain Schemes to Improve the Human Condition Have Failed*. New Haven: Yale University Press, 1998.

Secord, James. "Knowledge in Transit." *Isis* 95:4 (2004): 654–672.

Sellers-García, Sylvia. *Documents and Distance at the Spanish Empire's Periphery*. Stanford: Stanford University Press, 2014.

Sepúlveda y Herrera, María Teresa. *Procesos por idolatría al cacique, gobernadores y sacerdotes de Yanhuitlán, 1544–1546*. Mexico City: Instituto Nacional de Antropología e Historia, 1999.

Siracusano, Gabriela. *El poder de los colores: De lo material a lo simbólico en las prácticas culturales andinas. Siglos XVI–XVII*. Buenos Aires: Fondo de Cultura Económica, 2005.

Smail, Daniel Lord. *Imaginary Cartographies: Possession and Identity in Late Medieval Marseille*. Ithaca: Cornell University Press, 1999.

Smith, Mary Elizabeth. *Picture Writing from Ancient Southern Mexico: Mixtec Place Signs and Maps*. Norman: University of Oklahoma Press, 1973.

Smith, Pamela H., and Paula Findlen, eds. *Merchants and Marvels: Commerce, Science, and Art in Early Modern Europe*. New York and London: Routledge, 2002.

Solari, Amara. "Circles of Creation: The Invention of Maya Cartography in Early Colonial Yucatán." *Art Bulletin* 92: 3 (2010): 154–168.

Sousa, Lisa, and Kevin Terraciano. "The 'Original Conquest' of Oaxaca: Nahua and Mixtec Accounts of the Spanish Conquest." *Ethnohistory* 50 (2003): 349–400.

Spores, Ronald. "Mixteca *Cacicas*: Status, Wealth, and the Political Accommodation of Native Elite Women in Early Colonial Oaxaca." In *Indian Women of Early Mexico*. Edited by Susan Schroeder, Stephanie Wood, and Robert Haskett. Norman: University of Oklahoma Press, 1997.

Spores, Ronald, ed. *Colección de documentos del Archivo General de la Nación para la etnohistoria de la Mixteca de Oaxaca en el siglo XVI*. Nashville, TN: Vanderbilt University Publications in Anthropology, 1992.

Spores, Ronald, and Miguel Saldaña, eds. *Documentos para la etnohistoria del estado de Oaxaca: Índice del Ramo de Mercedes del Archivo General de la Nación*. Nashville, TN: Vanderbilt University Publications in Anthropology, 1973.

Steedman, Carolyn. *Dust: The Archive and Cultural History*. New Brunswick, NJ: Rutgers University Press, 2002.

Stoler, Ann Laura. "Colonial Archives and the Arts of Governance." *Archival Science* 2 (2002): 87–109.

———. *Along the Archival Grain: Epistemic Anxieties and Colonial Common Sense*. Princeton: Princeton University Press, 2009.

Strassnig, Christian. "Rediscovering the *Camino Real* of Panama: Archaeology and Heritage Tourism Potentials." *Journal of Latin American Geography* 9:2 (2010): 159–168.

Straznicky, Marta, ed. *Shakespeare's Stationers: Studies in Cultural Bibliography*. Philadelphia: University of Pennsylvania Press, 2012.

Sweet, David G., and Gary B. Nash, eds. *Lucha por la supervivencia en América colonial*. Mexico City: Fondo de Cultura Económica, 1987.

Tanck de Estrada, Dorothy. "Trips by Indians Financed by Communal Funds in Colonial Mexico." *Jahrbuch für Geschichte Lateinamerikas* 38 (2001): 73–84.

———. *Atlas ilustrado de los pueblos de indios: Nueva España, 1800*. Mexico City: El Colegio de México and El Colegio Mexiquense, 2005.

Taylor, William. *Landlord and Peasant in Colonial Oaxaca*. Stanford: Stanford University Press, 1972.

———. *Magistrates of the Sacred: Priests and Parishioners in Eighteenth-Century Mexico*. Stanford: Stanford University Press, 1996.

Terraciano, Kevin. *The Mixtecs of Colonial Oaxaca: Ñudzahui History, Sixteenth through Eighteenth Centuries*. Stanford: Stanford University Press, 2001.

Torre Revello, José. "Algunos libros de caligrafía usados en México en el siglo XVII." *Historia Mexicana* 5:2 (1955): 220–227.

Townsend, Camilla. "Introduction: The Evolution of Alva Ixtlilxochitl's Scholarly Life." *Colonial Latin American Review* 23:1 (2014): 1–17.

Trabulse, Elías. "Científicos e ingenieros en la Nueva España: Don Diego García Conde en la historia de la cartografía mexicana." In *Una visión científica y artística de la Ciudad de México: El plano de la capital virreinal (1793–1807) de Diego García Conde*. Edited by Manuel Ramos Medina. Mexico City: Centro de Estudios de Historia Condumex, 2002.

Traub, Valerie. "Mapping the Global Body." In *Early Modern Visual Culture: Representation, Race, and Empire in Renaissance England*. Edited by Peter Erickson and Clark Hulse. Philadelphia: University of Pennsylvania Press, 2000.

Turnbull, David. "Cartography and Science in Early Modern Europe:

Mapping the Construction of Knowledge Spaces." *Imago Mundi* 48 (1996): 5–24.

Ulloa, Daniel. *Los predicadores divididos. Los dominicos en Nueva España, Siglo XVI*. Mexico City: El Colegio de México, 1977.

Vaillant, George. "A Correlation of Archaeological and Historical Sequences in the Valley of Mexico." *American Anthropologist* 40:4 (1938): 535–573.

Valverde, Nurian, and Antonio Lafuente. "Space Production and Spanish Imperial Geopolitics." In *Science in the Spanish and Portuguese Empires, 1500–1800*. Edited by Daniela Bleichmar, Paula de Vos, and Christine Huffine. Stanford: Stanford University Press, 2008.

Van Young, Eric. *Hacienda and Market in Eighteenth-Century Mexico: The Rural Economy of the Guadalajara Region, 1675–1820*. Berkeley: University of California Press, 1981.

———. "Mexican Rural History Since Chevalier: The Historiography of the Colonial Hacienda." *Latin American Research Review* 18 (1983): 5–61.

———. "Material Life." In *The Countryside in Colonial Latin America*. Edited by Louisa Schell Hoberman and Susan Migden Socolow. Albuquerque: University of New Mexico Press, 1996.

Varey, Simon, ed. *The Mexican Treasury: The Writings of Dr. Francisco Hernández*. Translated by Rafael Chabrán, Cynthia L. Chamberlin, and Simon Varey. Stanford: Stanford University Press, 2000.

Varey, Simon, Rafael Chabrán, and Dora B. Weiner, eds. *Searching for the Secrets of Nature: The Life and Works of Dr. Francisco Hernández*. Stanford: Stanford University Press, 2002.

Wake, Eleanor. "The Dawning of Places: Celestially Defined Land Maps, *Títulos Primordiales*, and Indigenous Statements of Territorial Possession in Early Colonial Mexico." In *Indigenous Intellectuals: Knowledge, Power, and Colonial Culture in Mexico and the Andes*. Edited by Gabriela Ramos and Yanna Yannakakis. Durham: Duke University Press, 2014.

Wallace, Anthony F. C., ed. *Men and Cultures: Selected Papers from the Fifth International Congress of Anthropological and Ethnological Sciences*. Philadelphia: University of Pennsylvania Press, 1960.

Weld, Kirsten. *Paper Cadavers: The Archives of Dictatorship in Guatemala*. Durham: Duke University Press, 2014.

Whitecotton, Joseph. "Las genealogías del valle de Oaxaca: Época colonial." In *Escritura zapoteca: 2500 años de historia*. Edited by María de los Ángeles Romero Frizzi. Mexico City: Centro de Investigaciones y Estudios Superiores en Antropología Social, Instituto Nacional de Antropología e Historia, and Miguel Ángel Porrúa, 2003.

Widdifield, Stacie. *The Embodiment of the National in Late Nineteenth-Century Mexican Painting*. Tucson: University of Arizona Press, 1996.

Wiedemann, H. G., and A. Boller. "Thermal Analysis of Codex Huamantla and Other Mexican Papers." *Journal of Thermal Analysis* 46 (1996): 1033–1045.

Wilson, Bronwen. *The World in Venice: Print, the City, and Early Modern Identity*. Toronto: University of Toronto Press, 2005.

Wobeser, Gisela von. "La function social y económica de las capellanías de misas en la Nueva España del siglo XVIII." *Estudios de Historia Novohispana* 16 (1996): 119–138.

Wolf, Gerhard, Joseph Connors, and Louis Waldman, eds. *Colors between Two Worlds: The Florentine Codex of Bernardino de Sahagún*. Cambridge, MA: Harvard University Press, 2012.

Wood, Stephanie. "Pedro Villafranca y Juana Gertrudis Navarrete: Falsificador de títulos y su viuda (Nueva España, siglo XVIII)." In *Lucha por la supervivencia en América colonial*. Edited by David G. Sweet and Gary B. Nash. Mexico City: Fondo de Cultura Económica, 1987.

———. "Don Diego García de Mendoza Moctezuma: A Techialoyan Mastermind?" *Estudios de Cultura Náhuatl* 19 (1989): 245–268.

———. "El problema de la historicidad de Títulos y los códices del grupo Techialoyan." In *De tlacuilos y escribanos: Estudios sobre documentos indígenas coloniales del centro de México*. Edited by Xavier Noguez and Stephanie Wood. Zamora: El Colegio de Michoacán, 1998.

———. "The Techialoyan Codices." In *Sources and Methods for the Study of Postconquest Mesoamerican Ethnohistory*. Provisional Version (e-book). Edited by J. Lockhart, L. Sousa, and S. Wood. 1–22. Eugene: Wired Humanities Project, University of Oregon, 2007. whp.uoregon.edu/Lockhart/Wood.pdf.

Yannakakis, Yanna. *The Art of Being In-Between: Native Intermediaries, Indian Identity, and Local Rule in Colonial Oaxaca*. Durham: Duke University Press, 2008.

———. "Witnesses, Spatial Practices, and a Land Dispute in Colonial Oaxaca." *The Americas* 65 (2008): 161–192.

———. "Allies or Servants? The Journey of Indian Conquistadors in the Lienzo de Analco." *Ethnohistory* 58 (2011): 653–682.

———. "Making Law Intelligible: Networks of Translation in Mid-Colonial Oaxaca." In *Indigenous Intellectuals: Knowledge, Power, and Colonial Culture in Mexico and the Andes*. Edited by Gabriela Ramos and Yanna Yannakakis. Durham: Duke University Press, 2014.

Zeitlin, Judith Francis. "Ranchers and Indians on the Southern Isthmus of Tehuantepec: Economic Change and Indigenous Survival in Colonial Mexico." *Hispanic American Historical Review* 69 (1989): 23–60.

———. "El lienzo de Guevea y el discurso histórico de la época colonial." In *Escritura zapoteca: 2,500 años de historia*. Edited by María de los Ángeles Romero Frizzi. Mexico City: Centro de Investigaciones y Estudios Superiores en Antropología Social, Instituto Nacional de Antropología e Historia, and Miguel Ángel Porrúa, 2003.

INDEX

Page numbers in italic indicate material in figures or tables.

Dutch ink, 71

dyes/colorants, 64; indigo (*añil*), 6, 18, 46, 86–88; in maps, 63–74; red, 68, 71, 86, 89, 102. *See also* ink

dzoo cuisi (cloth; paper)/*dzoo yadzi* (cloth; maguey fiber), 84

east as indicated on maps, 25, *26–27*, 33, 45, 54 (*54*), 58 (*58*)

Echagoyan, Felipe de, 54

Eight Deer, 79, 128

El Camino de Etla, 87

El Camino Real (the Royal Highway), 18–19, 87

encomiendas (grants of Indian labor and tribute), 6, 9, 36

entailed estates (*cacicazgos*), 6, 19–20, 37

epidemics. *See* disease

"Epistle to Arias Montano, An" (Hernández), 64

Escamilla, Iván, 123, 144n1

escribanías (scribal appointments), 93

European animals: cattle, 17, 21, 38, 41–42, *43*, 133n2; horses/hoofprints on maps, 41–42, *43–44*, 47, 48, 56–57

everyday life pictured in maps, *61*

Fajardo de Aguilar, Pablo, 21–22

Fernández de Córdoba, Diego (Ruíz's attorney), 22–23, 30, 107

Fernández Franco, Gerónimo, 31

ficus (*amacuáuitl/amatl*) tree and paper, 76–77

Figueroa, Francisco de, 33

Florentine Codex, 86, *87*

Flórez, Andrés, 70

folds, crease marks, 79–83 (*81*, *82*)

footprints: discontinued in later maps, 56–57, 84; indicating presence and movement, 11, 36; unique for each painter, 36, *37*, 41, *42*

forced resettlements (*congregaciones*), 6, 10, 53

Forum conscientiae sive pastorale internum (Francés de Urrutigoyti), 83 (*83*)

"four-faced rock" on map, 108–110 (*109*)

Francés de Urrutigoyti, Diego Antonio, 83

Francisco Fernández de la Cueva, 22

fundo legal (space allotted to Indian communities), 10, 32

Gálvez, Conde de, 130

Geertz, Clifford, 16

Geográfica descripción (Burgoa), 76

"giant's tooth," 119

glosses on maps, 4, 25, 57–58 (*58*), 69

glue/adhesives, 59, 63, 75

Godoy Sotomayor, Melchor de, 97, *97*

Gómez, Jacinto, 31

González Echevarría, Roberto, 90, 91

grids, 9, 58 (*58*), 81 (*81*)

"grids of intelligibility," 115

Gruzinski, Serge, 2–3, 49, 99

Gutiérrez, Diego, 101

Guzmán, Juan, 20, 133n27

Guzmán, María de, 23

haciendas (landed estates), 16–17

Harley, J. B., 1, 2, 25, 27, 131n6

Haskett, Robert, 102

Hernández, Domingo, 91

Hernández, Francisco, 9, 63–64, 66, 70, 75–78, 86, 115

Herrera, Francisco Xavier de, 107–110

Herrera y Tordesillas, Antonio de, 105, 128

Herzog, Tamar, 32

Historia Chichimeca (Ixtlilxochitl), 36

Historia general de las cosas de Nueva España (Sahagún), 62, 66

Historia natural del reino de Guatemala (Ximénez), 68

History of Cartography, The, 82

Holy Family with Two Angels, The (Dürer), 50–51 (*51*)

horses/hoofprints on maps, 41–42, *43–44*, 47, 48, 56–57

How to Lie with Maps (Monmonier), 2

huanacaxtle (elephant-ear tree fruit), 66

Huave, 41

huitzquahuitl tree and ink, 68

Icíar, Juan de, 70–71

Icnotzin, Juan, 35

illicit manuscript workshops, 112

indigenous archives, 116

indigenous rights to land, 102

indigo (*añil*), 6, 18, 46, 86–88

ink: to authenticate maps, 69, 92; black and red, 57 (*58*), 63–64, 68–70; dangers of manufacturing, 71; European, 69–74; "hard balls," 71; *huitzquahuitl*, 68; iron-gall, 12, 69–70, *72*, 73–74, 89, 92; medic-

inal use of, 70–71; Mesoamerican, 62–69; and monochromatic maps, 63; *ocote*, 63; *ocotlilli* carbon-based, 64, 66; ritual use of, 63; "wood-smoked," 64. *See also* dyes/colorants

Into the Archive (Burns), 94

inventories, importance of, 117–118

"invisible social world" of maps, 2

iron-gall ink, 12, 69–70, *72*, 73–74, 89, 92

Ixhuatlán de Madero, 78–79

Ixtepec, 33

Ixtlilxochitl, Fernando de Alva, 35–36, 120, 121, 127–128

Jacinto, Juan, 19

jaguar logograph, 4, 41, *42*, 45 (*45*)

Jiménez, Antonio, 101

Johns, Adrian, 71

Juan Bautista, 97

Juárez, Diego, 19

Juárez de Zárate brothers, 56

Juchitán, 110

Junta, Juan de, 71

junta magna (Phillip II, 1568), 9, 92

Keating, Jessica, 118, 119, 144n3

Klein, Ursula, 66, 71

Laguna, Andrés, 71

Lagunas Portocarrero, Francisco de, 29

land grants, authentication of, 33, *82*, 90, 94, 101. *See also* authentication of documents

La Profesa archive, 123

Lara y Guzmán, Gerónimo de, 19–20, 23

legal writing, 90, 91, 94

Leibsohn, Dana, 2–3, 24–25

Lenz, Hans, 78–79

León Pinelo, Antonio de, 105

León y Gama, Antonio de, 106, 112–113

"lettered city," 93

Leyva, Manuel de, 21

lienzos, 5, 27, 84, 128, 130

linen maps, 27, 84, 118

literacy, alphabetic and visual, 2, 93

logographs/place-signs: decline in, 25, 47–48, 52, 56; in *lienzos*, 5; in Map of Mystequilla and Tegoantepec, 41–42 (*42*); in Map of Tehuantepec, 45 (*45*); in Map of Teozacoalco, 40 (*40*); in Map of Tepenene, 53 (*53*); in Map of Xoxocotlán,

Pacific Ocean (South Sea), 45 (*45*), 47 (*47*), 110

painter-scribes, 35–36

painters in New Spain: caciques as, 36–38; dealing with Spanish bureaucracy, 37–38; as elders passing on knowledge, 56; as geographic interpreters, 33–34; introducing European elements, 39; painter from Nochistlán, 36, *37*; painter from Tehuantepec, 33, 41–42, 46, 100–101; prestige of, 57; relationship of with patron, inspector, 51–52; traditional craft of, 34–36

Panes, Diego de, 130

paper: of Boturini collection, 118; European, *38*, 75–76 (*75*), 80–83; in indigenous books, 80–81; joined with glue, 75; of Map of Our Lady of the Rosary, 84–89 (*85*, *88*); Mesoamerican, 76–80; recycling of, 80–84; religious significance of, 77–79; shortages of, 80, 83; of Teozacoalco map, 75 (*75*)

Pask, Robert, 71

Pasto speakers, 102

Pearce, Susan, 1

perceptual versus conceptual illustrations, 50–51 (*50*, *51*)

Pérez, Ignacio, 70–71

Pérez, Juan, 31

Pérez de Salamanca, Juan, 21

perspectival drawing, 51

Philip II, 9, 80, 92

Piedra, José, 80

place-signs. *See* logographs/place-signs

Plano Parcial de la Ciudad de México, 123–125 (*124*)

Pliny, 71

plum trees issue. *See* Xoxocotlán, Santa Cruz

political genealogy, 40 (*40*), 126, 128

Portuondo, María, 105

power structure: native intermediaries and, 133n8; in Oaxaca Valley, 16–17, 20, 24, 36–37

printing press, 71, 80

quadrilinear urban grids, 9

Queguquilapa, 102

"Quispalapa" salt lake, 107–108, 110

quitichibi ("animal hide without hair"), 79

quitimani ("animal hide"), 79

rag-based paper, 12, 40, 80, 84, 118, 127

Rama, Ángel, 93

Ramírez, Cristobal, 103

Ramírez, Juan, 101

Ramos, Demetrio, 9

Rappaport, Joanne, 20, 83, 93, 102–103

Ray of Wind, 128

rectangular device indicating site, 33, *34*, 41, *42*, *43*, 46 (*46*)

reçute size paper cut, 80–81, 140–141n102

recycled paper, 80–84 (*83*), 117

red dye/colorants, 68, 71, 86, 89, 102

red roses tree issue. *See* Xoxocotlán, Santa Cruz

reinvention through reproduction, 137n64

Relaciones Geográficas survey, *3*, 10, 76; and cataloging inscriptions, 105; and instructions, questions for native informants, 49, 100–101; map of Tehuantepec, 45 (*45*); map of Teozacoalco, 39–41 (*39*, *40*), 44, 75 (*75*); results of, 104–106; use of, 105

Rendón, Antonio, 20–23, 30

reproduction of maps, 24–25, 30, 55, 61, 121–123

repúblicas de indios government, 6, 17

resettlements (*congregaciones*), 6, 10, 53

Reyes, Antonio de los, 35

Ricaldes, Sebastián de, 101

rivers, depiction of, 52 (*52*)

roads: depictions of, 36, *37*, 41, *42*, 87; and *ruta mixteca* trade route, *7*, 18

Robles, Antonio de, 83

Rodríguez, Joseph, 31–32

Rodríguez, Nicolás, 19

Romero Frizzi, María de los Ángeles, 18

rooftops, 41, *42*, 46–48 (*46*, *47*, *48*)

Roque, Juan, 110, 112

Roxas y Abreu, Antonio de, 117–120

royal interpreters, 127

Rublack, Ulinka, 76, 118

Ruíz, Bartolomé, 15, 22–25, 30–32, 134n42. *See also* Fernández de Córdoba, Diego (Ruíz's attorney)

Ruíz, Francisco, 22

ruling pairs, depiction of, *39*, 40 (*40*), 75

Russo, Alessandra, 49, 87

ruta mixteca roads, *7*, 18

Sahagún, Bernardino de, 62, 63–64, 66, 68, 70, 76–77, 79, 86

Salazar, Juan de, 54

Salinas, Francisco de, 49

salt lake map dispute, 107–108, 110

San Ana Zegache, 103

San Andrés Sinaxtla map, 57–59 (*58*)

San Andrés Tlacozahuala map, 56 (*57*)

Sánchez de Muñoz, Hernán, 80

San Dionisio del Mar versus San Francisco del Mar, 107–110 (*108*, *109*)

San Gerónimo Tlacochaguaya map, *43*, 60–61, 61

San Gregorio Atlapulco, 127

San Juan, Luis de, 22, 24

San Juan Chapultepec versus San Martín Mexicapan, 110–112 (*111*)

San Juan Teotihuacan, 127

San Juan Yuchayta, 110

San Miguel Cuestlavaca, map of, *37*, 50–51 (*50*, *51*), 53

San Pedro y San Pablo, Jesuit College of, 121, 123

Santa Cruz Olguín, Diego de, 97, 99, 101

Santa Cruz Papalutla map, *43*, 60–61, 61

Santa Cruz Xoxocotlán. *See* Xoxocotlán, Santa Cruz

Santa María Guelaxé map, *43*, 60–61, 61

Santa María Magdalena Mixihuca, Mexico, 127

Santiago, Joseph de, 56, 135n80

Santiago, Lucas de, 56

Santo Domingo Tepenene, 37–38 (*38*), 53 (*53*), 55, 73–74

schools, Mesoamerican, 35, 63

Scott, James, 51

screenfold books, 5, 79

scribes, 35–36, 93–94

Sellers-García, Sylvia, 87, 139n37

servants in indigenous households, 77

signatures: false, 110, 112; official, 12, 28, 92, 94, 97 (*97*), 105; unofficial, 36, 41, 47, 66

Simancas, royal archive of, 119–120

Smail, Daniel Lord, 93

Smith, Mary Elizabeth, 25, 27n21, 53, 135n74

sobresaliente (outstanding) indigo dye, 86

Sousa, Lisa, 112

space, Spanish view of, 87

Spanish bureaucracy, painters dealing with, 37–38

Spanish units of measure, *15*, 133n2

Spanish urban settlements, 6
Spary, Emma, 66, 71
stars, depictions of, 4, 54–55 (*55*)
state structure, 6
Stoler, Ann Laura, 115, 117
sun. *See* celestial/astral bodies
sun (east) as indicated on maps, 25, *26–27*, 33, 45, 54 (*54*), 58 (*58*)
surveying in Europe, 60–61
syncretic rituals, 9

tameme (porter), 18, 87
tasación (appraisal), 99–100
Taylor, William, 17
Tehuantepec region, 37; Africans and Afro-Mexicans in, 46; archives of, 116; caciques of, 37; complaints about alcalde mayor, 116; on El Camino Real, 18; indigo from, 86–89; jaguar symbol for, 41, *42*, 45 (*45*); maps of, *42*, 45 (*45*), 100, 108 (*108*), 110; painter from, 33, 41–42, 45–46, 100–101; topography, 7–8, 18; tribute records, 77
templates, notarial, 94, 113
Tenochtitlán, fall of, 36, 80, 128
Teotitlán map, 71–73 (*72*)
Teozacoalco map, *39–40*, 40–41, 44, 75–76 (*75*)
teptl (place-sign), 3, 53 (*53*)
tequitlatos, 100, 143n31
Terraciano, Kevin, 6, 112
tetlilli/"black stone," 64
Texcoco, 35, 125, 127
three-dimensionality, 50–51 (*50*, *51*)
"time immemorial" status, 18, 20–21, 106
tinta flor (flower ink) indigo dye, 86
titles to land, 17, 18, 20, 22, 103, 116, 130
título y merced (title and royal deed), 103
tlacehuilli (blue colorant), 86
Tlailotlaques, 35
tlaliyac mineral, 66, 68, 70

Tlapanaltepeque, map of, 47–48 (*47*, *48*)
Tlaxiaco map, 97 (*97*)
tlaxocotl (alum stone), 68
tlicomalli (jars for preparing ink), 64
Toltecs, 35, 121
tonalamtl ("book of days"), 121
Tonaltepec, *37*, *46*, *47*, *55*
Torquemada, Juan de, 126, 128
Torres, Joseph, 88
Torres de Lagunas, Juan de, 42, 45, 100–101
trade routes, colonial, 6–7 (*7*)
"transactional go-betweens," 38
traslado (authorized copy), 90
triangular rooftop (settlement), 41, *42*, 46–48 (*46*, *47*)
Triple Alliance, 120, 121
tutu ñuhu ("sacred paper"), 79
Tututepec, 80
tzacutli plant, 63, 75
Tzanaltepec, *37*, 45–47 (*46*), *55*

UNESCO, 1, 3
units of measure, Spanish, 15t, 133n2
untranslatable, the, 49

Vaillant, George, 35
Valadés, Pedro, 94, *95*
vaqueros ("cowhands"), 46
Varcarcel, Domingo, 126
Vargas, Gaspar de, 33
Vargas, Hernando de, 47
Velasco, Don Pedro Martín de, 102–103
Velazco, Andrés de, 22
Villafranca, Pedro de, 112
Virgin of Guadalupe, 114, 115, 125
vistas de ojos (site inspections), 91

Wake, Eleanor, 54
"war of images," 49
wheeled vehicles, 18, 87
Whitecotton, Joseph, 147n92

witness testimony, 30–32, 90, 101–103, 107–110, 117
"wood-smoked ink" (*tinta del humo de teas*), 64

Ximénez, Francisco, 68, 70
Xinmamal, Francisco, 35
xiuhquilitlpitzahoac plant, 86
Xoxocotlán, Santa Cruz: lack of written title to, 18; and Lara land purchase, 19–20; litigation over, 11–12, 15–16, 18; map and official copies of, 14–16, 18, 24–30 (*26*, *28*, *29*), 107; and plum trees issue, 22–25, 31–32; and red roses boundary *mojon*, 19, 21–22; and sketch of disputed lands, 19; *Xoxocotlán v. Antonio Rendón*, 20–22. *See also* Oaxaca, Valley of

Yanhuitlán, 49, 54, 56, 62, 83
Yannakakis, Yanna, 19, 24, 27, 31
yetze (Zapotec social units, ethnic states), 6, 17
Ystepeq and Zixitlan map, *34*

Zapotec poet, 125–128
Zapotecs/Zapoteca: alphabetic writing of, 49; importance of land to, 17; languages of, 102; and Mixtecs, 102, 128, 147n92; retaining irrigated lands, 41; terms of for schools and trade masters, 35; voluntary alignment of with Spain, 127–128
Zárate, Domingo de, 15, 24–28, 30, 36, 55–57
Zarazua, Juan Joseph de, 110
Zimatlán, 103, 106
Zixitlan map, 33, *34*
Zoque people, 41
Zorita, Alonso de, 121
Zuaso, Juan Ruíz, 41
Zumárraga, Juan de, 80